WAY BEYOND THE GRITS

SIDNEY KATE

Cover image by: Emily Robinson
Book design by: SWATT Books Ltd
Blurb by: Karen Williams
Interior Author Headshot taken by Yvonne Burns
Jacket Author Headshot taken by Nina Sartorelli

Printed in the United States
First Printing, 2025

ISBN: 979-8-9919097-0-9 (Paperback)
ISBN: 979-8-9919097-1-6 (Hardback)
ISBN: 979-8-9919097-2-3 (eBook)
ISBN: 979-8-9919097-3-0 (Audiobook)

Sidney Kate
www.sidneykate.com

"Don't worry about me if I do not answer the phone! I will be outside tap dancing."

Maredia Pace Bowdon, 2022

I dedicate this book to:

Maredia Pace Bowdon

"My Other Mother"

Born: July 21, 1927 in Iuka, Mississippi

Died: June 13, 2022 in Shreveport, Louisiana

and to

E.

"My Only Son"

Born: July 11, 1987 in Shreveport, Louisiana

Sidney Kate has created a playlist of songs to accompany her life's experiences. She wishes to pay tribute to these brilliant singers and songwriters whose music and lyrics have gotten her through the joyful as the depressingly challenging times. Music transforms and heals—learn from these lyrics and strive as Mama Cass would say, to "make your own kind of music"!

DEFINITIONS

GRITS—Girl Raised in The South

adapted from AcronymFinder.com

Grit—courage and resolve; strength of character.

Oxford Languages

Grits—is a food of Native American origin that is common in the Southern United States, mainly used in breakfast. It consists of coarsely ground corn. When made from hominy, it is referred to as hominy grits. It is sometimes called sofkee or sofkey from the Creek word.

Savannah.com/grits

Grits—anything seen as a necessity, e.g. money or sex.

Greensdictofslang.com

Kiss My Grits—A nice way of saying "eff you." It's a spin on the phrase "kiss my a**", written into a TV show from the 80s called "Alice". The saying was usually preceded by the name "Mel" who was the owner of the diner where Flo, the waitress who made the saying famous, worked.

Phrases.com

GRITS—also an acronym for the following, among others:
* Gentleman Raised in the South
* Guys Raised in the South
* Godly Revelations in Today's Society

adapted from AcronymFinder.com

CONTENTS

INTRODUCTION

I don't really want to become normal, average, standard. I want merely to gain in strength, in the courage to live out my life more fully, enjoy more, experience more. I want to develop even more original and more unconventional traits.

Anais Nin, Diary 1, p. 112

What is normal...in a not so normal world? This book is a memoir or, as I call it, a saga—a collection of my own life experiences as well as those of my flawed ancestors. These "flaws" have been passed down through generations of inheritance in terms of physicality, personality, and behaviors.

Growing up in the Deep South in the '50s, '60s and '70s, I certainly did not have a clue what was considered "normal." My stories are meant to show the extremes of real life, where shadows and darkness abound. They are about accepting all of one's life: the right and the wrong, the good and the bad, the happy and the sad. This book is about learning from the dark times which include toxic behavior beyond the acceptable norm.

I want to raise a smile and hopefully spark much laughter, although sadness is a reality of life that we cannot entirely escape. We all have experienced varying levels of pain and have wounds so deeply hidden that others may not know they exist—we are all the "walking wounded." Even though others may not see our wounds or feel our pain, that does not make them any less real.

Revisiting the past is the only way forward. I look back at my life with a smile as well as a noted sadness. To those readers who feature in these stories (and are still alive), I make the disclaimer that you know them to be true. So, get over it! Anyway, you should be too old to run for public office. To all others, just know I did not invent these stories—wild (and dysfunctional) stories from real life have always been around.

If we want to grow, we cannot continue to push away and refuse to face our own truths, our own pain, our own darkness. We can learn lessons from everything that happens in life. Our own truths and our own shadows are integral parts of our unique individual stories.

I must continually check my own boundaries and regularly attempt to recenter myself. After all, boundaries keep people out of as well as in your life. Hopefully you, too, will be encouraged to set your own boundaries.

This account of my life may not resonate with everyone—my hope is that by reading these stories, you will identify your own truth and be able to learn from it. Be your most authentic self and cultivate your own culture from your own experiences!

I also hope that reading this book sparks memories of your own unexpected thoughts that could be considered "way beyond" what is acceptable within the realms of your normal. Just know that we all have these types of thoughts, even if we do not act upon them. My hope is that you too will be able to get through the tragic experiences that forever change you and your outlook on life.

In writing this book, I have experienced a range of powerful emotions, which I must admit have contributed to my own growth. I have learned to embrace my shadow of personal darkness, with compassion and self-love; and to be comfortable with what makes me different. I will continue to stand in my own integrity and embrace my own individuality... to live my life *Way Beyond The GRITS*. My life's journey continues as I struggle to let go of what does not bring me positivity. My never-ending quest for love and happiness has been very painful but also very liberating.

I know it is scary, but I want you to find the light in the darkness and the possibility of TRUE love and happiness. There is HOPE for a better tomorrow—a future that involves acceptance of oneself, self-love, faith, and hope.

Sidney Kate

MY BACKSTORY

Nature, Nurture or a Combination of Both?

I have always been different than most and have known this since birth. I later learned to blame this in part on being named Sidney, the masculine form of Sidney not being a common female name in 1954. I come from a long line of female "Sidneys" with an "i," beginning with my great-grandmother.

I was born in the astrological sign of Leo under an Aquarius full moon. My *natal* chart reveals that this Aquarius full moon is located in my fourth house of home, family, roots, and ancestral legacies. My ascendant is in the astrological sign of Libra, leading me to seek continual balance.

The major theme of having an Aquarius moon in my fourth house is that I will *naturally* have difficulty expressing emotions and feeling normal. That is an understatement! The fourth astrological house teaches emotional intelligence; it is where we learn to *nurture* ourselves following childhood wounds and traumas, highlighting our time alone when facing our fears and loneliness. The *natal* fourth house in astrology is a strong indicator of the primary *nurturer* in our life, commonly known as our mother.

Having an Aquarius moon in my fourth house also means I am likely to be rebellious, continually seeking freedom and spontaneous change. I will have a progressive approach to life. Quite different from being *nurtured by* and *nurturing* others, I am likely to have an unconventional family life, including erratic and volatile relationships with my parents—especially my birth Mother. (For me, though, it was both parents.) The saving grace is that I appear balanced. My Libra ascendant continues to show me both sides of every story.

This explains what I was *naturally* born with—my *nature*—but it does not tell you how I have used these wonderful gifts. Let us start with my birth...

Friday the 13th

I was born on Friday the 13th in August. The record high that day was 106 degrees Fahrenheit.[1] Was there global warming in 1954, too?

My Mother told the story of my birth to anyone who would listen. Due to superstition, the other mothers avoided going to the hospital that day. Most tried to avoid giving birth. My Mother decided to take a chance on life and challenge the odds. She boasted that she had carte blanche at the maternity ward. It could have been worse—thank God I was born in a hospital and my birth was documented.

And more, I appeared with an amniotic veil over my full head of black hair. Oh boy, I was ugly! The hospital workers must have been very surprised to see me emerge like that. Stevie Wonder sings in "Superstition" about "When you believe in things / That you don't understand"—that sums up my birth and many years thereafter.

I believe my life story to be unique despite my unusual beginnings. I was born in Louisiana, in the Deep South—a cultural and geographic subregion of the Southern United States, which includes Alabama, Georgia, Louisiana, Mississippi, and South Carolina, according to *Merriam-Webster*. Louisiana is often considered the "most" Deep South of these states. The term was first used to describe the region that was most economically dependent on plantations and slavery.

History affects culture and culture affects history. From the Civil War to the Civil Rights Movement of the '50s and '60s, and even today, the Deep South retains many "remnants" of its Southern culture. Some still believe the Civil War was the ONLY war. Even so, the region continues to hold onto its traditional grace and hospitality, its culture remaining a beautiful tribute to life.

I was raised in Shreveport in a blended conservative family of seven children, with five brothers and one sister. Thanks to DNA testing services—and unbeknownst to my childhood self—I later learned that I was in fact the eldest of four, the only girl born to both my biological Mother and Father. My three younger brothers (identified as younger, middle, and youngest in this book) are my full "BLOOD BROTHERS."

My three older half-siblings (two males and one female) are genetic mixtures of one of my parents and someone else—all documented but one, who I call my non-sister. (I have another half-sister, but she is not part of this story, so I will leave her be.) I am the middle child, if you look at the clan of seven; and the eldest child, if you look at the children of my Mother and Father. This is my family tree—a lot of jumbled DNA.

Living Life on the Verge

I was born into a culture that was meant to teach me conservative behavior. Ultimately, though, I failed at completely internalizing this culture since it conflicted with my rebellious Aquarius moon. My personal revolt resulted in a boatload of not-so-conservative actions. I quote my longtime friend Holly when I say that I began and continue to live my life "on the verge!"

To this day, I outwardly appear to be progressive. However, the friends that really know me know THAT is a "crock of shit," since a small slice of conservative mentality is still ingrained within me. I guess this is why I can get along with those of various political persuasions. I can have hour-long conversations with my "liberal" friends, who truly believe I agree with them. All the while, I am secretly shaking my head and internally shouting "No, NOT REALLY!"

My progressive side includes an avid interest in the occult and the dimensions of the spiritual world. Why not? After all, I was born on Friday the 13th. In my teens, I participated in many seances and attempted levitations. In my thirties, I did readings with a renowned holistic astrologer. I have also consulted with other spiritual guides and psychic mediums and been involved in journeying and past life regression. I once owned a Ouija board, but its energy scared me. Recently, a younger male acquaintance called me a "unicorn" (for the definition, see the *Urban Dictionary*). Being relatively naïve, I have yet to figure out whether it was a compliment or a cut.

I have had many friends and lovers, while living independently in many beautiful places and absorbing their cultures (I particularly love the Northeast). I have made it to my advanced age without having had a true committed relationship—except on paper and for a short time, over 34 years ago, resulting in the birth of a male child.

I will always "love" the bad boy and run away from the nice guy. Consequently, I have found myself in a variety of diverse and sometimes overly complicated relationships—all fraught with unhappiness. Today, I search for a "bad boy turned good." Someone like that is not easy to find.

Almost all of my male relationships have been flawed with contradictions. I have looked for—but never found—a man with qualities representing what I loved in my Father. Hence, there were a lot of toxic relationships, because the qualities I sought were not always his good ones. I believe (and most psychologists would agree) that this tendency for unhealthy relationships must be partly hereditary, due to both my DNA and my environment, because it goes back many centuries. I learned a lot about unhealthiness from both my parents. Nature and nurture!

Over the years, I have experimented with very limited same-sex encounters, but I cannot commit to being more than a friend to another female. I have many close female friends in same-sex marriages whose stories and exploits I enjoy listening to. I decided long ago that I am purely directed toward interacting sexually with men; although I occasionally watch lesbian porn, out of curiosity.

I experienced a feel-up at a slumber party in elementary school, attempting to discover what extremely large bosoms felt like. I will not go into too much detail because my Southern girlfriend, who is happily married with children, would not appreciate me revealing this secret.

Over time, I have come to honor religion, especially during periods of extreme anguish and adversity, when I need a higher power to cry out to! In reality, I am merely a simplistic spiritual vessel who honestly wishes to spread my light.

My early childhood was full of different experiences that were "beyond the pale" or, in Southern terms, "beyond the GRITS." In spite of such extremes, however, I have always maintained a moral compass. Even as a young child, I knew what I saw was wrong, but my psyche, fueled by thoughts and emotions, took over. This need to fuel the psyche has persisted to a point, as I continually attempt to balance my moral compass and my innate dual composition. I have experienced a wide range of life experiences, from extremely pleasurable to not so desirable. Sometimes I have done the wrong things for the right reasons. Yet, through it all, I continue to seek the true Libran balance of my *natal* astrological chart.

I gravitate toward (and identify with) outcasts—those underdogs who beat the odds. As a young child, I made friends with the socially undesirable, the children who were made fun of and proclaimed to have "cooties"! It was not racial identity that made these children different because their color was white. Such proclamations would mostly be due to their obvious outward appearance of uncleanliness.

The root cause of this harassment would have been poverty, because my elementary school was predominantly full of white upper-middle-class children. On the outside, I may have appeared to fit in, but I was really somewhere between the two on the economic scale. I never felt like I belonged to the main circles, so I would sit with the "cootie" children at lunch and talk to them at recess. I was fascinated by the difference in their lives and wanted to hear their stories.

Was THIS really a false fascination? The only time I outwardly came close to their appearance—and understanding their plight—was when I fell into a puddle playing kickball before school. All the children laughed at me, covered in mud, pointing out my misfortune. I learned, for the first time, what the other children were seeing. I felt very ashamed and a little angry at their outbursts—but the real shame was the other children not seeing that they too had "cooties". The only difference was theirs were hidden deep inside.

I became friends with one outcast who invited me to sleep over at her house. I was curious to see how she lived; I accepted and anxiously packed an overnight bag. My Mother dropped me off one Friday afternoon and promised to pick me up the next morning. There would be no phone communication for the next twenty-four hours, because this family did not have a phone.

I walked through their welcoming door and found a barefoot family, including a beautiful mother holding an infant boy. The father was not present; I sensed he was away working. The large family, of at least five, quietly stared at me in awe. I looked around at the meek furnishings, including several twin beds. Their tiny house had three rooms in total—one large room, a kitchen, and a bathroom. The floor was tightly packed with dirt. Outwardly, I did not belong; but I was treated with respect and generously offered some of their meager supper.

I learned much about differences that night and vowed to myself that I would never compare myself to others based on outward appearance. I also vowed to continue being a friend to this girl, no matter what. And I did—but I noticed a few weeks later she was absent. I never saw her again, later learning that she left the school suddenly when her family moved elsewhere to find better economic opportunities.

I was probably the only child that cared about her. I wondered much later if she had been able to overcome her beginnings. I wanted her to—I wanted her to become an adult leader and make life better for others, because she knew what it was like not to have. Still, the experience was an early life lesson that I have never forgotten.

The only other time I experienced a similar scenario was much later, in high school, when the cheerleaders decorated the house of one of the football stars. You would never have known that this talented black athlete came from a poverty-ridden family, but the dirt floor was there again. These two experiences colored my opinions for life.

I still attract diverse souls of various ages from both extremes of the spectrum, accepting different responses, behaviors, and lifestyles. You could say I follow the "road less traveled." Every day is an adventure. My Aquarius moon drives my ongoing need for personal freedom, and even at my advanced age; I maintain a childlike curiosity about life's experiences. I still seek out people on the fringes of society—the "misfits"—and am genuinely fascinated by their lives.

I believe that powerful dichotomies exist between power and prestige, on the one hand, and weakness and struggle, on the other. Weakness encourages innovation. This theme was presented in the biblical story of David and Goliath.[2] Yes, underdogs and misfits are not weak and have the power to make change. I believe every person has unlimited potential. After all, as you will soon see, I am one myself—I am that underdog.

I am different—being named Sidney, being born on Friday the 13th, and having my Aquarius moon in my fourth house—only played a small part in my being unique. Yes, nature and nurture as well as experiences and struggles, have been important; but my beliefs, aspirations, and dreams are distinctive to me. Revisiting my past is my way forward. "I'll be your Louisiana / You'll be my Mississippi," as Blake Shelton sang.

Playlist Song #1:
"Honey Bee," by Blake Shelton.

Mississippi Mud

Although I have yet to find her real birth certificate, my Mother was born in rural Mississippi. She was given the first name Opal after the birthstone, which she hated. She was born on October 30, the day before Halloween. She was somewhat fueled by her dark shadow, reveling in the fact that I was born on Friday the 13th under a full moon period. "Mississippi mud" taught her many things, the most important being that the "darkness" does not forgive.

To me, she was passionate, intense, and draining. Although she was emotionally powerful, her quest for intellectual stimulation in an outside career stifled her. She became a true victim and remained one all her life, never overcoming it. As Southerners say, she "made a meal" out of her unhappiness. She may have tried to make a meal out of my life, as well!

My Mother never acknowledged her Daddy issues, but they came out in many ways, through her behavior and her attraction to what was familiar in my Father. She was close to a sister, my Aunt "I," who unfortunately only revealed this truth following my Mother's death. I now regret never asking Aunt I to reveal the sad details of my Mother's childhood. That was not something anyone ever spoke about, especially older generations. The dreaded cycle of emotional, physical, and most probably (though never confirmed) sexual abuse continued. I think my Mother marrying my Father allowed her to foster its continuation.

She married her first husband at an early age, having her first child—my older stepbrother—before her eighteenth birthday. I think it had something to do with a "falling out" and my Mother running away, probably from her father and his abuse. I believe she continued following this path so she could legitimately keep her distance from him. We rarely visited my maternal grandparents because she hardly ever went back to her childhood home.

I do not know much about my maternal grandparents, other than they were also born in Mississippi and were rural farmers. They later moved from Mississippi to run a small country store near Columbia, Louisiana.

It was relayed to me that my maternal grandmother, Hattie Mae, was quite the character. She was born in late October, in 1899. Rumor has it that she smoked, drank, and played poker. Her maiden name was Luna. I traced the name back to the Manx culture of the Isle of Man, to a distant great-grandfather with a last name of Looney, Dr. Looney. No wonder they changed it when they emigrated. My Mother revealed her grandfather was a bootlegger in Mississippi during the Depression, manufacturing his own moonshine.

I saw my maternal grandmother only a few times: she gazed at me fondly and called me "Little Maurie" over and over. She also called my Mother by her given middle name, Maurie. My Mother preferred Marie and changed it when she became an adult. She wanted to name me Marie, too, but was overruled by my Father and never got around to doing it.

I have a few vivid visual memories of my maternal grandfather— born in Mississippi, in 1893—semi-reclined in his Lay-Z-Boy, his rat terrier sleeping on his huge beer belly. He never said much to me.

I never witnessed my maternal grandparents having much wealth, but I got the impression that some land had originally been owned in Mississippi—maybe a small plantation. Certainly, there were slaves in our ancestry. My Mother told me she played with their children as a kid.

My Mother bragged that her father's ancestors had signed the Declaration of Independence and she was qualified to be a member of the Daughters of the Revolution. I believe this to be true; but this was one of many claims that my Mother failed to legally confirm.

We were also (and I think this is more legitimate) related to "Pretty Boy Floyd," a gangster connected to Bonnie and Clyde, with relatives in northern Louisiana. Bonnie and Clyde were hunted down and shot near Gibsland, Louisiana. I continue to research this fascinating ancestor using history books and ancestry.com.

Although my Mother was always relating such stories to me, she never spoke about her own personal misery. I think she wanted female companionship and a friend to listen, so she sought my audience. That was sad and dysfunctional, as I was not yet an adult who could process her complicated talks. I was "parentified," as they say, at an early age.

The few times my Mother reunited with her many brothers and sisters (I lost count after ten) tended to result in unhappiness. I think my Father, for whatever reason, encouraged her alienation from her family. After her death, I found several hidden pictures of some of my Mother's siblings in shoe boxes. It was clear that they communicated with her at least on a few special—and rare— occasions, in secret, without my Father knowing. I am not sure of the full extent.

My Mother spoke about most of them fondly in passing. She said one was "addicted to sex". This younger sister lived nearby. They met for coffee frequently. I bet those conversations were interesting. It was an extremely sad story, though, because her husband committed suicide. I wondered whether her sexual deviance caused his pain—and I wonder if this "sex" trait may be hereditary?

Louisiana Lagniappe

In many ways, my Father was also a victim with many childhood wounds. He definitely had Mommy issues as opposed to my Mother's Daddy issues, although he, unlike her, was not passive. He reacted to his abuse by being overly aggressive. My Mother told me stories about the lack of love in his childhood as though it was a badge of honor.

The importance of working and making money was instilled in my Father at a very early age, most probably from his mother. He got up at dawn every day, before school, delivering newspapers as a "paperboy."

My Father, without a doubt, had a problem with balance in his life. I now think he was a Peter Pan who had undiagnosed ADHD or was bipolar. He was not diagnosed nor medicated—and never sought help. Either would certainly have explained his extreme manic behavior, his highs and lows, and the long periods of non-laughter that I observed over the years.

He was a heavy drinker and smoker in his youth. When I saw a picture of him as a young man smoking, I was shocked—he looked very European. He resented my Mother's excessive drinking later in life because he, too, was an alcoholic. My Mother called this his "inside-outside" persona. My adopted mother—Maredia Bowdon, who I will tell you more about later; and who I dedicate this book to—concurred. In her infinite wisdom, she called it his "sidewalk" persona. Both women were born in Mississippi. Their observations mean the same thing—and, in my opinion, they are both right.

My paternal grandmother, named Minnie, was not quite five feet in height, but was a powerful matriarchal presence in our family's life. A "force to be reckoned with," she was born on June 1, 1894. This made her a Gemini from another generation. And, yes, I believe there was always an evil twin lurking within her, since she constantly seemed to be battling between good and evil. There were definitely two sides to her. She told me that she loved the smell of wine but could not drink it, because she was addicted to its smell (and, most probably, its taste, too)—a red flag for alcoholism.

Minnie was overbearing with my Father, her only son, and his two younger sisters. My Father kowtowed to his mother, out of fear or a very twisted love/hate relationship—or maybe even both. I am sure that my Father responded to her control by being a handful. My Mother told me that my grandmother would "wash his mouth out" with soap and lock him in a closet when he misspoke or misbehaved. Minnie may have done this to my grandfather as well. (I think she liked torture, having been raised in a strange abuse cycle, too, although she never spoke about it.)

As Minnie was not the maternal type, my Father was raised by Julia, his black "Mammy." Julia's mother worked as a housekeeper for my great-grandmother and helped to raise Minnie. They played together as kids. I believe she was one of her few friends, though not openly. Julia—short, with a soft round figure—appears in many early family pictures, usually standing next to my Father or grandmother, her hair neatly combed and wearing a crisp, white uniform.

She cooked and cleaned for the family for many years long before I was born. Her delicious meals, especially Southern Fried Chicken, which she cooked every Sunday dinner were something to forever remember. In the South, "dinner" is a heavy meal at noon on Sunday, while if you eat at night, that is called "supper."

Julia was a member of our family until at least the early '60s. She was an important part of our ancestral heritage, so she certainly deserves to be mentioned. She did not live with the family, coming over each day. She was paid to work and not enslaved. Much later, I learned that my grandfather bought her a house when her black (segregated) neighborhood was demolished due to gentrification.

It was not the Southern way to ask Julia her age, but I guess she was around my grandmother's age (born in 1894). Boy, she did not look that old! There is a saying in the South that "black don't crack"—that people of African descent tend to wrinkle less with age than those with fairer skin—or one could simply say "blacks do not show their age like whites."

Nuts of Many Varieties

Minnie was raised in the old family home on Buckelew Street, in what is now the downtown area of Shreveport. This large, white-framed structure was within walking distance of the family hardware business on Texas Street.

I am not sure of Minnie's relationship with her mother and father (my great-grandparents), only that her father died of a lingering illness around the age of 37. This is according to the obituary published in the *Shreveport Caucasian* (which later became *The Shreveport Times*) in April 1903. Minnie would have been around nine years old.

My Father was very close to my great-grandmother, whose name was also Sidney. He was the apple of her eye and they adored each other. She attended all of his baseball games and cheered loudly for him.

Minnie's youth is not clear to me. I know she was an intelligent woman, because she went to Mary Baldwin, a liberal arts women's college in Staunton, Virginia. I found records of her time there from 1913 and 1914. She was described as "a right smart piece" by her associates.

She majored in art and continued to dabble in it later in life. I particularly remember one watercolor and one pen and ink drawing (her two favorite mediums) showing blood dripping from a knife and a raven—which could have been alluding to unsavory family behavior. I know she loved to read Edgar Allen Poe. Maybe she was into her dark side, too—but, as I have been told, the dark side does not forgive.

Minnie left or graduated from Mary Baldwin College shortly after 1914. My Father was born in 1915, according to his birth certificate. I was not able to find Minnie and John's marriage certificate; I assume they were legally married before my Father entered the world, but until I find any evidence, I cannot know for sure.

She was a member of the Golf Club at Mary Baldwin, which I found interesting, as I never saw as much as a single club hanging around her house. I also never saw her exercising, aside from playing yard croquet or yard golf once or twice. It just goes to show there was much I did not know about her! She was truly a woman of many endeavors and an extremely hard "nut to crack."

Like my Mother, she also hated her first name. As one of her classmates at Mary Baldwin wrote in her yearbook, "If you were thoughtless enough to call her Minnie, all displays of wrath would be vented upon you!" I would not doubt the truth of this for a moment. I have thought the same myself when I am being teased and called Sidney by John, my eldest half-brother.

Minnie and my Mother never got on. It may have been their stubborn personalities and separate value systems; but there was a very real dislike beneath their fake Southern smiles, most likely due to jealousy over my Father. I believe their only commonality was their unfailing devotion to my Father.

In a lot of ways, my grandmother was the antithesis of my Mother. For one thing, she was not outwardly beautiful. My grandmother had a lifelong career as well as a marriage with three children. My Mother gave up on being a Doctor of Dentistry to become a housewife and raise six kids. I believe my Mother resented my grandmother and her career, since that was never an option for her. My Mother insisted that I get a college degree. Her dream of a professional career outside the home was much more important than I had ever imagined.

My paternal grandfather was also a character, although he was overshadowed by Minnie. He enlisted and was tough enough to serve in World War I, but I do not know any of the details of his service.

My Father, John Edward Junior, followed in his footsteps, starting in the Reserve Officers' Training Corps, early in school. He served in the army during World War II, training and commanding many men. I have a picture of him as a Major at the Jungle Training Center Headquarters in the Pacific. He rose to the rank of Lieutenant Colonel before the war's end, receiving the Bronze Star and a Presidential Commendation.

My paternal grandfather was tall and played basketball at Shreveport High (later C. E. Byrd High School), as shown in an old team photo. My Father, by contrast, was short, favoring his mother's side. Even so, he was a baseball catcher from his youth until college at Louisiana State University (or LSU), with many pictures in old yearbooks documenting his prowess. He did not complete college due to the war.

We, the grandchildren, called our paternal grandfather "Dump," poor fellow. I do not know how that name came about or why we called him that. I can only speculate. Dump hated having his picture taken and always covered his face—it was like he was playing hide-and-seek with the camera or maybe he was *in hiding*, period.

Dump always carried Lifesavers candy in his pocket—it was mostly mint but, on rare occasions, he had my favorite, butterscotch. I clearly remember focusing on his hand and fingers when he used his thumb to dislodge one mint at a time. He would go from one sibling to another, secretly giving each of us a mint, as though I was the only special one. I caught onto his game but continued to play along.

I always thought my paternal grandmother and grandfather were an odd pair. From what I could see, their marriage was odd, too. During their golden years, they slept in separate bedrooms, with twin beds. In the end, though, this seemed normal, since married couples on television, such as Lucy and Ricky Ricardo (from *The Lucy Show*) and Dick and Laura Petrie (from *The Dick Van Dyke Show*), also slept in separate beds.

My Mother told me that Minnie once learned that Dump was stepping out on her (most probably due to there being no sex or love in their marriage). She put an ad in the local newspaper, telling the whole town about his affair—and obviously not caring what the town thought about her. I liken her actions to Facebook drama today. I certainly found her thought patterns unusual and quite humorous. Others may find this story humorous as well. I am not sure Dump did, though. Minnie pretty much did whatever she wanted, when she wanted. She certainly lived her life somewhere "beyond."

I clearly remember that my Father did not get along with his father: he tolerated him, but I do not think he respected him. I never knew the reason for this, although my grandmother might have had something to do with the development of that attitude. My Father was a true "King Baby." In many ways, he was the flipside of my Mother: she was a "sealed book," while he was an "unchained melody." Interestingly, they were both born in late October.

Dump's family heritage was notable, his father—my great-grandfather—being called Henry or "Old Henry." Old Henry's father, my great-great-grandfather, who was called "Old Old" Henry or Henri, emigrated in 1837, arriving at Ellis Island from Alsace, France. Old Old Henry's parents were French and German.

Old Henry was born in Louisiana in 1859 and studied in Germany during his youth. He later became an attorney. For more than thirty years, he specialized in land claims in Louisiana. He served in the Louisiana Legislature as a State Representative for sixteen years and was also a Justice of the Peace. From 1916 to 1920, he also served as the Secretary of Treasury for the State of Louisiana under Governor Pleasant—who was the thirty-sixth Governor of Louisiana.

Before that, Old Henry authored a variety of acts as a State Representative under Governor Sanders, from 1908 to 1912. Some of these, mostly relating to business and transportation, were good for the state; but one was not—a legislative act of concubinage introduced in 1908, which later became law and defined concubinage in Louisiana.[3]

This law made it a felony for a person of white race and a person of black race *to live together*, with imprisonment for not less than a month and not more than a year as punishment. It also covered rights of inheritance and those of the children born from the union. Concubinage had a long history in ancient civilizations before being defined as such late in the fourteenth century.

Louisiana was not the only state to pass laws about black and white people *living together* during this time. Rightfully, this law and many other similar ones were abolished from the late sixties onward. There is a 1967 United States Supreme Court ruling, *Loving v. Virginia*, that repealed and made unconstitutional all state laws against interracial marriages. This landmark civil rights decision ruled that laws banning interracial marriage violate Equal Protection and Due Process under the Fourteenth Amendment.

I certainly always wondered why my Father would mention concubines. Historically, though, there were many unclear lines between my ancestors' relationships with blacks.

Old Henry was also a thirty-second-degree Mason (a member of the Caddo Lodge of the Masons), a Shriner (at the El Karubah Temple), a member of the Eastern Star, and a member of the Woodmen of the World—a fraternal organization founded in 1882, "after the Civil War". ("After the Civil War" is a Southern saying often used to establish a timeline—after all, according to some of my ancestors, there was only ONE war in the South).

This "fraternity" was concerned with helping others, promoting patriotism and civic responsibility, and providing financial protection for families. It also had something to do with private life insurance, which had grown since the middle of the nineteenth century. Although the concept of life insurance initially emerged in ancient Greece and Rome, only in 1875 was it available to the working class.[4]

Apparently, some members of the Woodmen of the World arranged for tree stumps to be erected as tombstones following their death, with thoughts of "a cleared conscience" and "a cleared forest" being synonymous. So much for the environment and the tree huggers! Such a comparison would be considered somewhere "beyond" today.

Old Henry died at the age of 68, following a sudden heart attack, with his funeral being held at the Scottish Rite Cathedral. He had purchased much land during the early years of the Depression. These purchases resulted in my family inheriting various landholdings that have survived today and have contributed greatly to our family legacy.

Family Legacy

As stated previously, Minnie was an artist and much of her legacy involved her art and writing. She was an avid genealogist, placing much more emphasis on her own family name than my grandfather's. This was before the computer so she traveled many miles to visit libraries and research everything the "old-fashioned way."

There was also a legacy of tradition. On Christmas Day, my grandmother phoned my Father (both using rotary phones) to say the words "Christmas Gift!" It was later explained to me that the greeting "Christmas Gift!" was a Southern holiday tradition from the early nineteenth century. This tradition involves waking up on Christmas morning and being the first to say "Christmas Gift!" to someone, who is then expected to give you a gift in return. It may have appeared in letters from Southern soldiers during the Civil

War, but the tradition became popular in upstate South Carolina during the '30s and '40s. This exchange between Minnie and my Father continued until she was no longer able to dial her telephone. It continues today between my brothers.

Minnie's other very important legacy—the family hardware business—was founded by her male ancestors in 1869. Once she became the family matriarch, after her ancestors had either passed or were no longer interested, she BECAME the hardware business. The hardware business subsequently became the meaning of her life. I believe her marriage to my grandfather began and ended as a business one. In any case, Minnie certainly wore the pants; when she held the reins of the marriage and the business. My poor grandfather never knew what hit him (the same being true for any other male relative within striking distance).

Dump was the President of the hardware business until his later years, my Father was the Vice President, and Minnie—or Dan Dan, as we also called her—was the Secretary/Treasurer. We all knew who the real boss was, though, and it was not Dump. My Father drove him to work every day. During the week, they took an hour or two for lunch at our house, which was a full-blown dinner meal. My Mother was a great cook, especially her pot roasts, which were accompanied by rice, green beans, and gravy. After lunch, my Father drove Dump back to the business, where my Father continued to work while Dump retired to his couch for a long nap.

Finally, there is a legacy of inherited traits, including physicality, personalities, and behaviors. Like lagniappe, my Father, along with his mother and father and their ancestors, were gifts that kept on giving. He was a genius and very complicated—too complicated for simple day-to-day activities. My Mother's organizing complimented my Father's lack of balance. She put his clothes out each day and made daily lists of important things, which he stuck in his hat as he went off to work. His work desk was definitely disordered, but he seemed to make sense of it. He instinctively knew where everything was and screamed the minute you took a piece of paper from it.

Looking back, I believe my Father inherited much of his extreme behavior from Dump, although Minnie definitely had her moments and passed on much of her special personality to a few lucky ones— both my Father and me.

———————————————————

PAINFULLY GROWING UP

The Apple Does Not Fall TOO Far from the Tree

I am a natural child of my Mother and Father: no in vitro fertilization, no adoption—I am a "unique genetic combination" of both. Unfortunately, I also carry their flawed genes, identifying with the feminine and masculine, the yin and yang, the light and dark—and, sometimes, the very dark.

I believe neither of them really knew how to love or what love is! How true is the statement "the sins of the Father are visited upon the children." I have often suffered from the actions of both of my parents.

I once read that the quote above means that God is "merely allowing the consequences of sin to run its natural course." I guess that is why my paternal grandmother drew pictures of daggers and had to stop drinking wine, because she "loved the smell so much." As I mentioned before, alcoholism runs rampant on both sides of my family.

Until the age of seven, I grew up in a small house on Elwood Circle in the Madison Park Subdivision of Shreveport. Outwardly, it appeared to be an ideal childhood home. We lived at the back of a quiet circle or cul-de-sac. I could have played for hours outside not worrying about the traffic, but I do not have any fond memories of doing so.

In August 1954, the Elmwood household numbered five: my Mother, my Father, two siblings—including Raymond, my adopted older half-brother, plus my (older) non-sister—and me. My younger, middle, and youngest "blood brothers" came into the world in 1955, 1957, and 1961.

It was behind the closed doors of this seemingly peaceful house— not the Elm Street of nightmares—that I was introduced to the darkness. I am not sure exactly when the abuse began; but I believe it was before I was born. It continued throughout my childhood and long into my adulthood. I was too young to figure it out or determine why; I only knew that danger was evident, so remained alert for the unknown violence.

I was cursed with remembering things, seeing and hearing many things my other siblings did not. I was, in a way, the first "chosen one." My headboard backed onto the wall of my parents' bedroom and I was a light sleeper. I heard yelling through their closed door and the sounds of physical violence—of fist hitting flesh.

Although my Father's childhood wounds may have been the root cause of his violence, my Mother's behavior, at times, would be the catalyst. She knew he was a man of extremes and she had ways of sparking his anger—a violent temper that would erupt without warning. My Mother must have known she was playing a dangerous game.

Still, my Father's violence cannot be condoned. Maybe he did not need an excuse. I eventually realized that the cause did not matter: his anger was always sizzling beneath.

It mostly occurred on the weekends, after they had gone out to dinner or been to a party. My Father would get mad at my Mother for drinking too much and feel jealous of her talking (and most probably flirting) with other men. He was extremely possessive and her behavior irritated him considerably. She was expected to be an obedient wife and mother. Maybe she just craved attention—she was a beautiful woman, after all.

Her behavior changed immediately when his anger emerged. Eventually, though, she appeared to become accustomed to the fear, as the abuse became oddly familiar. She had experienced it before and took it stoically. Did she feel a certain strength because she was able to take it? If so, the cycle was even sicker. That realization caused their past wounds and current power struggles to become most *real* to me.

As Martin Page put it in his song "In My Room," my Father would, "like clockwork, bring home drunken threats." Page sings that "he won't be pacified," and my Mother ultimately did not have the "strength to resist." Indeed, "I hear my Mother cry."

Playlist Song #2:
"In My Room," by Martin Page.

WAY BEYOND THE GRITS | SIDNEY KATE

My Mother and I never spoke about my "early listening," which is a shame. At the very least, I think it would have been cathartic for both of us.

On occasion, we as children bore the brunt of my Father's violence, too. I do not remember him ever hitting me. I managed to escape most of his physical actions, except for the occasional spanking (which never really hurt) or a whipping from a branch of the weeping willow in our backyard. It stung my skin, but did not break me. I never cried. The emotion was alien to me.

My brothers became targets if they tried to protect my Mother and got within his reach. And once a target, however young or old, and however unwarranted, the physical abuse would subsequently continue.

I tried not to become a target. I was always there, but quietly observing from the shadows, trying to keep away from the destruction. My scars did not show but nonetheless existed, as a rawness deep inside me. My hurt certainly fueled my own anger and definitely directed many of my decisions later in life.

What Is Good for the Gander Is NOT Good for the Goose

While it was not okay for my Mother to interact with other men outside the marriage, the opposite was true for my Father. He had a wandering eye, which took him to dark places with many other women, who saw him as a handsome and successful businessman. Outwardly, he was a dedicated family man; but inwardly, he was a philandering Casanova.

I was *younger than five* when I saw something I never should have seen.

One weekday, my Mother somehow found out that rather than being at the hardware store, my Father was entertaining a woman at the Camp on Bistineau, my grandparents' second home. My Mother had the brilliant idea to take me with her as she "caught" my Father in another woman's arms.

I watched the scenario unfold from start to finish. My Mother drove Raymond and I to the Camp, just in time to catch them naked in bed. I stood next to my Mother as I stared at my Father, not understanding why he was there without us and why he was lying naked on top of some strange woman.

Of course, I was confused by the scene! My young mind may have wondered whether this was normal—why else would my Mother take me there? I had yet to learn about sex.

It later became apparent that my Mother *wanted* my Father to see his little girl there. That was part of her plan: she wanted to shame him and let him know that there were other witnesses to his behavior. She wanted to demonstrate that she had some power, too, however unfair it was to me.

My Mother and Father exchanged a few heated words. I do not remember hearing my Mother cuss—she was too much of a lady for that—but boy, could she give a look. Outwardly, she remained in charge. Was this the trump card in a game?

Soon after, she threw me into the car, ordered Raymond to get in, and sped home. Thankfully, we did not have an accident. At the house, she tossed some clothes into her suitcase and gathered all of us—including my non-sister and younger brother—into the station wagon, with the *outward intention* of leaving my Father for good.

I cried, refusing to get in the car and screaming that I was not leaving "Daddy"! I loved my Father. I was certainly too young to understand this adult situation.

At about that time, my Father appeared, in a panic, without the other woman. I ran to him. He apologized to my Mother, telling her he loved her over and over and begging her not to leave. He professed he would not do it again and may have cried a little, for effect. Ultimately, he "sweet-talked" her into staying. Boy, was that some great acting. Watching and listening, I took him at his word. I, too, believed him to be sincere. I learned that words are not cheap. Words have the power to soothe; but also to excite, to destroy— and, in this case, to deceive.

At this point, my Mother was definitely not thinking like a mother. I do not believe she ever considered the situation from my perspective or had a single thought about how it might affect me. She was acting on emotions and reacting to the moment, with a singular focus on getting back at my Father in any way she could. She was trying to defend herself and maintain her perceived power.

She did not think about protecting me, although my non-sister was saved from the encounter, being somewhere else.

This destructive pattern of behavior continued, as I saw both parents fighting to influence the other's behavior. I began to see both sides of the inequity. Although "normal" society would have seen my young Mother as the *total* victim in an abusive relationship, she was *not* a total victim. Later in life, she became one, by her own choice. Theirs was a love/hate relationship, so the power struggles persisted for many years. Neither ever realized what real power each had within themselves. They were both very flawed.

Innocence Gone

I blamed my Mother for my loss of innocence that day. She could have let me be. There were many newspaper articles about husbands cheating at that time.[5] Like Minnie and her newspaper ad, I liken writing letters to newspapers in the '50s and '60s to modern "Facebook drama." My Mother should have sought professional help, but that was not something she would ever do.

I tried to let go of that day's memories at the Camp—or, at the very least, rationalize them and just accept them for what they are—in order to get on with my life. Truthfully, however, they still haunt me.

Being female, I related to my Mother first and foremost. I wanted to look like her and I wanted to be her. She sometimes dressed me up to look like her—I was her "Mini Me." I did the typical young girly stuff like wear her pill box hats and put on her make-up, including red lipstick that I thought would never come off. She was an avid fashionista and, many would say, a true outward beauty until the day she died.

"Mini Me" at Lake Bistineau, with my parents.

In my earlier years, my Mother bore the brunt of my inner anger, while my Father skated away. He remained blissfully unaware of the damage he had caused until later in life. When I was about five, I tried to run away from her, pedaling furiously on my bicycle. My Mother sent Raymond to find me and bring me home; which he did, even though I tried to hide from him. I was not happy; I knew that nothing was going to change.

Raymond was my Mother's original confidant, although I took over as soon as I was able to listen. From an early age, we were both treated like adults. Raymond was always an obedient son, as far as I could tell. I was an obedient daughter, up to a point.

Thereafter, for many years, I was on the receiving end of her many talks about my Father's behavior. After all, I was *his* daughter. I was now part of my Mother's "Special Club," as she confided her feelings and emotions to me.

My Mother was a stay-at-home wife and mom, who survived on a weekly allowance. Most women of the time did not work outside the home, so it was not uncommon for them to depend upon their husbands for monetary survival. That did not mean these women did not work, though. My Mother was our sole day-to-day caretaker, which, in my opinion, *was* hard work. My Father was the breadwinner; he held the "purse strings". To be honest, my Mother could not have financially supported us by herself.

Much later, as an adult, I asked my Mother why she never left him. She flatly replied: "because he would have abandoned his children. He would not want to take care of you any longer and you would have all been separated and given up to foster care." I do not know whether this would have been true—but, sadly, I still have not seen any evidence to contradict it. Who knows what my Father might have done? I wanted to think she was projecting. The Father I *knew* loved me. Why would he abandon me? Much later, I learned this could be partly true. He would abandon me, at least once.

From that day on, and for many years to come, I questioned their actions, deciding "if this is love, I do not want any part of it." Yes, I lost my innocence that day at the Camp. It scarred me then, and for many years thereafter, as I experienced my own hurtful relationships. To this day, I still see marriage as painful and run away from long-term commitment. Marriage can be a very flawed and broken institution.

Playlist Song #3:
"When I Fall in Love," by Nat King Cole.

Only later did I begin to remember other things about my childhood, seeing a past life regressionist in my twenties. At the session, I did not think the process worked: I saw only darkness, feeling that I was in a dark room or extremely large closet, where something bad was happening to me. I could never figure out what, exactly, but I thought of "the creepy room" in Minnie and Dump's house.

On many Saturdays, my Father took me to that house, for Minnie to watch me while he "worked." I know now that may have been an excuse to do God knows what with other women. I was just old enough to realize that my Mother attached me to my Father on weekend mornings to make sure he did not "run around"—but he soon found a way around that. Oddly, I do not have any good memories of baking cookies at my grandmother's house. Maybe I will remember some of the good someday, although I strongly doubt it. Maybe she did other things besides watch me but my defense mechanisms have prevented me from remembering them.

The "creepy room" was above the garage. I always felt that darkness or evil lurked there, remembering my grandmother's drawing of the bloody knife. Was that my imagination or a repressed memory?

After my Father died, I had a sexual dream in which my grandmother and a teenage boy were standing over me in that room. I saw much not-so-normal behavior before the magic age of six that was not a regression or maybe not a dream.

What Has Love Got to Do with It?

One day, as an adult, I was going through my childhood things and found "Sister Belle." She is a pull-string ragdoll made by Mattel toys, who said "I love you" when the ring attached to the line was pulled. Sister Belle was my friend. I took much comfort from her when I was a young child.

There was a problem with Sister Belle, though: she became damaged. I felt an overwhelming urge to cry (which I almost never did). Not only was she unable to talk anymore, but I had also drawn a black vertical line on each of her wrists. Did Sister Belle try to kill herself or had I repressed a memory of an attempted or—more distressing—actual suicide of someone else?

Luckily for me, Sister Belle did not kill herself but was placed in a box to be found much later in life. Sister Belle survived—and so did I, although Sister Belle had forever been prevented from telling the story I assume she witnessed hanging by my side—my little hand in hers—when she *could* say the words "I love you."

Vintage Mattel 1961 talking ragdoll—Sister Belle.

My siblings likely do not remember the following event, because they were not there. As "Mini Me," it seemed I was always near my Mother—attached at the hip. Of the many strange events of my childhood, this one haunts me the most.

At around the age of five, I was sitting on the floor of the room off the kitchen, adjacent to the living room, silently playing. It was Raymond's room, but he was not there. It was late morning or early afternoon, because my Father was not there—he was probably at work.

A female neighbor rang the doorbell. My Mother greeted her as a friend. She brought in a casserole. My Mother made coffee and they sat at the kitchen table. At first, it was very friendly, as they idly chatted about life. Suddenly their voices became louder. I knew they were talking about my Father, although I could not hear what they were saying.

Suddenly, Ruby, our black nanny, came flying out of the back room where the washer and dryer were. She had been listening and decided to take action, grabbing Sister Belle and me and placing us both in the coat closet near the front door. She wanted us out of harm's way, in preparation for what was about to happen. She left the closet door ajar so I would not be too scared in the darkness. My breathing quickened with my mounting fear.

I saw it all through the slit in the door. I can hear my breathing now, as I look down at my Mary Jane shoes. I was fearful about what was coming.

Ruby grabbed a kitchen knife and stabbed at the neighbor—there was a lot of blood everywhere. Emotions ran high as my Mother—who was never physically violent—looked aghast at Ruby's vicious actions. Who could fathom what she secretly thought!

I continued to watch as medical help was sought, my Father and grandmother being called. I remember my grandmother rushing in and whisking me away from the horrific scene.

I received no explanation as to why. I was too young to understand. Right! All of the players remained silent. My Father and grandmother took care of the neighbor's wounds. Later, I believed she was "paid off" in order to go away, or just maybe my Father continued to see her and supported her for the rest of her life. Who knows?

Eventually, I learned the rest of the Ruby story. My Father had been having an affair with the neighbor and had told her he was going to leave my Mother and marry her. This woman believed his lies, so she decided to confront my Mother, under the ruse of suddenly dropping by for a friendly visit. But her attempts backfired when Ruby—who, I later learned, had also had "relations" with my Father—overheard and acted on her own emotions. In a weird twist, I feel Ruby was standing up for my Mother.

Ruby was "let go" several years later, when she went after her own mother, Julia, with a knife. I remember her being a little too excitable and I think she probably had a mental breakdown. She had the most soothing Southern voice. I believe she truly cared about us kids. She never retaliated against the family.

I also learned later that my Father—a "King Baby" and a narcissist— would send his "mistresses" money and buy them cars. One day several years later, when I was in my early forties, I noticed he had transferred $30,000 to my checking account. I called him to thank him, but he said he had made a mistake and asked me if he could "take the money back?"

I should have said "No, too late!"—but I complied with his wishes, never asking him to explain himself. Apparently, he was sending the money to someone else and had sent it to my account by mistake.

It was certainly not earmarked for any of my brothers. Who knows what he was up to?!

His affairs and philandering continued until he was too old to "get it up," being reduced to "blow jobs" from the black housekeeper. I do not think my Mother liked oral sex much. Years later, I vaguely remember my Mother mentioning syphilis when I was in college. Maybe he did suffer, although he was certainly treated and escaped dying from this venereal disease. Either way, it would have served him right. My Mother stuck by him so he was never physically alone.

It was many years later that I realized how fundamentally these early memories affected me. As a small child, my mind would have had a hard time processing these events and the violence I observed. I am still working on processing it to this day. The witnessing of anger and violence affected all of us, but it produced some *very strange* behavior from me.

Do NOT Try This at Home!

As a child, I seemed shy, yet there was an underlying anger and aggression I dared not expose. It eventually came out in an interaction with my younger brother, when my small-minded patience was tested.

My younger brother is my Irish Twin: we are the same age for eleven days each year. He was born on August 2, before my birthday on August 13.

One of the things that ticked me off about my younger brother was that he was constantly demanding attention. He was always bragging that he was right about everything! Definitely a "know it all," from the time he could talk. He always took the opposite side of every argument: if I said it was so, he said it was not. He could have been a great lawyer like Old Henry, his great-grandfather.

My younger brother was smart enough to goad me with it. He was constantly causing trouble—and if I called him out on it, he argued his way out of it. I nicknamed him "The Professor," because he knew it all and was, at least in his young mind, always smarter than me.

One day, I had had enough of him. He was pretending to smoke a stick shaped like a cigar, puffing away and pointing out how good "the smoke" was, going on and on for several minutes.

Finally, I could not take any more—I reached out and tried to grab the stick, to make him stop. He clamped down on it, so I struggled to get it from his mouth, pushing it in and then out in an attempt to dislodge it from his lips.

I pushed too hard, though, and the stick went down his throat. All I remember is the extreme surprise on his face—his eyes as big as saucers! Suddenly, all this blood came rushing from his mouth—so much that I thought I had killed him.

My Mother rushed in, grabbed him, then hurried out of the door, leaving me alone with my perplexed shame, to face the consequences later. I did not go with them, because who knew whether I was going to attempt to finish him off during the car ride.

A very long time passed before he returned. I learned several hours later that he was treated successfully but had to have one of his tonsils removed.

You know what is ironic about all of this? He came marching in, proudly waving a small jar with his tonsil in it and proclaiming he was going to take it to "Show and Tell" at elementary school the next day. That was always a good way for teachers to learn what really went on behind a family's closed doors.

I did not know how he was going to explain these circumstances away: "my sister tried to kill me but LOOK what I got out of it!" I was sure he would think of something. He was good at making up stories, so I could only hope he would not incriminate my Mother for not paying attention to the negative behavior of her children.

The good—and bad—news was my younger brother lived to continue infuriating us. He eventually got me back for the tonsillectomy, in college, when he took my first car, a Pontiac Firebird, and jacked it up with big tires, painting it "pea green." I never saw the entertainment value in hot rods, but I guess tire size does matter. Fortunately for all of us, he is still alive today and makes my life much better.

My aggressive behavior came out in other ways, too—such as sticking mothballs up my nose, which my Mother had to tweeze out of me. I am surprised my nose still exists.

Although the following story is a minor one, it may be offensive to dog lovers. One of our dogs, apparently hungry, tried to grab a piece of food from my hand, but instead bit my finger. IT HURT! As my Mother told it, I "hauled off" and bit the dog back, causing it to whine loudly and scramble quickly away.

For some reason, my Mother got a kick out of telling that story. I really do not know why. Maybe she was proud of my aggression— my message was "don't mess with me, you silly dog." She was encouraging me to "bite back" at anyone or anything trying to take something from me. *Lesson learned.* The dog was afraid to come near me and never again tried to take any more food from me. So beware all dogs (dawgs), canine or human! Even today, I might "haul off" and bite back...

———————————————————

LEARNING LIFE LESSONS

Lake Bistineau

Not all my memories of Lake Bistineau involve my Father's infidelity. I learned a lot about life in general. Aside from my middle brother being bitten by a snake—prompting another emergency medical visit—I have many fond recollections of our time there, such as playing lawn croquet and grilling barbecues on July the Fourth as well as learning how to snap beans, pick mayhaw berries, and churn peach ice cream.

Mayhaw berry bushes and snapping beans at the Camp on Lake Bistineau.

There was also a lot of fishing for bass as well as swimming and water skiing on the lake with its moss-topped trees. I learned to enjoy the water and loved to jump in, feet first.

On one occasion, we were on vacation and took turns jumping into a swimming pool. My Father would catch us, before we would swim back, climb up, then jump in again. We had a great rotation going, but my Father became distracted while talking to someone else. I became impatient waiting for him, so I jumped in while he was not looking. I remained under the water for what seemed like an eternity, tugging on his swimming trunks and frantically trying to get his attention, before he finally looked down just as I felt close to drowning. It was a good thing that I was not jumping into the murky water of Lake Bistineau or he may never have found me!

Thankfully, my Father seized me with genuine concern. Of course, I ended up okay—or maybe not. I can still hold my breath underwater for long periods, having been conditioned from necessity early in life.

Nevertheless, my parents thought I needed some further aquatic education, so they signed me up for the swim team. This was an unpleasant and stressful experience. I was exposed to Coach Rountree, a loud "drill sergeant," who scared me into submission.

The practice sessions were at the Pierremont Oaks Swim Club, early in the morning—I cannot believe my Mother got me there on time! I think I was sacrificed so my parents could get a better deal on a new car, Coach Rountree being from the local "Olds Cadillac" car dealership family. One of many early negotiations by my Father: a child swimmer for a good deal on a car.

On to raising goats... One year, my Mother and Father decided we needed some farm animals at the lake property, so they bought a herd of goats. They justified this purchase by stating that the goats would eat—and therefore control—the weeds.

We all became goat herders! Most of my siblings chose the nanny or female goats; but I, being different, chose to get a billy or male goat. Maybe there was a little symbolism in the choice, too. After all, billy goats are the confident ones, which like to climb and stand tall above the others, driving themselves to become king of the mountain. I wanted to be like those goats. But there was one drawback, unfortunately: billy goats have a repulsive musk to them, so my goat "stunk."

In any case, the goat phase did not last for long: they did their job and opened up a pastureland by eating all the weeds. Today, we might have made a profit from goat yoga!

Lake Bistineau produced more than swimmers and goats, however. It also produced fruits from shrubs and trees, especially mayhaw bushes and pear trees. Minnie cooked and canned her mayhaw jelly from a recipe passed down by one of her ancestors. Dump maintained a massive pear orchard, which produced many delicious pears. Both Minnie and my Mother used his pears to make *their own individual versions* of pear jelly—another competition between them that my Father did not want to judge.[6] Both pear jellies were introduced to our Sunday morning breakfast of warm biscuits. To this day, I cannot eat a pear without thinking of Dump.

Dump could be outwardly gruff. Other than sleeping on the couch in his office, he spent most of his later years sitting in a lawn chair with a shotgun, shooting at any winged predator that dared to approach his prized pear trees. He guarded them ferociously.

He hated the woodpeckers—which he called "peckerwoods"— that bore into the tree's bark and damaged the fruit. But he also despised the crows, which swarmed the branches and vehemently feasted on the fruits and their seeds. They were easier to shoot than the woodpeckers, which were shiftier and less predictable. Although they are smart, they have long been thought to signal bad luck, so I guess the more crows he killed, the better luck he had.

When I was around seven, I found a bathing suit from the Roaring Twenties tucked neatly into an old armoire at the Camp. Little did I know what mischief Minnie would use it for later in life. When Dump passed away in the early '70s, while I was in high school, Minnie sold her house and moved into a condo. She had to deal with condo association rules thereafter. The group ruled on what apparel was appropriate for the swimming pool. Minnie took offense and marched over to the office in her bathing suit from the Roaring Twenties, which covered her body from her neck to knees, asking "Do I have permission to wear this?" I am sure it provoked reactions from all who witnessed the spectacle.

Bathing suit from the Roaring Twenties.

I did not inherit the bathing suit, but I still have a whole-body fox stole that Minnie wore in the '30s and '40s—a fox's body from snout to tail, which wraps around the shoulder, held together by a clasp. The animal rights people would have a field day with this stole today.

Business in My Heart and Hardware in My Veins

I have an affinity for business as well as much creativity within me. I inherited a little of both from Minnie. I am much more like my grandmother than I initially thought. There is also a degree of hardness in my blood which aligns with the hardware business.

Minnie was very frugal—much tighter than a drum, as we say. I initially attributed it to her Scottish heritage, but she was just plain cheap. I believe she always was. It certainly helped during the Depression, when she was forced to find alternative enterprising ways to make and save money.

She definitely had a keen eye for business. She had grown up around it. My cousin once told me that Minnie invented but was not given credit for the waffle cone. I later read that the waffle cone was in fact introduced in 1904, at the St. Louis World Fair, when Minnie would only have been ten years old. So, my cousin was WRONG! Unless, of course, the other news is fake! She may perhaps have invented a Southern version of the waffle cone.

That same cousin also told me that my great aunt invented the wring mop. I cannot find any evidence of that, either; but this cousin further mentioned she received patent royalties! Total bull, it seems to me, but this great aunt was wealthy, so she must have got her money from somewhere—perhaps even illegally?!

One Christmas, my grandmother gave me a tiny pocketknife. There was a gleam in her eye as she reminded me to "always remember your hardware roots!" Along with the gift was a note: "Keep me in your purse; I'll help solve your problems"—although I am not sure a small pocketknife could solve a young Southern girl's problems. Especially the ones I was privately facing. She also put a shiny penny in the box, so I would never "go broke." The knife is still in the original box, having never been used, but I have long since spent the penny.

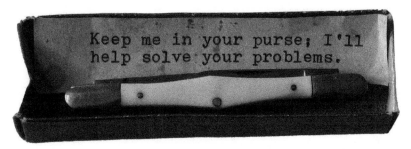

Pocketknife and note.

For Minnie, everything revolved around the business. As she advanced in age, and became "harder" emotionally, her obsession with the hardware business intensified. Boy, was she one cold fish. Let me tell you a little more about THAT VERY IMPORTANT HARDWARE BUSINESS...

The business shaped the lives not only of my grandparents and parents, but also of many earlier ancestors. It dominated my Father's life—when he was not being an army soldier or a philanderer—as well as the lives of my Mother, my brothers, and me.

Although it fueled many generations of independent spirits, it also did something to their souls along the way. The hardware business started on Main Street in Shreveport, in 1869. In the photo below, my great-great-grandfather, Wilbur Fisk and close relatives stand in front of it, surrounded by plows and other implements. I often wondered what it would have been like to have lived in the Reconstruction Era immediately following the Civil War. I probably would have been jailed for my independent spirit. If, in fact, I had been a woman—with past lives, you never know.

Outside the old hardware store in the late 1800s.

I have vivid memories of my younger brother and I exploring it, as we did almost every weekend in the late '50s, loving every minute.

I guess my Mother was becoming tired of having us incessantly underfoot, especially my younger brother, who needed to be disciplined every five minutes. It was my Father's turn to watch him while she got her downtime. I, on the other hand, was less active, but that did not mean I was an easy child.

The family hardware business had been established in Shreve Town on Texas Avenue, along the old Texas Trail—an overland route into the new independent Republic of Texas.[7] The downtown "store" was dated to just after THE WAR (Civil War). It has since been remodeled over the years. I loved drawing buildings as a child and it looked magnificent to me, consisting of several levels with high ceilings, long windows, and creaky wooden floors, which added to its charm as well as its eeriness.

I had many visions of "sugarplums" while drawing up my Christmas list. The 50s store offered bountiful products—all the goods sat on rows, the gadgets were on shelves in glass cases, and various implements hung from the walls and ceilings. It was packed to the hilt with everything from pin nails to baseball bats to plows and other heavy machinery, all in their own sections. I was particularly drawn to the bicycles and sporting goods, which I could relate to as a young child in the '50s.

Inside the old hardware store in 1914.

My younger brother was always getting into trouble, so I, as his not much older sister, watched over him while my Father "worked." Once my hellion brother had significantly disrupted the main floor, he decided he wanted to explore the basement. There was a dark and creepy staircase leading down to an equally dark and damp basement. It had the same ominous feeling as the bedroom over the garage at my paternal grandmother's house. The basement was off limits to us; mainly because we could be injured down there if unsupervised by an adult.

To prevent us from exploring, my Father told my younger brother that Rastas Jones, a dangerous criminal, was imprisoned there. Rastas was a crazy soul who would devour any child entering his world.

This did not scare my younger brother one bit, because he liked to push boundaries and reveled fearlessly in the danger (or perhaps he was smart enough to know that my Father was making everything up). My younger brother was hyperactive and very much like my Father, although he will emphatically state he is not! He certainly has his good qualities.

The building was kept in the family for many years, until it was sold and turned into a TGI Fridays. It is currently "The Blind Tiger"—a Cajun restaurant. The hardware business lived on elsewhere. It was expanded to several locations throughout the city during the late '50s and early 60s. All in all, my memories of the downtown store are good ones. As we say, life goes on...

Television: From Black-and-White to Color

The innovations of the '50s and '60s greatly affected my own history and day-to-day life in the South. One of the main things I remember, aside from the creation of five-digit zip codes in the '60s, was the onset of color television. The '50s saw the "Golden Age of Television," during which black and white televisions became more affordable—and more popular, experiencing massive growth. I believe this happened because the mass production of goods during World War II created a supply of less expensive products.

Most families could afford a black-and-white television set. Although color transmissions were broadcast in the '50s, color televisions were not introduced to the masses until the '60s.

Our set benefited our family life, mirroring our lives while also allowing us to escape. My Mother loved her daytime soaps, while my Father watched his detective and legal dramas at night. It was *General Hospital* for her and *Perry Mason* for him. I always thought my Father looked a bit like Raymond Burr who played Perry Mason. Maybe that was why I gravitated to the legal field—that and the fact I had it in my genes through "Old Henry."

My Father also loved watching Western dramas, both "shoot ups" and "shoot outs," when he was not reading novels by Louis L'Amour. His two favorites were *Bonanza* and *Gunsmoke*, the latter having been a long-running radio serial, featuring William Conrad as Marshall Matt Dillon. The subsequent television show included a colorful cast of characters, from James Arness, who played Dillon, to a young Bert Reynolds, who played Quint Asper. There was also Miss Kitty, "the sassy owner" of Long Branch Saloon in Dodge City, as well as a Chester and a Festus. (It is odd that the mother of one ex-boyfriend nicknamed me "Kitty"—looking back, I was Kitty.)

Gunsmoke was broadcast in black-and-white until 1966, while Bonanza's debut was broadcast in color in 1959. Until that point, most shows had been in black-and-white. *Perry Mason* continued to be broadcast in black-and-white until it ended in 1966. There was only one episode filmed in color. This episode was "The Case of the Twice-Told Twist".

Color soon dominated. *Mr. Rogers' Neighborhood* was one of the last black-and-white shows on network television. Mister Rogers was a Presbyterian Minister and his show was a favorite of mine, because he catered to children's emotional and social needs. I was definitely needy!

My Father bought many televisions as time went on. "A television in every room" was his slogan. A few of my brothers still adhere to this credo, the television having opened up a new world for us!

In the absence of a television remote, we had to get up and turn the dial to change the channel. It made sense for the lazy ones to sit nearby so they did not have to get up as often. I have several fond memories of sitting with my legs crossed in front of the television, eating a frozen dinner—most probably the Old El Paso Mexican one with tacos, beans, and rice.

Saturday and Sunday nights were my favorite times for sitting so close to the set I could feel the heat from the warming tubes radiating toward me. Who knows what cancerous vapors these tubes may have emitted? After all, I had already been exposed to the toxic and certainly did not need any more.

Life was less hectic on the weekends, as my Mother and Father relaxed a little and enjoyed life more. We turned on the television after supper and danced to the live music of the variety show *Lawrence Welk*. My Father allowed me to stand on his feet and hug his legs as he moved to the music, carefully, so I would not topple off and hurt myself.

Lawrence Welk was a leader of a big band whose music aired on Saturday nights from 1951 to 1971. The show was initially broadcast on the first commercial television station in Los Angeles, before being nationally syndicated on ABC in 1955. In 1965, it started broadcasting in color.

The Lennon Sisters first appeared on the *Lawrence Welk Show* for Christmas Eve 1955. This show opened with the sound of a champagne bottle being uncorked and bubbles floating around. The strange "beyond the" moment involved sound effects. Welk placed a finger over his mouth and then released it, making a popping sound and then a soft hissing sound that mimicked the bubbles escaping from the bottle.

The weekly show usually ended with a solo by the "Champagne Lady"—a gorgeous soprano. Welk called his performers his "musical family," who mainly performed "big band" songs as well as pop songs from the '50s, '60s, and '70s. His regular performers included the Lennon Sisters, but he also hosted Cole Porter and country singer Charley Pride, who made his first national television appearance on the show in 1967. Welk performed a "Salute to Cole Porter" in 1973.

By then, of course, I was too big to dance on my Father's feet. Instead, I was dancing to my own music at LSU.

Not Simply Black-and-White...

I also remember going to "picture shows" or movies, having especially vivid memories of the re-release of *Gone with the Wind* in 1961. This movie was first released in December 1939, to limited theaters. It was later re-released in the spring of 1942, then again in 1947 and 1954—the year of my birth—in widescreen format. A further re-release followed in 1961, premiering at Loew's Grand Theater in Atlanta, commemorating the centennial anniversary of "THE WAR."

Program from the Gone with the Wind re-release
in Metrocolor and stereophonic sound.

I was six years old when it came to Shreveport. The movie was so popular that we waited in a line to enter. I remember my Mother's excitement as she held my hand.

I noticed a line of people to the side and asked my Mother who they were and why they were standing in another line. She replied that they were the black people and they had a different entrance. I did not understand why, but I continued to look, feeling uncomfortable and knowing in my heart there was something wrong about it.

WAY BEYOND THE GRITS | SIDNEY KATE

These "black people" were not allowed to sit in the main theater alongside the "white Caucasians," having to watch the movie from the balcony. I wondered about their lives and turned my head to sneak views of them throughout.

I was too young to fully understand or question how they perceived their portrayal in the film. I simply watched the film for entertainment without considering the underlying racial implications.

The film was also suggestive of female empowerment. I identified with Scarlett O'Hara, a Southern belle, played by Vivien Leigh. I admired her driven spirit and daring approach to life. Little did I know she was a British actress who knew nothing of our Southern world! Damn, she was a great actress.

I loved her character's intellect as she sparred with Rhett Butler, played by Clark Gable, particularly when she tells him: "Sir, you are no gentleman!" His comeback line is priceless: "An apt observation. And you, Miss, are no lady." I laugh today because this line is a tribute to a *REAL SOUTHERN* woman—with whom I most readily identify.

I was also entertained by "Mammy" and "Prissy," played by Hattie McDaniel and Butterfly McQueen, respectively. I particularly enjoyed their few famous lines and exaggerated facial expressions. The lines of the former—such as "What a gentleman says and what they think are two different things" and "I ain't noticed Mist' Ashley axin' for to marry ya"—offered comic relief in contrast to the conceited Scarlett. Another favorite line is Mammy's remark about the character Ashley: "He'll be comin' to Atlanta when he gets his leave, and you sittin' there waitin' for him, just like a spider." Mammy was a wise woman; at all times, she was looking out for "her" Scarlett, which must have been exhausting.

For me, though, Butterfly McQueen's voice and comedic talent were unmistakable. One of the most famous lines in film history is a Prissy line: "Lawzy, we got to have a doctor. I don't know nothin' 'bout birthin' babies"—which she says only a moment after acting like she did, indeed, know how to "birth babies"! Much has been written about the underlying psychology of Prissy. Butterfly McQueen was widely "undervalued" at the time, but my take is that she was mostly in charge when interpreting "Prissy." If you look closely at the character, you can see her hiding aggression behind a false passivity and helplessness—that false passivity is so like Southern women, especially my Mother.

In my opinion, both Mammy and Prissy were wise beyond their time. Southern women of any race do not like to be seen as stupid. Mammy's wisdom was evident, even though Scarlett tended not to listen to it, while Butterfly McQueen's acting of Prissy prevented any such assertion.

Several years later, I read that the black cast members were prevented from attending the Atlanta premiere in a "whites-only" theater, due to Georgia's Jim Crow laws enforcing racial segregation in the South.

Mercifully, the film has not been banned and destroyed—it should still be taken seriously, for its value as historical fiction. Margaret Mitchell's novel of the same name was awarded the Pulitzer Prize for Fiction in 1937.

Another Lesson in the Racial and Gender Mix

During the '60s, television entertainment broadened my educational horizons and thoroughly expanded my very sheltered Southern world. No longer did I have to enter my imagination in order to entertain myself, since television introduced me to people of all ethnicities—people who, I originally thought, were so unlike me.

All baby boomers are likely to remember when The Beatles appeared on *The Ed Sullivan Show*, on February 9, 1964—a performance that was taped at CBS Television City in Hollywood. I thought being British was cool and was mesmerized by them singing the words to "She Loves You." Who would have thought "yeah, yeah, yeah" could prompt so much screaming?

Playlist Song #4:
"She Loves You," by The Beatles.

Sports fans also enjoyed that time. Other than my weekly dancing on my Father's feet, I shared special father/daughter moments watching football with him. I remember watching the first AFL/NFL Super Bowl, in 1967, between the Kansas City Chiefs and the Green Bay Packers (AFL versus NFL). It was broadcast by two television networks simultaneously: NBC held the rights to the AFL games, while CBS held the rights to the NFL games. The two teams vied for the new trophy before more than 61,000 attendees and more than fifty-one million television viewers. There were many celebrity sightings, such as Kirk Douglas, who starred in the movie *Spartacus*, in 1960.

Apparently, the game was blacked out for television in Los Angeles, since it was being played there. Both quarterbacks showed America real football in technicolor. Bart Starr, Alabama's finest, was the "most valuable" player, but Vince Lombardi—who never had a losing season as head coach of the NFL Green Bay Packers—was the real jewel.

Lombardi was ahead of his time in terms of discouraging racism. Displaying fierce opposition to "Jim Crow" discrimination, he supported acceptance; he treated his players as equals. He added black players to his roster at a time when civil rights were paramount. I once read his warning that any player would be thrown off the team if he exhibited prejudice in any way.[8] Similarly, he did not allow his team to stay in any hotel that did not equally accommodate *black and white* players. In 1967, the Packers were the only team to have a policy of not assigning hotel rooms based on race. It is thought that his racial views resulted from his religious faith and the prejudice he experienced as an Italian American.

I, too, adopted my belief in equality from an early age, never thinking of myself as better than anyone else.

———————————————————

WAY BEYOND THE GRITS | SIDNEY KATE

Side Work if You Can Get It

As we say in the South, "I was *not* born with a silver spoon in my mouth." I learned the value of a strong work ethic from my parents, who both worked hard. My family was not wealthy by any means, my Father only receiving a stingy salary from the business. Remember, my grandmother was a tightwad!

His salary alone was not enough to provide for our ever-increasing family. My parents were always looking for ways to make extra money. Like their ancestors before them, they were both smart businesspeople, though they were more progressive. Unlike their parents, they could not hang on to every penny, nickel, and dime, because our family would have starved. It became necessary for my parents to supplement my Father's income with what I call "side" work.

My Father began to buy houses at auctions—mostly duplexes—to renovate and rent out for income. This was progressive for the '50s and early '60s. He would sometimes buy houses in neighborhoods that were being demolished for gentrification, then move them across town to pieces of land that he squeezed out enough money to buy.

The average cost of a house in 1957 was $12,220.00.[9] Back then, making money from rental property was not conventional thinking, unlike today, where it is common, with an abundance of these types of properties and Airbnbs.

My Mother was similarly not afraid of hard work, being the organization behind my Father's financial successes—even dressed in dungarees, her natural beauty never diminished. I remember many days "helping" my Mother paint the interior walls of these cheap investment properties. I was cheap labor, willing and able to try.

This "side" work also shaped my creative future and eventually allowed me to supplement my own income. I have also made money from "renos" and acquired investment properties as "side" jobs over the years. I am a heck of a painter and color chooser!

Not Yet Our Time to Fly

Commercial airlines like American Airlines brought about the golden age of air travel. However, it was still a luxury for most travelers. Commercial aviation expanded in the '50s into the "jet age" of the '60s. I saw pictures of formally dressed passengers and glamorous stewardesses wearing white gloves serving beef bourguignon on fine china.

Airline stewardess aka flight attendant.

My family was not privileged enough to fly. Air travel boiled down to having money, which we were lacking. Consequently, we always traveled by car.

Road trips—mainly to the West, as my Father loved his Westerns—were a highlight of my youth. We also went east, to the beach towns of Mississippi, Alabama, and Florida, as well. One such trip was to a beach house owned by a friend of my Father in Grand Isle, a Louisiana barrier island on the Gulf of Mexico.

We traveled great distances in our 1960 Plymouth station wagon, which was coral and white. This car was eventually junked when my middle brother put sand in the gas tank. He claimed he was "helping out" because my Mother was always complaining about not having enough money for gasoline. Sound familiar?

Our road trips always involved Minnie packing individual "goody bags" for us, including crayons or colored pencils and coloring books, games, and snacks. These kept us busy for about five minutes, after which, like clockwork, my brothers started acting up in the rear seats.

In those days, the rear seats faced backward, so my brothers were always waving to truckers and pumping their arms, encouraging them to blow their boisterous horns. I now wonder what other things they might have got up to back there. Shooting the finger? Mooning motorists? Who knows?! My Father's rearview mirror did not offer an adequate view so they knew they had a green light for mischief.

My non-sister and I faced forward, directly behind my Father and Mother, the latter being in the passenger seat. We were in reach of our Mother's hand, which periodically came over the front passenger seat, trying to slap at us to keep us in line. It *never* worked for her. It just made her look foolish! When she was the driver, she adopted an alternative approach. She stared ahead with one hand on the steering wheel and the other hand reaching over the seat, swatting at us like flies. A fly swatter would have been more successful!

On the beach trips, we traveled with Ruby or another housekeeper. They did not accompany us to the Western states, mainly because these trips involved many days of travel and nights at hotels. They watched us when my parents went out at night or needed some privacy during the day. They did not swim, so the beach and pool were off limits during that time.

We traveled with Ruby on one trip when we had to stop at a motel for a night. My parents were surprised that Ruby was not allowed to stay with us because she was black. I was too young to understand why, but I think I would have broken the rules and snuck her into my bed, had I had the chance. In the end, my Father spent several hours searching for a room at a boarding house that allowed black people, most likely paying handsomely for the privilege. He left her to stay the night and picked her up again the next morning.

Driving with my Father was scary, given his inclination to drive recklessly fast. He was a daredevil, to put it mildly, and very impatient with the driving of other people. Notoriously, he played chicken with oncoming cars and trucks while passing long lines of cars on the narrow two-lane highways.

Tailgating was his forte. Once, he rear-ended the car in front, causing the car behind to slam into us. We were sandwiched between the two cars on a bridge into the small town of Breaux Bridge, Louisiana—the "Crawfish Capital of the World." The sudden action sent me flying to the floor. I ended up partially under the front seat. I was very small! Of course, back in the day, we did not wear seat belts. I am still not able to fall asleep in a moving car as a result of my fear and anxiety about an accident happening.

My Father frequently acted with audacity—or, as Dickens might say, "sassigassity"—and would not hesitate to drive through what we and others considered to be dangerous conditions.

When the gas tank of the Plymouth station wagon failed, my parents began driving a 1960 Cadillac Sedan DeVille. This car had an air-powered suspension system that, when activated from inside, raised the chassis off its axle.

On one occasion, during our travels to the West, we came across some high flood water. The other drivers, afraid their cars would stall, obeyed the policeman in charge and detoured around the high water. My Father refused to go around it like them. Rather, he pulled a lever under the dashboard; the car then made a revving noise and started to rise, before he slowly drove into the rising waters.

I can still remember the astonished looks on the faces of the bystanders—including the police officer, who stood shaking his head, dumbfounded—as we drove through the seemingly impassable water. Frankly, we were all amazed my Father had pulled this off, too!

Our cars.

Sidney Kate atop the trunk of our car in 1957.

Bartering a Papoose for an Indian Blanket

I was a young child—but out of diapers—when we first traveled to the West. I sat in my Mother's lap. My parents were not required to put me in a car seat. I often cried a lot; my Mother's lap felt safe and calmed me.

My active bladder literally drove my Father crazy on long road trips. He was just abusive enough to deny me bathroom privileges, purposely choosing not to stop. Many times, he also threatened to bring a portable potty for me, which only aggravated my shame.

My Mother had a clear memory of this story and told it many times in the following years. All my blood brothers remember it—even my youngest brother, who was not born at the time. As for me, I recall snippets, as most of it is buried deep inside my psyche.

One time, we were driving across the desert in New Mexico, when my Father became impatient with my crying in the car. We came upon some Native American women selling blankets and other paraphernalia beside the road. My Father pulled over, got out, and started bartering with these women for one of their colorful woven blankets.

He did not appear to be getting what he wanted from the negotiations. He marched over to the car and took me from my Mother's lap. I am sure she looked at him with a very puzzled expression! He walked back to the stand, held me up, and asked "The papoose for a blanket?" The women smiled and nodded, "Yes!"

My Father handed me over, took the colorful blanket, walked back to the car, got in, then drove away. All the while, my Mother screamed and protested against his actions.

The women immediately surrounded me, the elderly one saying a prayer over me. I felt the love being given. The prayer was much like the Ute Prayer for children, which reads:

Earth, Teach Me

Earth teach me caring—as mothers nurture their young.
Earth teach me courage—as the tree that stands alone.
Earth teach me limitation—as the ant that crawls on
*   the ground.*
Earth teach me freedom—as the eagle that soars in
*   the sky.*

My Mother continued to scream at him, grabbing at the wheel to get him to turn around and go back and get me. Eventually, he did. Had it not been for the caring of those loving women, I could have faced an abhorrence of evils.

I recently told a male friend from the Northeast this story. He looked at me with a questioning expression, before rationally quipping "I guess that is where the phrase 'Indian Giver' comes from?" I looked back at him and burst out laughing. In light of it all, the story was somewhat funny!

... but how about REAL abandonment?

To this day, I cannot think about that story without hearing the lyrics form Disney's Pocahontas, from the song, "Colors of the Wind", which go: "And we are all connected to each other ... in a circle, in a hoop that never ends ... we need to paint with all the colors of the wind."

Many years later, out of the blue, a psychic commented that I had a blue-eyed male Native American guide watching over me. That totally spooked me. I immediately thought of that tribe of women. The guide was probably sent my way by those women, who knew I was going to need serious help.

Two of my brothers then jokingly commented: "Just think, you could have been a wealthy casino owner or, even better, a famous little Pocahontas Indian wrestler?!"

Looking back, I cannot imagine what that life might have been like. I would most certainly have stood out due to the whiteness of my skin and the blueness of my eyes. Living with this Native American tribe of people or in foster care? Even though my life has been full of toxic behavior, I take solace knowing that neither actually happened.

A few years later, my family traveled to the West again, but my Father clearly avoided the blanket stand, or perhaps the business had since closed down.

One trip to Carson City, Nevada, is documented with a photo of myself atop a stuffed horse, with one arm waving a cowboy hat. "Ride 'em cowgirl!" Little did I know that there would be many other WILD rides to come.

First ride atop a fake horse—or was it a mule?

Lost and Found

On another occasion, we stopped in Salt Lake City, Utah, for lunch at a local hotel. I remember gazing over the salt lake in amazement after seeing a man floating on his back, reading a newspaper and smoking a cigar. I learned later that he was able to do this because the high salt content and dense water created his buoyancy.

We finished our lunch quickly. My Father wanted to get back on the road and head to our next destination. We hurriedly piled into the car and took off. About thirty minutes later, it became noticeably quiet and someone meekly asked "Where's brother?"

We all looked around but he was not in the car. My parents were a little afraid of being reported to child services. No cell phone—my Father turned the car around and sped back.

As was par for the course, my younger brother was sitting on the front desk, drinking a soda and talking with the hotel staff, who had not yet become sick of him. Apparently, he had not missed us.

I would never say this out loud, but I thought to myself "Why did we bother to come back for him? One less person, more for me." Yes, we should have left him to live with the Mormons in Utah, just as I could have been left with the Native Americans. He could have become a Mormon preacher instead of a Presbyterian one.

I guess I would have eventually missed him, deciding there and then that he was of value to me. Who would I have to argue and fight with? Now… I had to think of a way to get rid of the rest of them.

This was not the end of my younger brother's escapades, though, since he continued to make life miserable for all of us—especially my Mother—on many occasions.

For example, years later, my Mother was driving us down the street when we passed a 711 convenience store, then called "Pak-a-Sak." He cried out "Stop, I want an ICEE!" An ICEE is a frozen drink. Using her parental power, my Mother denied him; he continued pleading but she kept driving.

Suddenly, though, he opened the side door and jumped out of the car while it was moving. I do not know what he was thinking! Thankfully, my Mother was not driving very fast and he was not hurt.

It then occurred to me—how did he think he was going to pay for it? Unlike my youngest brother, who had a checking account as early as elementary school, my younger brother did not. It is amazing to think the neighborhood convenience store would take a check from such a young child!

My youngest brother is still good with money, taking after our paternal great-great grandfather, Wilbur Fisk, who started the hardware business. I do not think any of my younger brother's checks have ever bounced—unlike mine. Another reminder of that time: to this day, I have to catch myself when I ask for a "bag" at the grocery store. I want to call it a "sack"!

I have one last story about traveling to the West, from much later, when I was in my early teens. I call it our "Last Hurrah Wild West" road trip. It was an extended one, which involved traveling across the states of New Mexico, Arizona, and Utah, before ending in Nevada. My Father's endgame was to gamble in Las Vegas. His game of choice was blackjack.

During this trip, we stopped in Carson City, the capital of Nevada. The family sat for a group picture—a fake "wanted poster," showing mugshots of the group staring ahead with as serious faces as we could muster. My middle brother is wearing a beer t-shirt. No one in the family noticed it until my youngest brother pointed it out years later. Apparently, my middle brother loved beer even then. How often do you see a young child wearing a beer t-shirt? Oh well, it was the early '60s and a lot of things went unnoticed.

Saying Something More than Once Makes It True...!

"Louisiana IS God's country" according to my Father. He said it more than once to me and all the time when asking his customers for a "little lagniappe." They would smile in affirmation and open their wallets. It was in the late '50s to early '60s that Louisiana, especially southern Louisiana, was starting to become a hotbed for good Cajun food. More people were eating out at least once a week following the expansion of numerous restaurants, including already established national fast-food chains (or franchises) such as Burger King and McDonald's.

According to *Encyclopedia Britannica*, the first McDonald's restaurant was started in San Bernardino, California, in 1948, by the brothers Maurice ("Mac") and Richard McDonald. They are said to have bought appliances for their small hamburger restaurant from salesman Ray Kroc, who was intrigued by their need for eight malt and shake mixers. Kroc later opened the first franchise of McDonald's in Des Plaines, Illinois, in April 1955.

In order to fulfill the needs of these establishments, the demand for specialty hardware—restaurant equipment—rapidly grew. It was in 1962 that my Father and grandparents saw an opportunity to start a new venture, a restaurant supply business. The hardware business was already carrying food service equipment and sales had started to increase. It was a natural progression. The food service equipment business accordingly opened in six of the hardware stores, making the front page of the *Shreveport Journal*—the name of the newspaper had changed by then—on December 19, 1962.

The new restaurant supply business did exceedingly well. It was due to the increasing demand for specialty equipment at restaurants throughout Louisiana. It also expanded to some neighboring Southern states. I cannot discount my Father's role in its success; he had the business acumen and natural salesmanship to make it happen.

This new business also involved an adjunct ice machine business, called Scotsman Ice Machines. American Gas had developed the first Scotsman Cube Ice Machine in 1950, before Scotsman Ice Systems pioneered the development of affordable and reliable ice machines in the later 1950s. I believe my Father and grandparents incorporated this business because of the potential connection to my grandmother's Scots heritage. The ice machines were in demand at all types of restaurants, as well as in other food and service industries.

My Father made some lifelong friends in the restaurant business. The business of several original restaurants increased considerably during this time, especially that of Herby K's, a small dive or "hole-in-the-wall" restaurant. This landmark was founded in 1936, being named for Herbert J. Busi Jr., aka Herby K—a nickname he acquired at LSU. Although he was older, he was a friend of my Father's from

LSU, and I believe our ancestors knew each other for many years before that time.

Herby K's restaurant, Shreveport, Louisiana.

Herby K was known for his larger-than-life personality, sense of humor, and expert marksmanship—the latter being evidenced by a metal image, made from bullets, hanging behind the bar. The restaurant is also home to the "Shrimp Buster," a flattened fried shrimp, which was created in 1945.[10]

We ate there in the late '50s, when the restaurant offered drive-up service (similar to the Sonic restaurant today). I clearly remember a young "Jimmy" (a black waiter) running out to our car, attaching a tray to the open window, then taking our order. My parents would order a 21 oz. schooner mug of cold beer (or two). They would pass it around for each of us to take a sip, which sometimes became a swig. This began my lifelong love for beer. By the way, nothing was said about our underage drinking, if the restaurant employees ever saw us.

I presume the beer mugs were sold to Herby K by my Father as well, the hardware business being able to make special orders for a few restaurants like Herby K's. This was profitable for the business, since Libbey Glass had a local manufacturing plant in Shreveport, enabling my Father to buy from them directly, thereby saving on the shipping and freight charges that would normally eat into his profit.

Herby K's still has the uncomfortable bar stools that my Father sold them in the late '40s or early '50s.

Counter stools, 1949—photo taken as a result of my family's hardware business installation (unknown photographer).

I still love to eat a Shrimp Buster with Herby K's cocktail sauce—a catsup sauce with horseradish. It kicks a big punch, not unlike the many hot sauces on the market today. Louisiana hot sauces started with the original Tabasco sauce, which was created by Edmund McIlhenny on Avery Island, Louisiana, in 1868. The diet of the Reconstruction Era South was bland and monotonous, especially by Louisiana standards, so Edmund created a pepper sauce to give the food some flavor and excitement.[11]

I currently have a bottle of Herby K's cocktail sauce in my refrigerator. I much prefer to experience the real thing by sitting in a wooden booth in the bar area, not in the "beer garden." I get into town occasionally and never miss the opportunity to eat at this legendary restaurant.

Business Friend, Partner, or Foe?

My Father made many lifelong friends of hardworking restaurant and bar owners, who came in handy when I was in college at LSU in Baton Rouge. I called upon these friendships when I needed a good meal and had little or no money. Baton Rouge was then a college town where the legal drinking age was eighteen and "roadies" were still commonplace.

My Father had other acquaintances and potential business partners in the restaurant business who lived and worked outside of Louisiana, throughout the South. Some of them had unsavory backgrounds and ties to corruption.

Our family vacationed with the family of one of his business friends in the summers of the '60s, traveling to the beach with them. There were two sons and two daughters. The sons were around the ages of my brothers; one daughter was a little older than me and the other daughter was the youngest child. From the outside, they seemed to be happy and have every advantage.

My Mother and their mother kept in touch for several years thereafter; I believe they were friends. Their mother had proudly sent school pictures from 1970 to my Mother, which I found in a box following her passing. The beautiful handwriting on the back of each picture gave the name, age, date, grade, and school—a Methodist church school—and their mother had noted that the eldest daughter had turned seventeen in April.

Their father had a business partner and they had started a fast-food burger franchise called Colonel Dixie. As well as having good hamburgers, it was also home to the "Dixie Dog"; but the original business on Moffett Road in Mobile, Alabama closed permanently.

Colonel Dixie, "Home of the Dixie Dog."

Much later, in 1980, it emerged that my Father's friend had been indicted for the capital offense of the murder-for-hire death of his wife. It was later revealed that he was convicted in 1983 and sentenced to life imprisonment on the testimony of convicted felons.

An article in the *Mobile Press-Register* from 2019 stated that the wife of my Father's friend had kept a diary from 1975 to 1979. This story provided a "heart-rending" account of a woman in despair facing abuse, "feeling she had lost her husband's love" yet not also feeling able to leave him.

The article then recounts that this same man, together with another "trusty" as well as the warden and his wife, were all murdered by a "crazed inmate."[12] The story goes that he died heroically defending the warden and his wife. The story hints at the deep-rooted and long-lasting effects of abuse and how these issues can influence a person's choices later in life, causing them to become who they are. Ain't that the truth! Who knows how long that ancestral abuse pattern continued for in that family?

Most probably, my Mother and this woman shared stories of "jiggery pokery" about their own abuse in secret. My Mother may have been told secrets she never related to another soul. Maybe she had found another confidant. At least she saved me from those types of secrets!

I have often wondered what happened to the children of this family, who we had brief but pleasant encounters with. They would have been close to adulthood by then, but it cannot have been easy to lose both their parents in that manner.

"Uptown Girl"—Moving up in Life

Our financial situation improved with the success of the new restaurant supply business throughout the '60s. Positive events occurred before my young eyes. My Father had more authority and responsibility in the family business leading to a raise that allowed us to live more comfortably.

Our family happily moved from my nightmare on Elmwood Street to a large buff brick house with two stories and five bedrooms on Pierremont Road, a very busy street. Our social status improved: we had moved "uptown"!

Playlist Song #5:
"Uptown Girl," by Billy Joel.

By this time, I was seven years old and in the second grade at South Highlands Elementary School. The families attending this school were considered to belong to a higher social level. We were now living in the upper middle class; yet my Mother and I still walked to the corner grocery store and she paid for our groceries on credit.

No one knew this except for the store owner and manager. My Mother charged our groceries and paid a little off each month with her measly weekly child allowance.

These visits to the corner grocery store were a treat for me. There was a butcher who gave me a raw wiener or hot dog as we waited for the meat to be cut. I occasionally got the peanut patty candy that was pure sugar. However, the colorful candy suckers with a paper cord loop that you stuck your fingers through were reserved for trips to the pediatrician; who bribed us with them each time we needed a shot. The wieners were better for the teeth but worse for the body. I might have declined had I known what was in them— but it was the '60s and no one investigated the ingredients or wondered what was nutritionally best.

The house on Pierremont Road was much bigger and more difficult to clean, so my parents had to hire help. The housekeepers were treated fairly and most of them liked kids, which was pretty much a prerequisite. My Mother had to fire one because she caught her taking a "nip" of liquor or sometimes drinking whole bottles in our "washhouse" while working. Some others did not last more than a week for various other reasons.

The housekeepers spent a lot of time in the washhouse laundering the seemingly endless baskets of dirty linen we generated. Some were really hiding from my brothers, who would often get bored and act up whenever possible, with my younger and middle brothers tending to push the limits of these women's patience. These hard-working women would diligently clean the house only for my brothers to mess it up soon afterward, sometimes before they left for the night.

My brothers were always fighting, too—mostly roughhousing and breaking lamps. I do not think my Mother had one lamp that survived them. My brothers were always planning creative ways to ambush my non-sister and me. Sometimes destroyed property was the result.

Once, my non-sister, who was much taller than us, was walking to the stairs, when a dart flew out of the living room and into her leg. My youngest brother had thrown it, aiming for the dart board that was hung on the back of the French doors adjacent to the staircase. My younger brother, attempting to win by cheating, had opened the door at the last minute, allowing the dart to fly through the open door. My non-sister was simply in the wrong place at the wrong time.

Frustrated and hurt by their behavior, she chased after my *youngest* brother with the dart still sticking out of her leg. She looked like Frankenstein, with a strange grimace over her face. She finally caught him, but the one who had really caused the harm remained laughing hysterically in the background.

Moving uptown brought about new beginnings: I finally felt that I was beginning to live life rather than watching it happen to me.

———————————

Sunday Afternoon Sex Time

The shadow side was never far away, though. After an enormous dinner, Sunday afternoon was considered "parent" time, both of my parents being highly sexual people. I knew this because I made the mistake of walking in on them once—only this time, my Father was with my Mother. At first, I thought he was physically hurting her, but they were both naked and he was grinding on top. I do not know if she enjoyed it.

The incident fostered my sexual imagination. I was too young to understand sex and had not had the "birds and bees" talk. I never questioned my sexual or gender identity. I knew that I was female, like my Mother, the only twist being that I wanted to identify with the perceived power that my Father exerted over my Mother. I now know that I did not see my Father's deemed power clearly.

With five children under the age of ten, they had to schedule time for sex if they were ever going to have it. Needless to say, we were all relegated to our rooms for a scheduled "nap." My younger and middle brothers shared a bedroom to the rear of the house. My youngest brother, the baby, had his own room, which was tiny, more like a sitting room off the master bedroom. My non-sister and I had our own rooms, being separated because we fought constantly.

Of course, no one napped. This time allowed my brothers to think up creative ways of ambushing my non-sister and me, who rarely teamed up to thwart their efforts at attempting to invade our space.

Having my own bedroom allowed me some alone time on these Sunday afternoons. It was at the front of the house, off the porte cochère, which could be accessed from one of my side windows. I could not climb down it without a ladder, but I often thought about escaping to another family where I could be the only child. I had still not yet figured out a way to distance myself completely from my siblings.

My other daydreams were filled with fantasies of freedom and escaping from my own personal imprisonment. These vivid motion pictures saw me heading to Hollywood to become an actress and finding romantic love with a handsome prince, then living happily ever after. The same handsome suitor would climb up the porte cochère and into my bedroom, before ravishing me—whatever that meant! At the time, I was still too young to know. "Someday my prince will come..." I had clearly been reading too many fairy tales and watching too much Disney.

Even today, Sunday afternoons are a time for imagining lustful encounters. Who cares about societal mores now?

Playlist Song #6:
"Someday My Prince Will Come," by Adriana Caselotti
(from the Disney movie *Snow White and the Seven Dwarfs*).

Sitting in My Closet and Talking to Jesus

I felt alone and unloved on those Sunday afternoons. Imagining fairytale love and happiness only went so far in terms of soothing my inner wounds. Even then, I sensed I was different from my siblings and other children.

For some unknown reason, I was drawn to my bedroom closet, feeling comfortable there, as though I was protected and safe from both emotional and physical harm. Not unlike the closet in the Ruby story. I would sit there imagining different scenarios, some sexual in nature, for what seemed like hours. It was a personal space where I felt safe to explore the shadowy side of my imagination.

At times, I heard a faint voice saying "I love you." It was a soothing voice, like the voice of my doll, Sister Belle. I could not tell if it was male or female.

Many years later, I attended a Christian women's retreat in the mountains of North Carolina. I told this story to a Christian counselor who said it was the voice of Jesus. It now makes sense to me that Jesus was watching over me as a young child. It sounded bizarre but not entirely out there as I continued to mull it over in my mind.

Both Sister Belle and "Jesus" proclaimed that they "loved" me. I was feeling pretty good and learning but I was still not able to grasp what *true unconditional love* was.

The closet remained my primary escape from reality, even after seeing an episode of *The Twilight Zone* where a wall opened, before someone walked through it to another dimension. The image scared me so much I had nightmares for months, causing me to perform a ritual each night before climbing into bed. I looked under it and in the closet with my Mother watching to ensure no trap doors would open up and swallow me during my sleep.

Sometimes, my fantasies involved sexual curiosity, as I used my Barbie and Ken dolls to act out my imaginings of love and sex. It was clearly the sex of my imagination, though, as I had yet to learn the mechanics of the body's working. I only knew that my Father, being "dominant," was always on top of my Mother.

At other times, my fantasies included physical violence, as my poor dolls had to mimic the abuse between my parents. Looking back, I think I instinctively learned some self-help therapy through those dolls. Of course, I now assume that Jesus was watching all of this, too—or was the devil making me do it?

The sexual elements were more enjoyable: I remember an intense tingling sensation—was I too young to experience orgasm? I had stripped my dolls naked and had them interact with each other in different physical positions. Again, I had not yet learned how to "do it," exactly, and Barbie and Ken did not have the anatomical attributes to make that happen. I "came out of my closet" and experienced real female–male sex much later in life.

———————————————————————————

"I'm Going Home"

I fell ill with pneumonia when I was seven, shortly after playing outside in the winter snow, which did occasionally occur in the South. I stayed home from school for several weeks, which was okay for me, because I was a serious and introverted child. I preferred reading books and listening to music over outdoor play and social interaction. My Mother wanted me to play outside with my siblings, to "expand my lungs," as she frequently said.

I lived in my imagination through books and music. My favorite book as a child was *The Secret Garden* by Frances Hodgson Burnett. This book was eventually challenged and banned for its racial content. I loved it because it suggested how a child's love could heal emotional scars from the loss of her parents. It is about the power of thought, secrets, and developing independence—I already knew something about these secrets, but wanted to learn more. Adult's secret keeping only brings suffering and loneliness.

I spent hours listening to music on my small portable radio. I listened to the American Top 40 countdowns with Casey Kasem while my Father spent his Saturday nights listening to LSU football.

Back then, most pediatricians made house calls. My Mother knew our pediatrician extremely well (she would have his number on speed dial today). There were so many emergency visits! For this one, though, I sensed that even my Mother was very worried. She never left my side during my illness. Where was all this attention in my earlier years?!

My Mother's healing helped me through it, but I had apparently experienced fits of delirium caused by an extremely high fever continuing over a long period of time. Although I eventually healed from this one physically, I may not have healed mentally.

Still perplexed, my Mother asked me many months later whether I remembered going to the closet, picking out my clothes, and calmly stating "I am going home." After silently observing my bizarre behavior for several minutes, she asked me where home was? She then had to forcibly put me back in my bed after several repetitions. Apparently, I continued to perform this ritual over and over into the long night as well as some of the days that followed. What was I thinking? I could not say. Just another sliver of my weirdness emerging.

Secretly, I still believed I did not belong—and was unloved. I believed I was very different to the rest of my siblings, but you cannot tell that to your Mother or any adult, otherwise you might end up being diagnosed with a severe mental illness. Today, I could say that I am a "starseed," which I now believe to be true.[13]

A childhood friend of mine was committed by her parents to the ninth floor of Brentwood Hospital—a psychiatric facility in Shreveport—and she was never the same again. Today, it is a thriving facility that treats all types of mental diseases, but it was rare for *children* to be treated for them in the '60s.

Watching Mr. Rogers and *Davey and Goliath*—a clay animated Christian-based television series—helped me greatly during that period. The latter show featured Davey, a little boy, and Goliath, his talking dog. It aired on Sunday mornings and I watched it from 1961 to 1964. Two of my favorite episodes were "Lost in a Cave" and "All Alone," which taught me that I was loved and *not alone*.

Unlike the fictional Davey Hansen, Mr. Rogers was a real man who helped a lot of children face their fears and various mental issues. He had such a calming voice. His storytelling had a soothing effect on me. His stories taught me how to face my issue of feeling unloved. He once said that "Love isn't a state of perfect caring. It is an active noun like 'struggle.' " To love someone is to strive to accept that person exactly the way he or she is. I later realized Mr. Rogers was one of my many angels on earth.

Seeking Validation in Merit Badges

The Girl Scouts taught me the value of community service. I still have my Girl Scout sash with all of my merit badges sewn onto it. I became a little plump from eating too many cookies, but the Girl Scouts of America helped me to feel valued. I joined the troop at South Highlands Elementary School—our hut was located in a little house on the corner of the school lot, which we shared with the Cub and Boy Scouts.

Girl scout sash with merit badges (including coffee cup badge aka hospitality badge), from 1963 onward.

In order to earn the hospitality badge, I had to follow a recipe from start to finish, then serve the food to an adult, who was required to taste it and confirm it was edible. I asked my Mother whether I could use a recipe from her *Betty Crocker Cookbook*. She gladly agreed but was, I think, curious about what I had planned.

I decided to make Southern breakfast biscuits for my family. I woke early one Sunday morning (no church or Sunday school that day) to prepare the ingredients and gather the cooking utensils in order to make these important biscuits. I was excited because I had never cooked anything by myself before.

I followed the recipe perfectly and baked the biscuits without burning them. I was about to serve them, proud of myself for my accomplishment, when my Mother noticed that the flour had weevils in it. She was not much of a baker, so she had not replaced the flour in months. But it was too late—I had already cooked the insects into the biscuits. My siblings found out and refused to eat them.

My Father felt sorry for me and made my siblings eat the biscuits, because I would not get my badge otherwise. Well, they say insects are good for you! I wonder if that was the "first taste" my siblings had of *him showing favor toward me*? Although it could also have been considered abusive, as well, since he made them eat the biscuits that were clearly full of cooked bugs.

We could have lied to the Girl Scouts, but my Father, wanting to appear as an upstanding citizen, told the truth, with the result that I was known thereafter as the Weevil woman. This story is almost as good as this next one...

One day, my Mother and younger brother brought home a small green turtle from the pet store; but soon after could not find it, despite looking everywhere. A few days later, my Mother cooked a roast for my Father's and grandfather's lunch, subsequently discovering the partially frozen turtle in the bag with the roast.

She set the "frozen" turtle on the kitchen counter, thinking it was dead—and most probably wondering how to explain the situation to my younger brother. Several hours later, when my younger brother came home from school, the turtle had thawed out and started to walk across the counter.

My Mother was saved from yet another unpleasant moment. As luck would have it, my younger brother had another great "Show and Tell" moment about the rebirth of amphibious reptiles.

The Girl Scouts required me to sell cookies in the spring. I thought I could be a good salesgirl, even though I was so shy I barely spoke. Even so, I was excited to walk through our affluent neighborhood of families who, I imagined, would either buy the cookies or give me some money to go away.

My Mother was busy and decided she did not have the time to "walk the streets" with me; so she allowed me to sell the cookies by myself, but only on our immediate block. After all, what could happen to a small girl in broad daylight on her own street block? Well, a lot!

It was a long city block and our neighbors, unlike us, had large and manicured lawns. I crossed the street at the light and walked in my full Girl Scout uniform toward the six houses on the other side.

I was excited yet anxious as I approached the first house; my extreme shyness started to emerge. I told myself "I can do this" and envisioned selling a hundred boxes to the first wealthy patron. I walked the long driveway to knock on the door, expecting a woman or housekeeper to answer. There was a long moment of silence, so I knocked again.

I was about to leave when the door flew open. I was faced by a creepy old man. I know I looked surprised when I saw his half-naked body and, in particular, his wrinkled penis. Trying to sound professional, and attempting to look at his wrinkled face, I asked him whether he would be interested in buying my cookies. Thankfully, he said "No" and slammed the door, bringing our interaction to an end.

I immediately hightailed it out of there, shaking uncontrollably. That was the end of my outing, as I was not able to go any further down the block. It just goes to show there are perverts in all social classes: a valuable lesson to learn. Thankfully, I was safe, although it could have been worse.

WAIT, It Will Disappear!

My girlfriends and I have gotten up to much mischief over the years, from elementary school onward.

One time, three of us—including Leesa, my best friend—tried out a science theory on an unsuspecting participant. Really, it was more a dare than a science experiment. We were at Leesa's house, which was across the street from the mall. It was always busy at the mall, especially on the weekends.

We had procured the substance in question from a local toy shop and agreed that one of us would approach a complete stranger in the parking lot and squirt the liquid, "disappearing ink," over their clothing, then watch it disappear.

The chosen friend was neither Leesa nor myself, so we watched excitedly while she selected her prey in order to complete the mission, executing it perfectly. Only, it failed because the so-called "disappearing ink" did not disappear.

The chosen friend pleaded with the unwilling female participant over and over: "Wait, it will disappear... I promise!" The woman was not pleased, revealing "This is my new $32.00 dress."

The ink ended up ruining the woman's clothes and the chosen friend had to make good on her promise. Of course, the minute she was in trouble, Leesa and I ran to a neighbor's house, as we did not want the victim to know where Leesa lived. We then snuck back along the back fence and hid, randomly peeking out of her front window, so as not to be seen. In other words, we abandoned our friend to her own devices. How loyal we were!

Apparently, disappearing ink has been used by various countries for decades, as part of their covert operations. Guess who was at the "leading edge" of its development? The Germans, of course! The breakthroughs occurred during World War II: "it became a veritable 'invisible ink' arms race, with each side trying to outdo the other and come up with that holy grail of invisible inks."[14]

Further advancements came from the "well-staffed laboratories of intelligence agencies" in the '50s and '60s. In particular, the Soviet KGB and East German Stasi developed the dry transfer method, with a message being transferred from a top sheet of paper to the one below by means of chemicals. This method was also used by American prisoners of war in Vietnam to include secret information in their letters home.

Invisible ink became almost obsolete when developments in computer technology and the digital transmission of sensitive information came into play. Invisible ink was no longer in a "spy's bag of tricks."

Instead, it became a product for magicians, pranksters, and children. Our invisible ink was of a synthetic nature and obviously not meant to be spurted on fabric. We learned a valuable lesson that day!

The woman did not press charges—our prank could easily have been construed as a malicious attack on her person in today's world. Had she filed charges, our chosen friend would have had a juvenile record for life.

*Example of the disappearing ink that was sold
in the 1960s (taken from eBay).*

The Famous Pillbox Hat and the Creepy Christmas Elf

My elementary school years were full of entertaining and *not so* entertaining moments as well.

One positive experience was the time I played Susan B. Anthony in a second-grade play. We were required to participate in these productions every now and then, to ensure we grew into "well-rounded" adults. In any case, it helped me to begin to overcome my fear of public speaking! My teacher obviously saw something in me, as I was chosen to play this famous women's rights advocate.

I have long since forgotten my lines—except for "I am Susan B. Anthony"—but I know my words emphasized the strength of women and their right to vote. I am sure my teacher chose something that was not too hard for me to remember. One of her unforgettable lines was from her "Declaration of Rights" speech of 1876, which read: "Men, their rights, and nothing more; women, their rights, and nothing less."

My Mother was excited to dress me in a slender pencil skirt, white shirt, and her famous pillbox hat (which she eventually gave me). When my turn came, I marched out and recited my few but powerful lines. I believe I was a big hit—or, as Dickens would say, a "whizz-bang" (*The Pickwick Papers*).

It was meritorious, especially with my Mother and all the other mothers in the audience. I do not think there were many men— "they were all working," right?

My third-grade Christmas party was not a hit, though. I had started to realize that my Mother's attention was no longer on me, but elsewhere. After school, I stood alone in the school driveway, waiting for my Mother to come and pick me up long after everyone else had left. I could have walked home, but I was not allowed to after the fiasco with the cookies.

Her extreme lateness—verging on humiliation—occurred so frequently that the principal, seeing me standing all alone, came outside to ask why no one had come to get me. There was no childcare after school, nor did I have a softball practice or Girl Scout meeting to attend. Ironically, the thing my parents most feared could have happened while I was waiting alone, with no other adults around.

This was not the only embarrassment caused by my Mother's chronic inattention. Each year, my class would have a Christmas party before the holiday break. Such parties may not happen now, due to today's public schools being more diverse. In 1963, though, my teacher passed around a hat full of carefully written names—heaven forbid someone had been left out! Each child drew a name from the hat.

That year, I picked my early childhood crush, of all people. I had secretly had my eye on him for quite a while and was so excited, pleading with my Mother to buy him an expensive gift—one he would never forget. I was anxious with excitement for the big occasion. I had fantasies of my crush opening the present and being so happy he would grab me after school and jump my bones, lathering me with attention. Yeah, right?!

The night before the party, I asked my Mother whether she had my present. She replied: "Oh, I forgot all about it!" Seeing the look of disappointment on my face and my mawkish crying, she then reassured me: "Don't worry, I will wrap up a gift and have it ready for you to take in the morning."

It did not matter—I went to bed that night feeling very forgotten and thinking that what I wanted was not important. After all, I had no money to buy this boy a gift; I did not receive an allowance, as my parents could not afford to give us money each month.

Well... I woke up to a present lying at the end of the bed, nicely wrapped in Christmas green foil paper. I placed a name card on the package, then put on my prettiest Christmas dress, before skipping merrily out of the door.

When I got to school late, as usual, all of the others had put their presents under the Christmas tree. We gathered around to begin the exchange. I was so excited, anticipating what "boy" gift my Mother had come up with: a race car, a truck, a train, or maybe even sports equipment (I think he played "flag" football, as all the boys did)? The possibilities were endless!

When it was my time, the teacher called out the name of my crush. He stepped forward with excitement in his eyes, ready for his Christmas present. Well, he got it—in the form of a creepy Christmas elf. Not an adorable one, like the Elf on a Shelf, but one with a sinister smile. Everyone laughed. I was mortified and he became the laughingstock of the party, looking at me, with hurt in his eyes and asking "Is this a joke?"

I do not remember what I did next—I knew I had to disappear and get out of there. I probably asked to be excused and went to the bathroom to cry. The teacher came to my rescue, however, giving him another gift and telling him it was a mistake on her part. I was grateful to her. I do not believe he ever knew otherwise.

After that, though, my trust in my Mother's judgment waned. I never went on a date with him nor did we ever become friends, thanks to my Mother's foolishness. She did not think how it might embarrass me in the eyes of my peers. It was a tribute to her not thinking about my feelings and not caring how others saw me. I was not important!

After all, I was a female born in the South, whose worth could easily be devalued. Or at least that is what I thought, not seeing much evidence otherwise. I now know it was much more than that.

Booklets and Basement Drills

Making booklets was a learning tool that was supposed to foster creativity. One teacher *really* stressed their importance. I made more than twenty of them in her class. Creating these booklets taught me how to research a subject and present my findings in an organized form. I was more comfortable writing than speaking, so I was very good at creating booklets. Thankfully, I did not have to present the material orally. This was the most terrifying thought imaginable.

The booklets I created were on a range of subjects; from current events to geography. I wrote about the assassination of JFK and, ironically, the northern New England states of Vermont, New Hampshire, and Maine. My interest in the Northeast has always been alive!

I liken making booklets to modern-day scrapbooking with historical and geographic twists. These booklets were at the beginning of a learning curve that ended up teaching me the skills necessary to research, write, and photographically illustrate a book.

It was overall a pleasant experience. I always got "A"s, because I was a "most promising writer and a good little student."

Playlist Song #7:
"Duck and Cover (Atomic Bomb PSA),"
from Old Time Radio Commercials (originally 1951 Civil Defense Film).

The bomb shelter drills in the '60s were unpleasant. I was in the second and third grades at this time, aged seven and eight. The drills still haunt me today and I get anxious whenever I hear a warning signal or buzzer, like the one you hear from the emergency alert system on your television. Loud sounds in the airport are the worst.

Back then, following the sounding of a special alarm, our class headed robotically into the basement, where we would duck and cover on the floor until we got the "all clear." We then did the reverse, marching back to our classroom and acting like nothing had happened for the rest of the day.

"Duck and cover" drills were so named because the individual would "duck" down or lay face down and "cover" his or her neck. These drills were implemented under President Truman in the '50s. The earlier drills required a child to get under a school desk. They constituted a preparedness measure, a civil defense response to a nuclear attack.

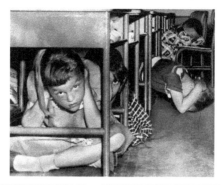

Duck and cover.

According to the *Encyclopedia Britannica*, this procedure was practiced in the '50s and '60s, during the Cold War. Numerous "fallout" shelters were constructed, and children practiced taking "immediate refuge," so they would know how to act in the event of an atomic bomb explosion, which, we were told, would be "signaled by a blinding flash of light."

These were preparedness drills; actions to be taken to be ready for a potential disaster. In a real emergency, the doors and windows would be closed for several hours, until the civil authorities confirmed there was no lingering radioactivity.

We were told not to look directly at the light that would accompany the bomb. That alone was a frightening thought (a lot more frightening than the "creepy" elf). Looking back, that one drill may have caused more instances of mental illness or what we now call post-traumatic stress disorder, due to the extreme fears of the unknown being triggered in the minds of young children.

As I previously suggested, I often wonder whether these drills did even more harm to a child's mind because, let's face it, the damage from an atomic bomb would be extreme no matter how well we prepared. What were they thinking? I, personally, would rather NOT have known.

On the Righteous Path?

Minnie appeared to be a devoted Presbyterian; but she did not always display her Christian charity toward others. She loved church on Sunday—and some would consider her religious—but I never heard her sing a hymn. My Father sang many times, but never a church hymn. Come to think of it, I never saw him as religious at all.

He always referred to Louisiana as "God's country," but he avoided all church activities like the plague. I think he said those words often so those he did business with would think him religious—a "God-faring" not "God-fearing" man in the "Bible belt" of the South. Who knows? Or maybe he thought saying the word "God" aloud was enough to make him a believer. His "outside" personality made him believable, especially to a few. For much of the time he was too busy "working," anyway, benefiting from my Mother's organization with the lists he stuffed into his hat.

My Mother would take us to church or Sunday school on occasion. I often wondered why it was called Sunday school—it was not really a school, but I guess we learned some things about the Bible. We were Presbyterian, even though, at first sight, given the size of our family, most would have thought of us as Catholic. I attended vacation Bible school during the summer. I enjoyed this even though I knew it was an inexpensive babysitter for my Mother.

Like most Southerners, my Mother was raised as a Southern Baptist. Her parents smoked and drank—I am not sure how *that* was received in their church community. They were not the average Baptist teetotalers, BY FAR!

The only other time I remember my Mother taking us anywhere near a church was when we went (I have no idea why) to a Catholic convent. My Mother, younger brother, and I stood on the grassy lawn, waiting for I am not sure what. We suddenly heard a bell ring. A few seconds later, a great number of nuns swarmed in unison down a much larger hill toward the church chapel, apparently going to Mass. This massive group was moving in unison, with billowing black robes and habits. It was an ominous sight. Out of the blue, my younger brother promptly screamed "Momma, look at all the witches!" He never lived that one down in my mind; even after he became a Presbyterian minister later in life.

Personally, I had a strong intention to follow a righteous path when I signed up to sing in the children's church choir. I missed too many Sundays, however, and was eventually kicked out. I always felt inadequate; I did not believe my voice measured up musically.

In 1966, it was time for me to make a religious decision. Everyone my age had joined the Presbyterian church and professed their faith in the Lord. I also wanted to join the church, but I would have to go through the required confirmation class first. I diligently studied the Bible and passed the class. Remember, I am a good student!

The important Sunday finally came around, when my class would be presented to the congregation. I was required to be at the church for the 11 a.m. service on Sunday. Unfortunately, that did not happen. This faux pas of not showing up could not be blamed on anyone other than my parents. I was only twelve years old. I was at the Camp with no ride into town.

I felt guilty, to a point, about not making it to my church debut. The minister, being forgiving, allowed me to join anyway; sending me a nice note with his prayers, the program for the day (which included my name) and an engraved New Testament Confirmation Bible. His prayers were appreciated, but I wondered whether he felt I would need more than his prayers, because who knows why I did not show up to church on that important day?

Looking back at the church program now, which I still have, I shake my head, because right below my name is that of Jimmy Mac, who came into my life several years later. I am shocked to see he actually joined the church on that day. Even back then, we were obviously on the same path. I find that very comical, for reasons you will find out later.

What I do know is that I learned many life lessons during this time. I grew immensely during this time, "way beyond" my true age of twelve years old. I made friends through activities I participated in outside my home; and witnessed more reality, some of it harsh, as I started to immerse myself in my Southern environment. I wish I had been ready to experience more challenges. Most of my wounds were still deeply hidden from the outside world.

MY TEENAGE YEARS

From Rapid Learner to Rapid De-Learner

On my first day at Youree Drive Junior High—now Middle—School, I soon became aware I had been placed in the "Rapid Learner" program. This was a rat race involving pressure and competition; which I, being shy and quiet, feared.

There and then, I decided this program was not for me and asked to be transferred into what I called the average student class. I consciously decided I did not want the academic pressure. Yes, I still studied, but I wanted to be more outgoing and walk among the majority of the school's population.

I made a few new friends and began "socializing" more. I was testing my feminine charms upon the males, going to (still segregated) male–female dances, and volunteering for worthwhile civic organizations—in that order. In retrospect, I do not remember doing much dancing.

I became a fashionista and even started to wear a little makeup, learning how to apply it slowly and carefully—especially the various shades of pale or light pink lipstick over my thin lips.

My wardrobe consisted of hand-me-downs from an older cousin. I was so happy to have some new clothes. I did not think of them as regifts. Apparently, Minnie regularly gave her daughter's children new clothes. I guess she believed they needed them more than we did, since my Father was being paid a salary. She assumed that he could afford to buy us new clothes.

She was wrong; we were barely scraping by each month at our new home. My Mother shopped at the Centenary College Thrift Shop, which had some great stuff donated by wealthy patrons. I was happy to have anything "new" and wore it proudly. My favorite hand-me-down was a plaid "kilt-like" skirt from my cousin.

One day, this cousin and a few of her friends approached me while I was talking to my friends and loudly exclaimed "That is my skirt!" She did not say it looked good and it almost sounded as though I had stolen it from her. I was mortified. My few friends looked closer and started laughing. I must have glared at my cousin with hatred: how could she be so insensitive?

I ran home and told my Mother about the incident. Soon afterward "all hell broke loose," as my Father would say. To this day, I have reservations about wearing other people's clothes and still think about the incident every time I see my cousin, even though many decades have passed.

———————————————————

The Ranch

My parents acquired what we call "the Ranch" in a trade-plus for the Lake Bistineau property, ironically—and karmically—from the same family whose son was my elementary school crush in the "creepy elf" story. It is located in Keatchie, Louisiana, near the Texas border. At first, I was very upset. There would be no more swimming or boating, since it was not close to a lake or a large body of water.

I came to understand it was a great financial deal—being worth much more than the lake property—and it eventually produced future riches and many blessings. My parents soon filled the more than a thousand acres with Red Poll cattle.

These cattle were first imported from England in the 1880s. They are considered friendly. I once thought they were charging at me in a pasture; but I soon realized they had merely heard the hay wagon in the distance and were running to the feed stall. I simply happened to be in the way.

These hornless, dark red creatures are known for the quality of their beef. A registered breed, each had its own name and certificate from the American Red Poll Cattle Association—like a family tree, but for cattle. My Mother kept these documents in several spiral notebooks. Each animal wore a colored plastic numbered tag stapled to the ear, which looked like an earring. It was a colorful sight to see them all raise their heads as we approached.

I received my first lesson about the birth process when watching the delivery of a calf. It caused me to become apprehensive about the prospect of childbirth. My Mother registered each calf, noting whether it was a heifer or bull. Some of the latter would be castrated steers and slaughtered for meat. Others would father several calves. I always wondered how those decisions were made.

My Mother had a book of baby names from which she pulled out weird combinations. Later, during high school and college, she started naming the bulls after my old boyfriends. Kingly Stuart and Mighty Fine Marshall were two names. There might have been a future Roaming Regal Richard. I did not like this at first, but eventually did not care; because two of them were my exes, after all, and we had discarded one another.

None of these names came close to those given to the dogs, which had much more common names, like Lulabelle. Right? Unlike the cattle, the dogs were all mutts.

My Father had a soft spot for his animals. We often thought he treated his dogs much better than his wife and children. Later in life, he became a collector of dogs rather than women. He picked up strays from the side of the road and took them back to the Ranch for my Mother to feed and care for them. Of course, this made things a lot harder for my Mother, who had to drag large bags of dog food from the grocery store. What lucky dogs to have been chosen by my Father!

The only drawback was that his dog "pickups" were never considered for life inside the house. There was a true caste system, the first and older orphaned dogs being higher up the hierarchy. My Father did not discriminate on his Saturday drives, though, taking all dogs out in his smelly Ford Bronco.

This vehicle stank of wet dog and who knows what other smells. It was covered in dog hair. I wanted to put on a hazmat suit whenever I rode with him. Anyone with an allergy would have gotten sick just smelling the air! He became a scarier driver the older he got, so I always put my seatbelt on. The Bronco did come in handy for putting out fires; as I will reveal later.

The Ranch gave me a newfound love for horses. My parents decided to buy some for us because the child of one of my Father's business partners was into them.

My middle brother had a Shetland pony named Prince, who was always trying to dislodge him by running under an old white house at full speed. My middle brother had to jump off, otherwise he would be slammed into the house. My non-sister had a strawberry roan mare named Sheba. I opted for a male paint horse, who I named Caesar. He was originally used to round up cattle, but loved chasing them instead, so was put out to pasture by his previous owner.

Friday nights were reserved for another new love: competitive barrel racing. Caesar had a wild streak; but he took the cue for a lead well, so I decided to make him into a fine barrel racer. He learned easily. He reigned in and was perfect for the sport. The business partner's daughter was faster and more skilled, but I managed to place competitively a few times. It was fun! I never lost my love for horses, but teenage life—and boys—soon took up the majority of my time...

On the Yearbook Staff

One of the greatest academic achievements of my youth was working on the yearbook staff in my last year of junior high. It was a big deal. I was soon noticed by all the students, who were vying to get their pictures into the yearbook.

The staff was drawn from ninth graders, who were chosen primarily for their writing abilities. The English teacher, Mrs. Freeman, invited me to be a staff member and put me in charge of the ninth-grade section.

Once the school year had ended, she wrote me a note encouraging me to continue my writing, as she thought I was gifted. I was elated! This made a lifelong impression on me, as you can see. That is why she is the one of the few teachers I name in this book.

Being involved in the yearbook made me very popular—and my parents very proud. I was excited that my work would be published in a book that would live on forever in the hearts and minds of my fellow students and teachers.

I wanted to contribute something that had not been done before and was pleased to create a collage, bringing together photographs of numerous students on a single page. Usually, only one student got the spotlight. I attempted to make it a piece of art; I wanted it to show real student life, not the usual posed photographs of academia or athletics. I included several students performing school activities ranging from the serious to the amusing.

I was relieved that I did *not* get into trouble for using pictures showing students acting up. It had to be censored by Mrs. Freeman and the rest of the staff before it was printed for posterity.

Stabbed in the Back

Another incident from junior high still stays with me—I am reminded of it on a daily basis, as a pain in my lower back. It was a hot day in early fall in the mid '60s, between classes. The bell was surely about to ring. I was standing in a long line for the water fountain. The complete integration of public schools had yet to end, but water fountains were no longer segregated.

The boy directly behind me became impatient, like the others behind him. He had a spiral composition book and a sharp pencil in his hand, which was pointed at my back. The pencil lead went into me when he was pushed from behind. It hurt and started bleeding, so I went to the nurse's room. They put a band aid over it and gave me an aspirin. Many years later, I still have pencil lead in the middle of my back.

Otherwise, my self-worth grew as I got older, taking personal satisfaction from other accomplishments. My Mother was visibly proud of me when I started wearing a bra and experiencing the menstrual cycle. My Father's behavior evolved into understanding: his little girl was growing up. *He* started treating me with kid gloves. There was still a wounded child deep within but I was becoming unblocked. I started to see a certain beauty in life emerge from the ashes.

My First Boyfriend

Moving from junior high to high school was anxious yet exciting. The first day of high school was a combination of speed dating and neighborhood watch. I have a montage of memories from this period, involving: stupid underage drinking, fighting off sexual advances from boys after stupid underage drinking, and near-death experiences resulting from stupid underage drinking. I also started to gradually build up delicate but positive lifelong friendships with other females.

I met a handsome boy about a week after our August birthdays. Leo became my first boyfriend. This was prior to the first day of high school in August 1969, when the autumn colors were becoming a very beautiful sight.

Leo had moved in down the street. His mother bought the only house for sale on my block—a redbrick house of two stories, four houses down, on the same side. His mother had recently become widowed, and he was transferring into public school. Leo had attended a private school. She may have wanted her eldest son to be near her during her grief or it could have been that she simply did not want to pay the exorbitant costs of private education.

He started showing up frequently at our house. There was one immediate drawback, though: he was a year older, my non-sister's age, and she had instantaneously developed a huge crush on him. I did not do anything to encourage him; but he chose to dog me, which increased the rift with my non-sister.

I went on a few car dates with him before he gave me a promise bracelet. This was a bracelet with the girl's name engraved on one side and the boy's name on the other. It signified a promise of being in an exclusive relationship. I accepted it before realizing that I did not want to be in such a relationship. It was jewelry, after all. Later, I heard his best friend had given several girls promise bracelets at the same time, so maybe I was *not* the only one.

He became semi-obsessed with me afterward. Eventually, being next-door neighbors became uncomfortable, as he would show up at unscheduled times when I had other dates. He was jealous and I think he thought he owned me. There were several times when I had to rush other dates away because he wanted to talk to me on the spot.

He was a good kisser, but he wanted more than kissing, increasingly asking for oral sex—which I was not inclined to offer him. I similarly disregarded his demands to "go down on him," to pleasure him. I had no concern for his sexual desires. If he did not like it, he was welcome to move on to the next girl.

I did not once consider what other girls could offer him. After all, he was not only handsome, but also from a rich family. He eventually had many other offers and possibly initiated many pregnancies. If so, he kept it under wraps (at least from me), because it never got around, as did the stories of other later loves.

I began to wonder if I was a prude. He finally moved on—and to drug use as well—but that was not the end of our physical love.

———————————————

Instant Attractions

I was attending the first football game of the season at a rival school, Captain Shreve, when I felt an instant attraction I could not ignore. Jeff was standing there with a group of my peers, his presence noticeable to all around him. I looked at him and wondered "Who is that incredibly handsome boy?" I say boy, but he looked grown-up to me.

I had never met him before. I thought I knew everyone, as I had gone to elementary school with one group, middle school with another, and—thanks to a line change relating to school districts—high school with a third. Well, I thought, "High school is going to be very interesting if this beautiful male is part of the mix!"

Someone in my peer group introduced us. He asked me out. I soon became enamored with him, so we started dating. Jeff was the first who caused me to lust, reminding me about the feelings my Barbie and Ken dolls had initiated long ago. With his patrician features, he reminded me of Michelangelo's David or a Greek God. He was an Eagle Scout and spent his summers in the wilderness, getting tanned and buff.

I had recently gotten my learner's permit and drove my Father's Ford Galaxy 500 to the game. This car was used by local law enforcement because it could go from zero to sixty in a matter of seconds. I also enjoyed the thrill of freedom behind the wheel.

On that night, though, I was stopped by a cop for speeding through the school zone on my way home. I had snuck so many people into the car—probably over the legal limit—I was likely to be in big trouble.

My passengers scattered as soon as they could get out of the car. The policeman looked at my permit and first name but did not believe it was me. Not only did my name appear in the male spelling, with only a middle initial but the permit also did not have a photograph. One could not tell whether I was male or female.

I really perplexed the young officer as I pleaded that, yes, I was that person. None of my friends knew that Sidney was my first name, since, like everyone else in my family, I went by my middle name. I disliked it and tried to hide it whenever possible—this incident only made me loathe it even more.

I was finally given a warning and let go. Thankfully, I was not (underage) drinking and driving that night. No police stations or jail time for me! My middle brother, however, was not so lucky...

Looking for My Hands

My middle brother later rode in the "Police Paddy Wagon" after drinking too much and looking for his hands in the cement sidewalk in front of a small neighborhood bank. Many years earlier, we had all been taken there by my Mother to memorialize our existence, kneeling down and putting our little hands in the fresh cement.

She wrote our names and the date for posterity. It was similar to the Tributes to the Stars at Grauman's Chinese Theater and the Walk of Fame in Hollywood.

On this particular night, a police officer found my middle brother, after many beers, kneeling on the cement once again. He made a big mistake when he stated he was "looking for his hands"—a comment that resulted in a police escort to the local station. He clearly smelled of alcohol and could have been arrested for underage drinking, as he was considered a juvenile.

I am not sure whether they offered him a breathalyzer test (which had only recently been invented). He was subsequently released after a call from my Father to the local Sheriff, a friend who he had financially supported in a recent election. It pays to have important connections!

My brother escaped a "juvie" record. I was secretly envious of his adventure and repressed the impulse to continually ask him "Well, did you ever find your hands?" I am now known as the "Weevil Woman" and he is the "I Can't Find My Hands Man"!

Drive-ins and Playing Putt-Putt

Jeff was the dream boyfriend—and he is still a real Southern gentleman. He was the one that Leo feared the most and that was certainly justified, poor boy! Like Leo, though, he never made it far with me during high school, likely because we were rarely alone.

Many times, Jeff picked up my little brother to play "putt-putt" early on Saturday mornings. He could have been sleeping in instead. Sometimes, my youngest brother accompanied us to the drive-in theater, too.

I felt an intensifying ache whenever I was around him. Jeff had an athletic masculinity that could not be ignored. We continued to date throughout high school and sporadically during college, but we lost touch for many years afterward. He was frequently around, though, even when we each had other dates.

He was a popular kid and a football player—and, oddly, he was paired up with me as my escort on the Junior Prom Court. I do not know whether God or an overzealous teacher did that! After all, I soon discovered I had a knack for finding, dating, and making some of my boyfriends kings and bulls, if only by name.

It was important to me at the time that Jeff liked to hunt, which was a plus in my book. I invited him to stay a weekend at the Ranch to hunt for rabbits.

My Father and Mother both hunted. I remember as a young child, on rare weekends, hiding quietly in the bush while they shot at ducks. We were threatened with submission and silenced so as not to scare their precious fowl. Surprisingly, my Mother was a very good shot, which made me wonder why she did not *ever use* that talent.

My Father hunted ducks, owning several rifles and handguns following his service in World War II. He had a yearly duck hunting lease in Gueydan, Louisiana, whose motto is still the "Duck Capital of America." Like the ducks, he *flew* south each year with his hunting comrades and my younger and middle brothers (once they were old enough) to hunt. I guess you could say he had his own "Duck Dynasty."

I was so distracted I am surprised I did not get SHOT that weekend. I was also surprised I kept my virginity, because I was so turned on by Jeff's athletic body and his expertise with a shotgun. Of course, we were chaperoned the whole weekend, with separate bedrooms in separate houses. I do not think we got many rabbits that weekend.

Once again, though, he was the perfect gentleman—at least on the surface!

Jeff has always been hard to read emotionally. Outwardly, he is the "coolest" man I have ever met. Inside, there is a rare deepness that he seldom shows. He is the only previous boyfriend for whom I hold a quiet flame of love and friendship many years later.

Recently, Jeff told me a story about high school that I found very amusing. He had found out that Leo was bad-mouthing him behind his back, perhaps because of me. Of course, being a man's man, he did not "take it lying down." Instead, he found out where Leo lived, got his phone number, and called him up from a pay phone. He told Leo to meet him outside his house in 15 minutes, so he could "beat his ass."

I am sure this scared Leo "shitless," as he was a pretty boy and did not want anyone to mess up his face. He was also very wily and able to talk Jeff down. Jeff was and always will be reasonable.

Saturday Steak Night

Saturday steak night was a tradition in my family. Each Saturday night, we would celebrate by cooking choice steaks and spending quality time together. It was more about sharing a meal together than our previous dancing.

It was an honor for my chosen date to be invited over for steak before going out. We had a substantial "supper" of steak, baked potato, and barbeque beans with a sourdough roll. The roll helped to soak up the impending alcohol consumption!

My Father cooked the steaks so tender and the taste so delicious that no red-blooded meat eating male could pass up the invitation. I was soon given the nickname "T-bone" by a good friend, partly because of these steaks and partly because of my rear end.

My boyfriends all relished this event, especially if they were asked to help cook the steaks. My Father had a way of quickly making them feel inadequate. Most were secretly afraid of him; and became nervous about making a mistake and ruining the meal. They should in fact have been afraid of my Mother, since she was covertly taking down their names for her bull registry. Each meal was courtesy of one of those dearly departed steers.

"Ode to a Broken Date"

My Father had an odd way of taking everyday sayings and making up his own version. For instance, "fish or cut bait" would be reworked as "better have bait if you are going to fish." Speaking of cutting bait, I certainly was doing a lot with my revolving door of dating.

I was pursued by a range of boys who were not yet men and had so many offers I could not keep up with them. One was particularly persistent. Keats kept asking me out, even though I kept saying no. Eventually, I relented, concluding that I had to say yes at least once. I was not interested in him, but I thought going on a date might curtail his interest in me. He had been awaiting an opening and asked me several weeks in advance, so I could not think up an excuse.

As it happened, I had another offer from Barrett, who I was interested in, to accompany him to a playhouse dinner event that same night. I said yes, forgetting I had other plans. I was in a big dilemma; I was not going to cancel what I saw as the better offer. I needed a twin or clone to go on the date with Keats. I nervously called him and made up some lame excuse.

On the day of the supposed date, I opened the door to a dozen roses and a poem, "Ode to a Broken Date." My John Keats, a very crafty guy, had written me a beautiful but cutting poem. I saw him in a different light and felt enormous guilt. How would I feel if someone did that to me? I felt even guiltier about lying to him. The date with Barrett was nice, but did not go any further.

The rejection kept him at bay, preventing him from asking me out again. Many years later, I wondered what happened to him and how successful he must have become. I certainly would have appreciated his talent today—he was one unique individual.

I had a few blind dates, although I tried to avoid them at all costs. They were called "blind dates" for a reason: one goes into the date blindly, for better or for worse, sometimes knowing nothing about the other person. We could not look at a photo or read a bio or choose by swiping left or right.

My first blind date was with someone whose name began with "D"—I cannot remember and did not care to. Let us call him Dexter. He was harmless, as far as I could tell. We were on a double date with one of his buddies, who was very cute. They both went to boarding school or military school but came home during the holidays.

I do not remember how the following events came about, only that Dexter proceeded to drink too much, before pulling a "non-sister move" and robotically walking around the kitchen (perhaps chasing me—who knows?). He eventually dropped to the kitchen floor, passing out with his face in the dog water.

I penned my own story that night—"Adventures of Dexter and the Dog Water"—and later left it to my girlfriend Jo in the "Wills" section of my senior high school yearbook. We ended up putting Dexter to bed soon after. The night turned out okay. His "very cute" buddy asked me out while driving me home and we had many more positive dates thereafter.

Skipping School

I had other dating adventures during high school, but one stuck out more than the others. I was still seeing Leo from time to time. He had a nice ski boat; he frequently asked me to skip school to go water skiing on Lake Bistineau.

I was game for adventure and eventually said yes. I had never skipped school before and, unbeknownst to me, my Father had asked the school to notify him should anything seem amiss with me. Apparently, his business dealings caused him to fear that I might be kidnapped for ransom, so my not showing up would be a definite red flag.

Leo also had a partner in crime, who was also a pro at skipping school. Leo picked me up in the school parking lot, where I had left my car, and we went off to frolic at the lake.

The one previous time I had gone water skiing on Lake Bistineau was during a date with a popular and talented golfer who went to Captain Shreve, a rival school. One day, he got into big trouble for stealing from a beer truck parked at a general store on a road leading to Lake Bistineau. Thankfully I was elsewhere that day.

I was not so lucky on this occasion. We had a great time skiing and soaking up the sunshine, before making sure we were back at school for the bell sounding at the end of the day. The only problem was my Father had called the cavalry when he was notified that my car was in the parking lot but I had not shown up for school.

They were waiting for me when we drove up. I had a lot of explaining to do. Boy, was I in trouble! Needless to say, I never skipped school with Leo again. My Father probably had one of his "talks" with him.

Election by Forgery

My Father demonstrated his need for control in other ways, attempting to prevent me from trying out for cheerleader in the spring of my junior year. Apparently, Minnie had said something about "cheerleaders being loose girls," so he adamantly refused to sign my permission form.

My Mother listened quietly to the whole ordeal; she dared not cross my Father directly, fearing another physical beating. She surprised me by sneaking into my room with a forged signature on the wrinkled permission form, which she had dug out of the trash can.

Despite being done in a sly manner, my Mother had nonetheless rebelled against his power. I think she saw something of her younger self in this situation. I was even more surprised when I looked at the form, since she had done an excellent job at forging his strange handwriting. It even made me wonder whether she had done this before?

By the spring of 1971, our segregated school had recently experienced forced busing as a result of racial integration. Forced busing was defined as the practice of assigning and transporting students to public schools within or outside their local school districts. The purpose was to diversify the racial makeup of these schools. There was an influx of new students and the school wanted the cheerleading election to be "fair," so every student had to vote using a central voting machine.

I used a corny slogan that Jan, my artistic girlfriend, helped me come up with, painting a banner that read "It is in your fate to vote for Kate." Being different, I wore a blue jean dress that I had created for the occasion: it was tie-dyed with a darker blue indigo ink and had a circular skirt. I was good to go!

I ended up making the *all-girl* cheerleading squad, which was a change from the previous year, when it was composed of three girls and three boys. Owen was one of the male cheerleaders from the previous year's squad. He looked somewhat like the famous actor, Owen Wilson. We had met and started dating in the spring before the tryouts. We continued dating throughout the summer. The prior cheerleading squad was responsible for training the new squad during the summer for cheerleading camp.

We saw each other during morning practice and became close friends. Owen was witty and funny and we laughed throughout the summer, driving around in his convertible MG. But we were never intimate and there was no sex between us. I had not yet lost my virginity and was not attracted to him in that way.

By late August, I had turned seventeen and was about to begin my senior year. Owen was getting ready to go off to college. Our relationship was heading toward its end, when he revealed a big secret to me, out of the blue. He took me aside and quietly yet officially proclaimed that he had padded the ballots in the cheerleading election so I would win. He did not say how.

I looked at him in disbelief, unsure whether he was telling the truth, since he was known for his mischief. Was this a last-ditch effort to keep me going out with him or did he just want me to be grateful enough to let him into my panties?

Ultimately, his revelation of the "ballot padding" only made me wary of trusting him in the future. I went on to be elected to Homecoming Court and a Senior Favorite without his help, so I naturally later questioned whether he was lying. I was not in love with him like Jeff—or Dude, who would soon show up in my life. I am not sure if he is still alive, but if he is, maybe I will one day ask him to tell me the truth. Perhaps he lives in Georgia and monitored the voting machines for a past major election.

We Are the Jackets!

Cheerleading offered fresh experiences—and, on rare occasions, embarrassing ones, such as when I forgot my cheer briefs or bloomers or "purples" (as I called them) and could not perform the jumps. Even so, I enjoyed my senior year as a cheerleader and being part of Finuf's troop.

Miss Finuf was our cheerleading sponsor, and she was one cool number. She was so different from my overbearing Father and treated us as though we were adults, pretty much allowing us to do whatever we wanted. I secretly envied her independent spirit.

Our colors were purple and gold, our mascot being the Yellow Jacket. Our school cries were "Who are the Jackets?" and "Sting 'em, Jackets!" We were also famous among the student body for our pep rally skits, which were mostly authored by Pomeroy, who was seriously talented and very funny.

I will always remember a pep rally spoof of an *I Love Lucy* episode, titled "Vitameatavegamin," which originally aired in 1952. In this episode, Lucille Ball performed a funny commercial to sell this health tonic, which included meat, vegetables, vitamins, minerals … and, most importantly, 23% alcohol. In order to sell the product, she swallowed a spoon of the tonic, which was supposed to give her vitality and make her popular. After ingesting a spoonful for each of the many commercial takes, she ended up grimacing at the taste and becoming intoxicated, due to the high alcohol content.

In Pomeroy's version, the name was something like, "Veta, Vita, Vegiman," and the tonic gave the user the special power of winning a football game. The humorous subject matter of the original television episode was not lost on those of us who wanted to be more popular and, of course, those of us who were underage drinkers.

I enjoyed acting in those skits. The auditorium was packed with students each week, usually performed on the day of a football game. These skits helped me to become more well-rounded and overcome my fear of public speaking, like the plays in elementary school. One skit cast me in the role of Maredia Bowdon, the Journalism teacher, who later became my Other Mother. Maredia was known for her exuberant spirit. I smiled a lot and performed "herkie" jumps in her purple dress and yellow high-heeled shoes! No wonder my feet are so messed up now...

High school football spirit ribbons—against the
Westlake Rams and the Carroll Bulldogs.

On certain days, Miss Finuf allowed us to leave school for swimming and a long lunch at the house of my good friend and fellow cheerleader, Delma. Her parents had a beautiful landscaped house with a swimming pool. They also had a great housekeeper, who was part of their family, as Julia was part of our family. She fed us great lunches when we needed a break from our studies.

Delma's boyfriend had a friend with an old mail van, which was used to transport Finuf's troop to all out-of-town football games. We took a nap on the long road trips to Westlake High School in Lake Charles, to play the Rams, and to Carroll High in Monroe, to play the Bulldogs. These were our most memorable road trips.

We were unchaperoned on these trips and given a little too much freedom—as one might say, genuine "jailbait"! Sometimes things got pretty wild. Our only other unchaperoned trip involved riding a bus to cheerleading camp at Sam Houston State College in Huntsville, Texas. This was after we had trained all summer with the previous year's cheerleaders.

It was a C. E. Byrd tradition that we were expected to win the "Spark Plug" award for spirit each year—and we did not disappoint. We spent the whole week cheering loudly with smiles on our faces everywhere we went. We cried "Jacket spirit ain't never gonna die"—and we never did let it! At least for that week. Our squad managed to get home without injury; except for one cheerleader, who fell and got a bump on her head after attempting a handstand incorrectly! Otherwise, we were extremely tired by the end, plus my face hurt from smiling so much.

Our other road trip as a cheerleading squad was for a weekend glamping trip at a local lake in the summer after graduation. This adventure included our adopted friend and cheerleader mascot, the Postman. He was always hanging around with jokes and friendly banter and we all enjoyed his company.

The Postman's family owned a used car dealership, so he showed up in a different car every outing. The cars looked good on the outside, but I once drove through a car wash with him and one of the rearview mirrors fell off.

On this occasion, he drove to the campsite and took us all to a local drive-in movie. One or two of us snuck in—without paying—in the trunk of the car.

I will never forget the night he came over to my house, late, after partying with us earlier. He staggered through the front door, which was never locked, looking a bit like Jack Nicholson, and said loudly "It's the Postman." I liken the incident to a scene from *The Shining*, where Nicholson says "Here's Johnny!" I cannot envision this image without seeing the Postman's face transposed upon Nicholson's. Sorry Jack!

The house on Pierremont Road—"Our door is always open!"

Blame It on the Fact She Is from Minnesota

Our high school football team was boosted by the acquisition of several talented black players when the forced busing occurred. The introduction of all the new students seemed to go well, especially with the addition of these star football players.

Our cheerleading squad was never advised how to treat these new students; we simply welcomed the diversity and adapted. It was going to be a new and exciting experience for all of us. I did not hear any racial remarks from any of the players or any other student, for that matter. We merged together in the classrooms and even attended their churches on occasion, which I found very interesting. My Presbyterian church offered a more passive experience—a sermon with a little singing—so I was charmed by the vivacious interactions of the black congregations.

The music of Isaac Hayes, particularly the theme from *Shaft*, echoed through our academic environment. For once, the spirit of our school sparkled. The new players seemed happy and we were all excited that we might have the opportunity to win the state title that year!

One of the cheerleaders was a little too happy when we finally won a big game. She had a custom of hugging and kissing the players after a big win, so it was second nature for her to continue the ritual. She was congratulating the players at the end of one game. One of the most talented of the new shining stars waited patiently for his hug and kiss. She performed as usual, but it was a little awkward.

We did not want to make it a big deal—but clearly it was! We were not yet consenting adults, although we were all the same age. It was the first time *any of us*—from either background—had been exposed to such a situation. The results of our interactions—the outcome of the forced mix—would emerge later. One thing was certain: that moment opened a door onto a new world of male–female relationships. My great-grandfather's law from the early 1900s was so "way beyond" obsolete. In the meantime, there were many more awkward moments to come.

The Dog Did It!

Drinking too much alcohol and then throwing up became my trademark. I should have known that I was not meant to drink heavily—being only five feet and two inches tall and just under a hundred pounds in weight did not help.

My first neighborhood boyfriend, Leo, had a party one weekend (yes, he was still in my life). His mother had gone on vacation, leaving him alone. Everyone knew about it and several irresponsible people showed up uninvited, trashing his house. There were also several sexual encounters in the bedrooms. Not me, not yet.

I drank too much, though, and threw up on my date's new Cutlass—he was so proud of that car and I had ruined it. He was unable to get rid of the putrid odor for many months, despite having it fumigated many times.

Another night, I had a date with a senior, who I will call Ham. We went to the Bossier Strip and guzzled down various rum drinks, which always resulted in stomach danger. On the way home, I got sick and passed out in his car. He became rather anxious, not knowing what to do with me or how to get me safely home; but he remained the perfect gentleman.

Ham later related that he drove into my driveway with the headlights off, walked into the house (the door was never locked), and slowly crept up the stairs as quietly as possible, whispering my non-sister's name hoping she could help get me into bed.

This was an impossible task, since there were many closed doors and Ham did not know which belonged to my non-sister. He therefore walked up to each closed door, whispering her name. Of course, my non-sister was sound asleep and did not hear, but my Mother, a light sleeper, did.

She headed to the landing, saw the strange boy standing in the hallway, and freaked out. Ham then calmly explained the situation, so as not to awaken the BEAR that was my Father. They were then able to get me into my bed, where I slept it off for at least twenty-four hours.

I got away with a lot of foolhardy behavior in high school, but one of the funniest moments—to me, at least—was when, having drunk too much and feeling sick to my stomach, I ran through the unlocked front door and headed for the nearest bathroom. I did not make it, throwing up near the bottom step of the main staircase.

I went upstairs to my bedroom and passed out, not recalling anything the next day. In the recesses of my memory, I can remember lying in bed and hearing a faint conversation between my Father and Mother about the dog throwing up on the carpet.

That poor dog took the blame for it all those years, because I never told another soul it had been me, until now.

Living an Alcohol-Induced Life of Sin

My alcohol-induced life of sin did not raise any hopes for my Christian redemption. By this time, my Irish Twin younger brother had given his life to Christ and was watching my non-religious behavior closely. He, too, was about to give up on my lost soul.

I did not feel Jesus was near—he had certainly quit talking to me in my closet. I rarely made it to church, except for major holidays like Christmas and Easter, and even though I sang the hymns, the sermons did not resonate with my life. There was no longer a vacation Bible school in the summer nor an occasional day of Sunday school to encourage me to "follow the good path."

Indeed, I missed many Sunday school and church days due to my alcohol-induced ways. One Saturday night, I was on a date when we wanted to buy booze. We were underage, so we drove to a liquor store in a remote part of town.

We asked the first drunk who walked past if he would buy liquor for us. Boone's Farm was our drink of choice, primarily because it was cheap. We pooled our money and gave it to the unknown man. Just when we thought he had absconded with our money, he came out of the front with our purchase. Mission accomplished!

That led to a successful night of drinking. Long story short, I was always way too hungover to get out of bed on most Sunday mornings. I had not yet explored sex, but I was truly a lost sheep. I did not open the Confirmation Bible until I was in my thirties, at a time of marital struggle, and it was only in my early fifties that it became apparent I needed Jesus and my faith more than ever.

"Knocking on Heaven's Door"

I actively chose to date another football player who was a year younger than me. He was handsome and caught my eye in the winter of '72, my senior year. I asked him to a senior party—these were held by groups of girls in a large venue with a decent dance band. These parties included much underage drinking.

The month of February always seems to involve extreme unhappiness or extreme happiness for me. I got married in February, I met my first "Northern Star" in February, and I started writing this book in February. I also experienced a tragic event on February 5, 1972 that almost cost me my life.

This handsome boy escorted me to the home of a friend whose parents were nowhere to be found, which was always the first sign of a drinking party! We actively explored the alcohol in the liquor cabinet. The plan had been to meet up, drink heavily, then drive to the senior party, where we would sneak in some more liquor before heading home.

Taxis—a sure sign we had had too much to drink—were an option, but we were legally underage and could be arrested, so we avoided them at all costs. Most of us drank, so there were no designated drivers. When it was time to go to the party, we all piled into separate cars, without thinking that drunk driving could be very dangerous. We would follow each other there—"the blind leading the blind," as they say. My friend, Dude, was in the lead.

His good friend, Pat, and his date, nicknamed Lollipop, a good friend of mine, were in one of the following cars. We were laughing and revving our engines and acting as though we were in the Indy 500. We started racing, going faster and faster, until we encountered a ninety-degree curve—but we continued straight ahead and hit a telephone pole at an extreme speed.

A small grassy incline, seat belts, and a few inches saved our lives. The incline mitigated the impact, so we ended up hitting the pole at a slightly lesser speed. To the right of the pole was a cement wall. Had we plowed into that wall, we would have been history.

Even so, we were far from being okay. I woke up in the emergency room (ER) where, sprawled on a sterile table, I looked around and saw my younger brother staring at me. I was a little loopy (either due to the concussion or the heavy drinking) and told him that I loved him.

This was the brother from the tonsil incident, who I had seriously wanted to do away with when I was younger. He was much more serious now that he had grown up, though. Several minutes later, there was an uproar, and I realized the senior party had decided to come to the ER. My friend, Lee, was also being treated for an injury from hitting his hand into a wall.

The next thing I knew, my parents were standing beside the table. My Mother later told me that my Father had wanted to shave, despite the call from the hospital, as though it was a normal day. She had to yell at him to "Stop it—we need to go now!"

Thankfully, Dude and I survived both the accident and the wrath of the FATHER (as well as our own two Fathers). I ended up with a broken jaw and sore muscles, while he had whiplash and a broken spirit. I was never punished or given a talk about drinking and driving. In today's world, Dude could have been arrested for driving under the influence—and it would have been the responsibility of our parents, because we were both underage. We both knew we were very blessed because our accident could have been fatal. Thankfully that did not happen. Everyone involved was relieved— my parents were very thankful that we were both alive. Maybe they both said a prayer?

I lived to drink another day. You would have thought I would have learned my lesson, but no, I continued my drinking activities way beyond college. I still drive by the scene of the accident whenever I visit Shreveport. It looks the same as it did in 1972 and reminds me to remember the true blessing I received that night and to say a little prayer to thank the God, the Father, who spared both our lives that night.

The Postman with wrecked Cougar, February 1972.

He Broke My Jaw and I Fell in Love

Dude and I continued our relationship after we had both mended. We were friends at first, before our relationship grew into something more, perhaps because he felt guilty at disrupting—and possibly ending—my life.

Dude is a beautiful writer and wrote me many letters. He is witty and funny and his writing reflected this. Being a writer myself, I appreciated his words and wished I had kept his many letters.

Speaking of writing. I had many visitors during the months of my recuperation. Everyone who came by was escorted to my bedroom, where I lay in my bed in my nightclothes. What was my Mother thinking?

I had broken my jaw in the accident, so it was wired shut. Someone had gotten me a guestbook, as though it was a wedding reception, so there was a documented record of these visitors. I still have the book. Each person signed their name and the date was noted. Some made entertaining comments, as though they were signing my yearbook. There were many comments, mostly positive ones, and it still surprises me, even now, how many "friends" came to see me.

I had to write down what I wanted to say, because I could not speak clearly enough through my wired jaw for people to understand. On the other hand, I could hear them without issue. Most did not appear to grasp this. There was nothing wrong with my hearing, but almost everyone took out the pad and wrote back to me as though I could not hear them as well. It got so frustrating that I started making up my own sign language and signals! I also cupped my ear or pointed to it to emphasize that I could still hear. In other words, talk to me! I had a brief taste of what a deaf person's life might be like.

I am glad I have that lasting record because I was drinking liquid codeine, an opioid, for the pain. The days became blurred. Thank God I never got addicted to that drug!

Dude was a frequent guest. Because of the uniqueness of our first date, we became kindred spirits and our friendship became the basis for a budding love story. I was accustomed to dating older guys, or guys my own age, so this relationship took me down the uncharted path of dating a younger male.

Eyes Wide Open AND Jaws Wired Shut

Following the recuperation period, of about six weeks, I got back into the swing of things by—you guessed it—more partying! I was in my senior year and had walked away from something that could have killed me. I had the mentality of an invincible teenager and I was going to live my life to the fullest. I did not once think about changing things.

My motto was "I just want to celebrate another day of living." Ironically, this was shared by other students in my senior class, because "I Just Want to Celebrate" by Rare Earth was later voted our graduation "senior song."

Playlist Song #8:
"I Just Want to Celebrate," by Rare Earth.

I was voted senior favorite, even though Owen was not around to mess with the votes. I must have been the only senior favorite in the school's history to have been photographed with my jaw wired shut. It was not my most flattering shot!

Time moved forward quickly. Dude and I continued to see each other. My feelings for him were growing stronger each day, but I kept them at bay by seeing a few other male friends who remained just that—friends.

One of them was Jimmy Mac, who had joined the Presbyterian Church with me as a child. I had not really had much interaction with him before that. He was very smart yet had a wild side, too. I believe he lived with his father, who never seemed to be around, so he was mostly unsupervised. I do not know about his mother.

We planned to get a group of friends together to celebrate our graduation in the French Quarter of New Orleans. I am not sure how I did it, but we ended up going without my parents knowing. I am sure they never found out. I told them I was staying at my girlfriend Jo's house. She was a good friend and had started dating Lee, a male friend. I liked her because she did not care what people thought of her and she told people off frequently. Jo was a great person to have in your corner.

I was still not allowed to eat solid food unless it had been ground to mush. I certainly could not eat a hamburger, which I craved daily. By then, my prescription of liquid codeine had come to an end—it might have been dangerous to mix that with alcohol.

Addictions came in all forms. Jo's weakness was drinking Coca-Cola or soda—or "pop," as the Canadians called it. She always had one in hand and "guzzled" several a day. So much sugar! Another male friend, who I called Old Pop, drank Dr. Pepper for breakfast and called it his "belly wash." I always thought both addictions were more than funny.

By then, I was super skinny, thanks to my lack of solid food and diet of codeine. Even though I was nearing the end of my recuperation, my jaw was still wired shut. The surgeon continued to tighten the wires regularly to help my jaw heal properly.

The carefully planned weekend soon arrived. Jimmy Mac and I drove to New Orleans in his Chevrolet Corvette—it was a pleasant ride, because he made sure to drive safely, to avoid a rerun of previous events. Our first stop was Pat O'Brien's in the French Quarter. I still have a picture of that weekend in New Orleans, which I treasure, along with my Pat O'Brien Mardi Gras doubloon.

I do not know how I skirted the issue, but no sex was involved. I am sure having my jaw wired shut helped kill any romantic buzz, plus we both passed out after drinking too many Hurricanes. I cannot speak for the rest of the group. We got home safely, without incident, and had a GREAT time!

There was only one hitch. The following week, at my doctor's appointment, my surgeon commented that my "jaw opened enough to get a hamburger in." My Mother looked at me with a questioning look, knowing I had not eaten any hamburgers on her watch. He shook his head and tightened the wires. I laughed inwardly because I had indeed had a McDonald's Happy Meal just a few days before, on our way home from the Big Easy.

Playlist Song #9:
"House of the Rising Sun," by The Animals.

Can We Go Get a Whopper and Fish Filet Sandwich Now?

The summer after my senior year, I was getting ready to go to college and coaching the new cheerleading squad each morning, to prepare them for cheerleading camp in Texas. My jaw had healed and I was no longer eating baby food. Finally, I could kiss boys. Life was free and easy.

My first sexual experience was far beyond serious. Heavy touching and kissing only went so far. My "Virginia" was turned on 24/7 and I *needed* to experience the real thing. I had hoped to lose my virginity to Jeff, but Dude and I had become very close friends. I felt I could trust him with the "gift." I was due to turn 18 soon, the age of legal majority in 1972, when I would no longer be a minor in the eyes of the world.

We began planning our big night, when Virginia and Dude would connect in living color. We did not choose the respectable Hilton or Marriott—God forbid someone might know our prominent parents or recognize us.

Dude picked the most "no-tell motel" in Bossier City he could find. I remember pulling up to the Barksdale Highway Motel—or perhaps it was the Barksdale Motel (named after the nearby Air Force base)—and thinking "You have got to be kidding?!"

He went into the office to check in, probably under an assumed name, playing up the clandestine encounter. He came back smiling with the keys to the room. I assumed he had paid cash and was anxious to see what his money had bought.

I was somewhat surprised at the gigantic king-size bed that took up the whole room. I remember looking for the vibrating bed or "Magic Fingers Vibrating Bed," as it was called, which was a highlight of most motels from the late '50s to the '80s. Many years earlier, I tried to jump on the bed while it was vibrating. What an experience that was!

Magic Fingers was a box with a coin meter and timer that was attached with wires to the mechanical vibrator in the box springs of the bed. The guest fed the box with quarters, like the air machine for tires. Well, my tire was about to be inflated! I later read that the "Magic Fingers" company fell to the wayside, after losing lots of money from patrons damaging the boxes and stealing the quarters.

Magic fingers.

Back to the task at hand... We nervously proceeded to take off our clothes, to touch each other in places we had not yet dared explore. We had only one goal in mind: for him to penetrate—or "do it"—and for me to lose my virginity.

As we proceeded to disrobe, I noticed for the first time that his penis changed shape as he got more excited. I had felt it through his jeans when we kissed, but WOW, to me, it was huge! Or at least I thought it looked HUGE. I had never seen an aroused penis before (except the shriveled one of the old man when I was a Girl Scout). That context made it somewhat confusing.

Now I was really in trouble. How in the world was that big thing going to fit in my small hole? Well, I decided there and then it was not going to—not that night, at least. I told him so in not so many words. I was not ready.

We laughed about it and got dressed. Once the mood had changed, we suddenly realized we were both hungry. He left for about thirty minutes to get a Whopper for me and a Fish Filet sandwich for him from the nearest Burger King. When he came back, we sat on the bed, eating our food and watching television. We both laughed at ourselves and our "would-be" encounter. After all, he had already paid for the room.

What a buzzkill! Although our physical relations were by no means over… I later termed the experience my first SEXUAL learning experience, as I learned something about the male anatomy I did not know before.

Playlist Song #10:
"This Hotel Room," by Jimmy Buffett.

I should point out here that I do not know what others thought of me during my three years at high school. I can only assume they thought I was putting out, as I was popular with the boys and had way too many suitors asking me out on dates. I did not show I cared, at least on the outside.

Who knows, maybe frustrated Leo was spreading wild and untrue rumors (as he frequently did) behind my back?! Whatever was going on, I left high school with fond as well as ugly memories and most probably lots of sexually frustrated males in my wake. I was moving on continually living, learning, and growing up.

THE SALAD DAYS

The Kappa Alpha Theta Sorority

I went to college in the fall, to LSU, whose football colors were also purple and gold, like those of C. E. Byrd. College was the beginning of my "salad days." I wanted it to be a time of carefree pleasures, youthful dalliances, and idealism.

I pledged Kappa Alpha Theta (KAT) during sorority rush, at the beginning of my freshman year. Dude's mother, who I respected and loved, had been in this sorority and wrote me a glowing recommendation. During sorority rush, as it was called, the incoming freshman would go from house to house and socialize with the sorority sisters. You hoped you would be chosen by a sorority at the end of the week. Some girls were chosen by several sororities, while a few were not chosen by any. KAT was considered a smart sorority, but I think being chosen was more about looks and personality. KAT had a beautiful house on University Lake; we were able to live there during our sophomore, junior, and senior years if we wanted to.

I continued seeing Dude for the next year or two. We still had much laughter. Our spark had dimmed due to the distance between us. I still cared about him and thought that one day, after both experiencing life, we would come back to one another and remain together for good. It was a romantic notion, I know. Fiction at its best!

By this time, he had graduated high school and gone to college in another state. I flew over one weekend, staying in his freshman dorm room. He had joined a fraternity and was living the college life. I was starting my next journey.

I Hurt in Places That I Did Not Know I Had

Dude and I decided to date other people; he found solace in other women during my absence. Not much later, he got one pregnant and soon married her. I clearly remember the day I found out—I was devastated.

Playlist Song #11:
"Hurt So Bad," by Little Anthony and The Imperials.

I remember wondering "Why didn't they use protection?" I thought all people used some form of contraception! I had tried hard NOT to get pregnant with him. I loved him and that was the last thing I wanted for him. For once, I had acted like an adult. Looking back, though, I often wonder whether that decision was a good one.

It was so hard to walk away, but I did, until a few years later. By this time, Dude was strolling a baby and changing diapers. I was finishing my last year at LSU, having strayed to the University of Texas (UT) at Austin for a year. He had finished his undergraduate degree and was in his first year of law school at LSU, Baton Rouge, on a path to practicing law in Louisiana.

He knocked on my door late one night. I opened it to see him smiling on the doorstep and my heart melted. It was a beautiful yet painful moment. I had invited him over on the premise that I would return his engraved St. Christopher, which was a gift from his mother.

I planned to say goodbye to him forever and tried to keep it friendly, but I knew the night held much more. We had unfinished business. By that time, I had experienced sex with other males and had many other relationships with college boys; but I was still in love with him. A physical relationship started that night, which thereafter continued sporadically.

Several years later, I saw him briefly while I was working in Houston. We shared a common bond of love and law. But it was sad, mainly due to what we could have had. Even so, we had much laughter and continue to have a true male/female friendship.

He was meant to be a family man and is a good father to his children. I am a proud supporter of all his life achievements. There are, as they say, "no hard feelings." We are and always will be special friends with no benefits. He also introduced me to the Bowdons, who would later take me in and save my life.

I would only experience these types of feelings—of what could have been—again much later, in my sixties, when I met another unavailable man who unintentionally stole my heart.

Playlist Song #12: "
I'll Get Over You," by Crystal Gale.

Newfound Freedom... I Think?

College opened many doors for me, and I was going to take advantage of all the opportunities presented to me. LSU was a party college; I was ready and willing for the freedom but not yet ABLE.

I was over the legal age of 18 but had yet to experience the true freedom of being an adult. My Father still kept close tabs on my actions, "for my protection"! I called my Mother one weekday while my Father was at work, for a girls talk. I asked her if she could do anything to help me, since the other girls had much more freedom than me. Freshman students were required to live on campus but were segregated into male and female dorms.

About a month after my conversation with my Mother, the Dean of Women sent a message asking me to come to her office for a little chat. I rushed over as soon as possible, feeling confused. What had I done to warrant this meeting? Was I getting kicked out of school already?

I sat anxiously as the Dean presented me with a legal document that I had never laid eyes upon before. It was a permission slip signed and dated by my Father prior to my arrival. She then handed me another form, which appeared to be exactly the same, but was dated much later. Was this a test?

I was confused, as I had never seen either form before. Then I looked more closely. The first form was the permission slip signed by the head of the household upon admission. It was signed by my Father, the parent who paid the bill.

It suddenly became clear that my Mother had struck again, signing the second form. She had taken matters into her own hands and used her little power in the hope of giving me the freedom I had requested. This time, however, she had been caught.

The forms outlined the three options for the female dormitory. The first required me to sign in by 10 p.m. The second allowed me to stay out until midnight. The third gave me the freedom to stay out all night, preventing the Dorm Monitor from sending out the authorities when my room remained empty.

On the original form, my Father chose the first option. But on the second form, my Mother chose the third option, mastering my Father's signature perfectly. My face remained stoic, but I secretly smiled. Maybe my Mother felt she was covertly stealing from my Father—a twisted thrill of power. I was too busy keeping my cool to try to figure out her motive, though.

It quickly became obvious that the Dean knew the first one was not the forged one. My Mother and I had been outed. But did she think I had forged the signature? I was not about to blame my Mother—after all, I might need her talents later!

The Dean told me she had phoned my Father and he said he had not given permission for the third option, which I had been already utilizing every weekend, being a card-holding member. As a result, the Dean tore up the second form, placed the first in my folder, and asked me to hand back my current pass. She put me on probation and forced me to spend time in study hall, to appease my Father.

Did I learn my lesson? Not by any measure. Yes, it foiled my plans of partying and possibly sleeping with boys. But the fact I was imprisoned after 10 p.m. did not stop me from rebelling—I simply did it during the day, before 10 p.m.

Indeed, it was time to make a choice: I chose to begin a major in adult acting out—a destructive pattern of personal rebellion that involved heavy drinking and eventually spiraled into my "fuck all men" stage. I now know it was a noxious response to repressed toxic memories.

Memories of my Father's infidelity and my Mother's perceived powerlessness had lingered below the surface long enough. Learning about my first love's forced marriage and realizing my own lack of power to make my own choices brought my underlying anger into everyday reality.

It was time for payback: I chose to "fuck" with the heads and bodies of as many men as possible. I was hoping to have some fun along the way, too. But, damn, I hoped I would never have to realize how very much it would hurt me...

Panty Raids Galore...

"Panty raids," as they were called, were a weekly treat for those observing as well as participating. It was very entertaining, like Mardi Gras, but instead of throwing out colorful beads and shiny doubloons, it was every size of underwear imaginable.

Each week we scoured department stores for the largest and most colorful "granny" underwear we could find. We made bets on whose underwear would fall the fastest or whether it would be large enough to float wistfully above the masses. Yes, it was a sight to see! There were many boys waiting with "bated breath" and open arms. I often used my binoculars to scan the crowd for my next date.

Our dorm building was several stories high, but we were allowed to open our individual windows just enough to throw out all shapes and sizes of lingerie. In hindsight, those windows were probably installed as a safety precaution, to deter the jumpers, who considered suicide on a weekly basis.

It was always a hoot to see who would show up begging for a treat; it was mainly males, but the occasional female would unexpectedly appear.

I certainly had an unpretty pattern of behavior. Although I enjoyed using my creative mind in classes that interested me, such as English and Architecture, my grades in other subjects were sinking. I only went to those other classes to learn enough to pass the exams. I was hoping to major in architecture because I was fascinated by buildings. I drew buildings incessantly as a child.

I frequently skipped my 8 a.m. history class. This was a required class and it was not uncommon for freshmen to have such early times. I suspect it was planned to keep us out of bars and on track with our studies.

This class was so large the teacher did not take the roll, so I flew under the radar and was never missed. I thought the teacher was boring as well; he sounded as though he was reading the phone book verbatim. I had to drink three cups of coffee to stay awake. The only comic relief was that he legitimately looked like a walrus.

I got really drunk the night before his exams and performed stand-up in the common area of the dorm. I never experimented with LSD or other drugs in college, so the Walrus Comedy Show helped me escape many nights of college boredom.

Playlist Song #13:
"I Am the Walrus," by The Beatles.

One of my architectural achievements was designing and building a houseboat—which, surprisingly, floated—in my freshman architectural class. University Lake was in a residential area surrounding the college campus. The design of the houseboat was unique. It folded up while it was afloat and expanded with a deck when it was docked. It was a big hit, with a picture appearing in the LSU yearbook. Ahoy, matey!

Playlist Song #14:
"Freedom Was a Highway," by Brad Paisley
and Jimmie Allen.

Speaking of mates, I have some other funny memories of my freshman year that did not involve building houseboats or not attending required classes. I met some very interesting girls in my dorm, who I called my "hallmates."

One, Tatum, spoke with a New Orleans drawl and had a favorite saying—"Where you at?" She looked like a cupie (or Kewpie) doll. Her roommate came from a wealthy Southern family, her father being a politician from Mississippi. She drove around in a luxury Continental we nicknamed the "pimpmobile."

Both hallmates were always up for mischief. One Friday, we piled into the "pimpmobile" and headed to the beach towns of Mississippi for a long weekend roister. We sported our Ray-Bans, had our cocktails or "roadies" in hand, and loudly sang along with the popular songs on the radio.

Playlist Song #15:
"Born to Be Wild," by Steppenwolf.

We were high on life, driving fast and wildly to Bay St Louis and Pass Christian. The road trip was all interstate, allowing my hallmate to take advantage of the horsepower under the Continental's hood. Suddenly, though, we saw flashing lights in the rearview mirror. OH SHIT, we were in trouble, especially since we had to guzzle down our roadies or throw them out. Neither was a pleasant option.

We quickly hid what we could not finish under the seat, but we did not fool anyone as we sat up straight, trying to look prim and proper in our sauced circumstances. The officer walked up to the driver's window. Our Mississippi hallmate was nervous and attempted to roll down every window except the one facing him. The officer waited patiently as she performed this feat.

She finally rolled down the appropriate window, smiling embarrassingly and shrugging her shoulders. Those few anxious moments seemed much longer. I held my breath as I waited to hear what "Southern spiel" she might concoct as she handed the trooper her driver's license and smiled prettily.

He studied it closely, looked up and smiled, then asked "You related to...?" She relaxed, smiled back, and said in her sweetest Southern voice "Why, yes sir, I am, Mr. Officer!" He shook his head, returned her license, and warned her to slow down.

Obviously, he had deduced who her father was when he ran the plate before getting out of his squad car; but I could not believe we did not get arrested there and then. It just goes to show that political clout goes a long way in times of trouble. We thanked our lucky stars the police officer was not of the other political persuasion and did not have a grudge against her popular father.

Trying out for College Cheerleader

Playlist Song #16:
"You Are the Sunshine of My Life," by Stevie Wonder.

For some reason, in my sophomore year, I thought I was good enough to try out for the college cheerleading squad. It was not my first rodeo, but I was being delusional, since I had not followed my exercise routines and was in bad shape due to too much partying.

Since I am an impulsive individual, I made my decision at the last minute, choosing to perform to Stevie Wonder's "You Are the Sunshine of My Life," because I loved the song. The beat was not conducive to a cheerleading routine and I looked silly standing in one place, swaying to the music and shaking my purple and gold pom-poms. It made me dizzy—and did not make any sense, like many things in my life at that time.

The only good thing was the judge that day complimented me on my choice of music. Or was he secretly making it a joke? Marnie, my sorority sister and future roommate, WAS good enough. She had a cheerleader smile, which aided her chances—and, interestingly enough, she ended up marrying that same judge...

The KAT House

I remained in the KAT sorority for my sophomore year. I was good friends with my sorority sisters living college life without worry. I had passed the final exams of my freshman year, so had to decide which direction I was going to take for my major. I wanted a major that would not cut into my demanding social life too much, so I decided that Architecture was a little too time-consuming.

During this time, I had some great adventures with Marnie, who knew how to party. She was from New Orleans and we went there often, meeting two boys who attended Tulane University. My date was from Wichita Falls, Texas. They were so different from the LSU boys—more studious and yet so much fun.

Whenever Marnie drank heavily, she would put a wet washcloth or "cold compress" on her forehead before going to sleep. I finally asked her why. She said it helped cure the hangover. After thinking about it, I decided "that makes sense" and followed suit.

It must have looked like a spa day as we lay in our beds with wet washcloths on our foreheads! It happened so often it became a ritual. It was difficult for me to keep mine in place, as I moved around a lot in my sleep. Marnie, however, lay perfectly still all night, having acquired the knack of doing so. I envied her. Idiosyncrasies make life interesting, and this was hers—a real "beyond the GRITS" moment.

Marnie is very intelligent and we had many great conversations. Although I have lost touch with her, I have vivid memories of the fun of our many road trips to New Orleans and I still smile when I think of her "hangover" washcloths. As for the boy from Wichita Falls, I visited his family once and enjoyed the weekend, but it never progressed into anything more.

Playlist Song #17:
"On the Road Again," by Willie Nelson.

Food's Out

The KAT sorority had recently finished the yearly rush—I was doing the "rushing" this time, not being "rushed." We had done our jobs and pledged some beautiful and intelligent recruits to mentor throughout their college lives.

Living in the KAT house was fun. We got up to all kinds of mischief, especially after a long week of intense study. It was our way of letting off steam. Late one night, after many hours of study *and* drinking, we got the munchies. A sorority sister came in and tipsily announced that her car key opened the locks on the refrigerator doors.

We were forbidden from eating from the refrigerator after hours. All the refrigerators had locks on them. Some even had chain links through the handles. I guess that was where all the good food was. Our elderly housemother, Mrs. Craft, made sure they were locked each night so we could not take any food from them.

The sister motioned us to follow her, so we did, quietly heading down to the kitchen so as not to awaken the housemother. We waited patiently for her to perform her magic. And she was correct. Unbelievable! How she ever compared the two thoughts is still a mystery. She was very smart and her brain was a little quirky.

This gave us all kinds of ideas, most of them not good. We grabbed some of the good food, since our true mission was to soak up some of the alcohol. It was like we won the lottery. Noticing that some containers had lard in them, we decided to play a prank on the rest of the house. We placed them on the dining room table, with plates and silverware, to give the appearance of a buffet dinner. I am not sure whose idea it was—most probably my housemate from Fort Worth, who was a little dramatic with a deviant mind.

We pressed the button on the intercom and Fort Worth proudly announced "Food's out," imitating Mrs. Craft. Actually, she sounded just like her! Surprised by the announcement, the whole house stampeded down the stairs, only to find loads of lard ready to dish up.

By that time, my two housemates and I were hiding in the shadows, laughing our asses off. The one in big trouble hid on top of the toilet seat in one of the bathroom stalls. The other housemate and I jumped into our beds and lay still under the covers, as though we were asleep.

Mrs. Craft woke up and hobbled up in her gnarly bedclothes and slippers, yelling a name over and over. She forgot it and got it backward, so no one answered. I almost laughed aloud but knew I would be yanked out of the bed and disciplined should I utter a sound. There was no telling where our errant housemate was— probably out for a drive with the magical car keys.

Several weeks later, we were still on good behavior... but apparently the rest of the campus was not, especially the Delta Kappa Epsilon or "DEKE" fraternity, as we called them.[15] Five presidents had been DEKEs: Rutherford B. Hayes, Theodore Roosevelt, Gerald Ford, George H. W. Bush, and George W. Bush. The DEKEs were steeped in Southern heritage but very controversial at times.

Streaking in the '70s

mostly dated Sigma Alpha Epsilons or SAEs, who we fondly referred to as the "sleep and eat" boys. They frequently—and not so fondly—referred to us as "I ate a Theta."

I had no wish to date DEKEs, but I did date one. His last name rhymed with "VROOM," which was particularly fitting as the story unfolded. The early '70s was a time of experiment, and this rowdy chapter of the fraternity was not afraid to try anything, as I can attest from firsthand experience.

On the outside, this particular DEKE appeared to be shy and reserved—not, in other words, a normal DEKE. I was willing to give him a try because he was cute and well spoken, not loud and boisterous.

One Friday afternoon, I was sitting on the veranda of the KAT house with my fellow sorority sisters, talking about our plans for the upcoming weekend. It was a warm and sunny afternoon. We were in a party mood, looking out across University Lake, and getting ready for the weekend by catching up on the week's news.

My "would-be" date suddenly appeared before me—I was surprised to see him, having accepted a first date with him the following night. He was acting a little weird but spoke to me directly, saying "Wait here, I will be right back!" The comment was strange but intriguing. I waited patiently yet distractedly on the porch, anxiously making idle conversation with my sorority sisters.

We then saw a lone runner heading toward the sorority house, entirely naked except for a pair of socks and tennis shoes—quite a surreal sight! He soon appeared in full view of all the sorority sisters.

Of course, our eyes focused on his male appendage, swinging in the wind—I put my hand over my mouth in shock at the sight. I was not ready to see that part of him yet, especially not before the first date.

He continued jogging and waved to me as he passed. At first, I thought he might have been made to do it, as part of the fraternity hazing. I decided there and then that he was history, since he was definitely acting like a "DEKE." According to an article I later read, there was a streaking trend on college campuses in the late fall and winter of 1973, where "streaking" was defined as "running naked through a public place."[16] Unsurprisingly, it was popular at warm-weather schools.

The article goes on to relate that at that year's Academy Awards ceremony, David Niven made the following quip after a naked man ran across the stage behind him: "Just think, the only laugh that man will ever get in his life is by stripping off his clothes and showing his shortcomings!" That raised many laughs from the audience as well as those watching on television. This DEKE's "shortcoming" did not get my laugh!

Streaking in the '70s.

Apparently, some of the fraternities on the LSU campus proved the perfect conduit for this "counterculture movement," which was mainly driven by young white men. According to a later article, many considered streaking to be a reaction to the social justice movements that were emerging on campus at the time.[17]

As for me, I think it was bound up with the "zeitgeist" of the era; for those who sought freedom from established norms. I was certainly living that in a personal—rather than public—way. Streaking was a seemingly harmless way of forgetting the woes of the day while also releasing some self-exhibitionist tendencies. The craze died down at LSU in 1974, when students started studying for finals.

Playlist Song #18:
"The Streak," by Ray Stevens
(especially the YouTube version—Ray Stevens aka Harold Ray Ragsdale definitely thought "way beyond").

Wetting the Bed in the Presidential Suite

I had many other adventures in my sophomore year with two of my sorority housemates, who I am calling Mandeville and Fort Worth. None was quite as memorable as the night we spent at the historic mansion of the Louisiana Governor. This mansion was built in 1963.

Mandeville dated the eldest son of a famous "colorful and powerful" four-term Louisiana Governor, Edwin Edwards. This Governor was known for his charm and was very much a "ladies' man."

The mansion, as we termed it, had a spacious chef's kitchen that even my Father, in the restaurant supply business, would have drooled over. I learned that the staff included prison inmates—displaying "good behavior"—from the local penitentiary in Angola, Louisiana. I later visited this prison in my senior year, on a field trip for my Criminal Justice class. I cannot imagine feeling comfortable living in the mansion in such a situation.

One night, we were invited to spend the night at the mansion after several cocktails, when we were "three sheets to the wind" and unable to drive home. The kitchen prepared a late-night breakfast, before we were escorted to the Presidential Suite. We climbed onto the biggest mattress I had ever seen—much larger than the mattress at the "no-tell motel." All three of us fit very comfortably and the sheets were soft and silky. I fell asleep immediately.

Slightly before dawn, I heard Mandeville exclaim "What?! Who wet the bed?" Fort Worth, who slept in the middle, confessed to doing the deed, having been too drunk to head to the bathroom. The center of the mattress was soaked, as were the sheets, which now reeked.

Now what were we going to do? All the dignitaries and even the President were invited to stay in this room, yet Fort Worth had made her mark like a dog. Mandeville was a fast thinker and we hightailed it out of the back door as soon as we could.

Later that day, after many hours of sleeping off our hangovers, Mandeville told us that her boyfriend had called. Housekeeping had discovered the puddle. It was assumed one of the young grandchildren had climbed on the bed and done the damage. Just like the story of the dog and the vomit. We were off the hook, which is all that mattered; but I am not sure how they managed to clean that mattress.

Governor Edwin Edwards went on to win several gubernatorial races in later years—including one in 1991, as an underdog. Lanny Keller a journalist from a local newspaper had suggested "the only way he could win was if he ran against Adolf Hitler." Never say never: he ended up in a runoff against former Ku Klux Klan leader and "neo-Nazi" David Duke.

Governor Edwards joked with the press that he only had to "stay alive" to beat Duke, also boasting to the public that they had "only one thing in common"—namely, they were both "wizards under the sheets." The Louisiana voters loved him. He claimed an "unprecedented" fourth term as Louisiana Governor, winning the runoff with a landslide majority.

In later years, though, Governor Edwards got into all kinds of trouble for political corruption, being found guilty of racketeering charges and sentenced to ten years in federal prison. He was released in January 2011, after serving eight years. He died in July 2021, at the age of 93. I, for one, will miss his spirited banter.

Working "The Porters"

During my time at LSU, my Father continued to be a workaholic lothario: he worked at the store during the week, and at the Ranch on the weekends. I am sure he always had time for sex in between and on the side.

The Porters were a group of loyal black men, who worked in the warehouse as store employees during the week and as ranch hands on the weekends. They were paid through the business for their work in the week and paid separately for their labor at the Ranch. In other words, they worked every day. All but one—Rev, a church reverend, who was allowed the day off by my Father to work for the Lord on Sundays. It was now the '70s, so these employees received benefits such as health insurance and also had the option to participate in profit sharing.

My Father paid the wages for the weekend work with his custom Ranch checkbook, which he kept in his Bronco. This checkbook featured a Red Poll cattle head on each check. Whatever needed to be done, the Porters came to the rescue—putting up fences, helping with the cattle, cutting timber, and other odd jobs.

My Father also demanded the respect of these men, who called him "Mr. Honeysuckle," either because they could not pronounce his name or because they, like Prissy, secretly made fun of him. He was definitely not "sweet-smelling" like the flower of the same name.

The only time I conversed with them was when I drove my Pontiac Firebird to the business to fill it up with gasoline. My Father had installed a gas pump near the warehouse—the delivery trucks could fill up their tanks and he could also save money by filling up the many family cars. I do not know how he managed that one.

It was easy for me, as a "helpless Southern woman," to pull up, get out, and let one of the Porters fill up my tank, while I chatted with "Daddy" inside.

I would walk through the warehouse and greet each of the Porters by name as I headed to my Father's office. One of them would smile and say "You are so much like Mr. John!" Looking back, I often wonder if they were in on the BIG secret that I only found out about much later, when I was in my sixties.

Morning Milk Coffee

Playlist Song #19:
"Wake Up Sunshine," by Chicago.

invited my sorority family to the house on Pierremont Road several times during breaks and holidays.

We observed the traditional rituals of milk coffee as well as Saturday night steak. The tradition of morning milk coffee started before I was born. I do not remember all the details; but I loved my morning milk coffee, which I have drunk since I was a very small child. I do not know if this is a Louisiana tradition or one started with my Father and grandparents.

My Father loved his morning coffee. Ours was milder than the popular New Orleans French Quarter chicory coffee. He liked a little sweet, too. It was not a beignet topped with powdered sugar; rather, he preferred a blueberry cake donut, which crystallized into delicious crunchiness when heated under the oven broiler. It tasted very good with the milk coffee! No wonder he struggled with type 2 diabetes later on. He continued the tradition when my son was born, in the '80s: my son loved waking to the food, but received milk instead of coffee with his blueberry cake donut.

Here is the ritual in a nutshell: my Father woke early, made the coffee, placed the cups on a tray, then came around to each of our beds, waking us and serving us our coffee in bed. He was our human alarm clock! We woke up and drank the milky substance. He originally used small demitasse cups when we were young, but the cups got bigger as we grew older. He would sometimes impatiently leave mine by the bed—and I, in rebellion, would take a sip and go back to sleep immediately, adamantly refusing to get out of bed.

In high school and college, these wake-up calls were sometimes accompanied by the occasional sight of a cattle prod—an implement with a voltage similar to a modern-day stun gun that was used to steer cattle. He never actually used it; but it amused him to warn me about the consequences of not waking up and getting out of bed.

Drinking the coffee was especially painful when he came around at 6 a.m. and forced me to take a sip after a night of drinking. Eventually I had conditioned myself to go back to sleep even after drinking a whole cup of his delicious coffee, continuing to rest for many hours after he headed merrily off to work.

One weekend, while home from college, Mandeville and I were sleeping off a night of partying when he came around with the coffee. Thankfully, without the cattle prod. This quirkiness was not for the world to see. The outburst "Look at the head on that one!" followed, causing my sorority sister to start laughing.

Apparently, she had "bedhead" hair, but her nightgown had fallen from her shoulder, so she was not sure which head he was referring to. Let us hope it was the former. Even today, Mandeville remembers this as though it was yesterday, as does Leesa, my other long-time best friend, who experienced a similar scenario many years before. Hers was definitely the former.

Jigger a Minute

Most summers, I came home from college to work part-time at the store and vacation with my family. My adventures continued, even as I transitioned from more freedom to the prison of living at home. Of course, it was much more difficult to date when I was, once again, expected to be at home before midnight.

One day, I heard from Jimmy Mac, who was having a party at his father's house, who I had never met. Jeff would be there, too, so it seemed harmless—a good time to renew high school friendships and celebrate the end of one more year of college.

We met up and immediately started to play a drinking game called Jigger a Minute. I do not remember the alcohol of choice. It probably depended on what was available in the liquor—or "medicine"— cabinet. As the name implies, Jigger a Minute requires each participant to consume a jigger (roughly one and a half ounces) every minute. The winner is obviously the person who consumes the most jiggers. I think we bet on this, so the prize was probably money. A jigger a minute for an hour works out at ninety ounces, which is well over three bottles of whiskey—alcohol poisoning at its worst. Of course, no one would have gotten that far and lived.

We started the game at about nine and I had passed out in Jimmy Mac's bed by ten. Sleeping soundly, I woke up to banging on the front door sometime in the night. I heard Jeff talking to someone who was speaking very loudly at the front door. He then came into the bedroom and tried to shake Jimmy Mac awake. I was not aware that he had lain down beside me sometime during the night (I do not believe he was into "nocturnal sexsomnnia").

I doubt he even attempted to give me a kiss. Had he tried, he would have gotten nowhere. I struggled awake, only to hear Jeff say that my Father and younger brother were at the front door. Many years later, Jeff revealed that my younger brother most probably saved his life that night. He told my angry, gun holstered Father that Jeff was not with me. My Father believed him and backed down.

Holy shit, I was in big trouble! I had driven over in my car, so my Father must have looked for me all over the neighborhood when I did not get home before midnight. Then again, my Father might still have been having me tailed, for all I knew.

Needless to say, he was very angry with me and Jimmy Mac, picking me up and flinging me over his shoulder, before marching rapidly out the front door with my younger brother in tow.

I was definitely grounded, although I was clearly over the age of majority. That may have been a record for a college student back then! Most parents emancipated their children when they turned eighteen, which was the legal age in Louisiana until around 1985. I was definitely much older than eighteen at this point.

That said, Louisiana was the last state in the nation to raise the drinking age to twenty-one.[18] Before that, one could buy and consume liquor between the ages of eighteen and twenty, which was known as the "drinking-age loophole." There were "loopholes" in the new law, too, since an individual under the age of twenty-one could enter a bar and drink if they were "with a parent or guardian" or they were "attending a religious celebration or a non-profit event."

So those who were religious and charitable—or make-believe religious or charitable, of which there were many—could drink to their heart's desire. Also, could a guardian be your close friend or buddy if they were over the age of twenty-one? There will always be ways to get around the rules if you have a creative mind.

Not only was I deeply embarrassed at my debacle, but I was also forever considered the "black sheep" of the family after that. No other sibling came close. It was torture! Jimmy Mac tried to contact me several times, but the house phone was being monitored 24/7. His calls were blocked the old-fashioned way, my parents taking my phone from my room.

My Mother was instructed by the "Warden," my Father, to answer the house phone and hang up if a male asked for me. My Mother never expressed any opinions about this situation, again probably fearful of my Father. There would be no dates for me for a while.

Jimmy Mac finally sent me a message through one of my girlfriends, whose calls were not blocked. We finally met up several weeks later, at Betty *Virginia* Park—how ironic.

Sitting on one of the picnic tables, we discussed the possibility of a continuing friendship. I never considered Jimmy Mac for a romantic relationship, so we pretty much parted for a couple of years, until picking up our friendship story in Austin.

Jimmy Mac was always very bright. I heard he went on to work for NASA several years later. I would like to see him again to learn about his life after college—and, hopefully, laugh about our post-adolescent stupidity. Perhaps at a future reunion...

Thank God Jeff and my younger brother were able to talk my Father down so he did not shoot either Jeff or Jimmy Mac. That would have most assuredly put me in a mental hospital and ruined my life.

The Chevy Malibu from Hell

It is also worth mentioning another longtime and non-romantic friend, BIG. I have known him since kindergarten. I could be wrong; but I think he got his nickname when he was very young, because his head was not in proportion with his body.

BIG was the KING of getting into trouble and known for his "landscaping" adventures. Landscaping was akin to "rolling" someone's house with toilet paper, but far more destructive. One waited until the night following a big rainstorm, picked a victim—usually someone who had wronged you—then drove into their front yard, creating deep ruts in their manicured lawn.

You could get very creative with the circles and curves, even spelling out words, depending on how much time you had. It would be best if you picked a night when the victim and their parents were out of town. I never participated in a landscaping event, but BIG did it frequently, according to his boasts.

You never knew what you would get on a date with BIG, but I reluctantly accepted his invitation. He picked me up one night in his Chevy Malibu, with some fireworks in the back seat—mostly Roman candles. He had carefully planned everything: I would drive the car, while he shot Roman candles from the rear window at passing and oncoming cars.

This was before he had had a few drinks! Alcohol consumption did not seem to be a factor in BIG's behavior. His creative thinking had no bounds even stone sober. After a few near misses, I put a stop to my involvement in this escapade, before it escalated to something more extreme. BIG definitely had a case of rebelliousness, especially against authority and the police.

In my junior year, I accepted a date to a senior party on Cross Lake with a friend of BIG's, doubling with BIG and his date. My date was the designated driver—a respectable and responsible individual. In his usual form, BIG became disruptive and began calling the security cops "pigs," being arrested shortly thereafter.

My date tried to help BIG and even called his father for help. BIG spent the night in jail, after his father—who was called Scoob or SCUBE—told the police to leave him there and refused to help BIG with bail. I guess this was just one of many calls he got from his son and he wanted to teach him a lesson. But I think it only fueled the fire within BIG, prompting further impulsive and destructive behavior. How he has managed to escape prison or death eludes me to this day! He showed up to our 50-year high school reunion recently, single, but in rare form, despite the wear and tear of aging.

At this same reunion, I found out that Spinks, another friend of BIG's, had passed away from heart disease several years ago. Rather than firing Roman candles, Spinks was known for his overzealous "mooning" out of rear windows, which occurred more frequently than the "every now and then" of intoxicated behavior.

In case you do not know, "mooning" is the act of pulling down your pants or whatever covers your ass, thereby exposing the latter to the world. It was done in a variety of locales. Spinks was quick and his timing was impeccable, always seeming to moon others who laughed it off as adolescent fun. He never faced an angry individual threatening to sue him for indecent exposure; and, like my childhood girlfriend, he never earned a juvie record—at least, not that I know of...

Making Terrible Decisions

Soon after my sophomore year in college, I was knee-deep in my "fuck all males" phase. My life started to spiral even more, however, as I experimented with multiple sexual partners. At first, it was all college boys. The hookups that had started in college then continued throughout my twenties, as I made many terrible decisions, induced by alcohol, sleeping with whoever I found attractive at the time. There were many—SO MANY!—that I do not even remember their names or their faces... And there are some I do not wish to think about, even in my deepest fantasies or nightmares.

The only saving grace is that most were one-night stands, so I did not have to see them again, let alone develop a love relationship. I do not know how I managed to avoid anal or oral sex with any of them. It is hard to remember, since that part of my sexual life is so different now.

I especially detested the men and women in long-term love relationships, I sought to destroy that trust by sleeping with "their" boyfriends and encouraging sexual infidelity in the weaker ones. I was rarely attracted to anyone who was looking for a caring relationship.

A big part of my "fuck all males" stage involved late night "booty calls." In particular, I had one encounter with a boy from southern Louisiana who I had met at a Baton Rouge dive bar. He looked like Boz Scaggs—a popular singer-songwriter with a unique sound "in the blue-eyed soul genre."[19] I chose him for that very reason, although I doubt he could carry a tune, especially because he was always too drunk to perform adequately. To this day, every time I play the Boz Scaggs album *Silk Degrees*, I think of him.

I gleaned that the real name of *my* "Boz Scaggs"—aka Big Scallywag—was an aristocratic one, with a "III" behind it. He dressed in button-down shirts and khaki slacks, very "uptown and preppy." I hooked up with him a few times, mostly late at night, when he would call or show up at my door in a drunken stupor with his heavy New Orleans accent.

Playlist Song #20:
"What Can I Say," by Boz Scaggs.

I had become what I would term "my worst enemy"—certainly a women's enemy or non-professional whore, who chose the "who, what, when, and where" in each of my encounters. In all honesty, though, I do not know how I maintained my double life of inside and outside personalities, while making my way through college, into an esteemed sorority, and later into a prestigious law firm. It was a feat beyond measurement.

I guess I learned it from the best—my Father! It was a miracle that I avoided dating married men. Anything long-term was out of the question and something I dodged at all costs. After all, that would be bound up with the chapter of my life involving "Father issues" and it was a pattern of destructive behavior I did not want to *consciously* explore. There was some discrimination, though, and in lucid moments I managed to go on dates that did not end with sex. I made a few long-term male friendships along the way.

The Tragedy of Michael G.

Michael was a nice boy who I grew up with, mainly seeing him on Sundays at the First Presbyterian Sunday school. Of course, I only went to Sunday school occasionally; I think he went every Sunday. We may have had a few dates as friends, but only in high school and college. He was also an SAE and was friends with all the boys I dated and/or slept with on occasion.

One night he and two other boys were driving home in someone's vehicle—name unknown. All three were in the front seat, Michael having fallen asleep or passed out, when they drove into a utility pole. Michael never woke up: his neck was broken. I was devastated when I heard: I did not understand why the Lord had chosen to take Michael and not me. I guess I experienced what is called "survivors' guilt," as I remembered my own encounter with a telephone pole only a few years earlier. They always say the good die young. Well, that did not say much about me!

About a month later, I was on a date with one of his fraternity brothers, whose grief over Michael's death was still apparent. I heard a song that reminded me of Michael—and when I thought about what I had been through in the past, the loss and grief became extreme. I burst out crying. I hardly ever cried and to perform this public display in front of a boy I barely knew was embarrassing.

I had grown up thinking crying was for babies. This was *my* conditioned response, having learned early in life that crying was not okay, since it only made my Father mad. It was only much later in life—thanks to the love of Maredia and her husband, Jim—that I learned crying was in fact okay and even necessary. The date turned sour after my outburst and I had to go home, but the memories of Michael's death survived long after.

I remained friends with this one-off date, but later reverted to my prior ways, hooking up in a parked car with his best friend and fellow fraternity mate, who I will call Don Juan. He was a handsome rogue. There had always been a physical attraction although he was in a long-term relationship with another woman. Apparently, I was still into breaking up lasting commitments. It was a one-time thing at the wedding of someone I cannot remember—and do not care to.

———————————————————

Tell Him It Is His and Get Married

All this time, I was on the "pill" and protected against unwanted pregnancies. But it DID NOT, as the label explicitly says, protect you from sexually transmitted diseases. I managed to avoid most of the dreaded ones, like gonorrhea, syphilis, hepatitis, and AIDS. I guess it was sheer luck in my choice of males that I never went down that path.

I did not, however, avoid pregnancy. My first boyfriend, Leo, was still in the picture, hovering like a helicopter. I had managed to avoid sex with him previously. He was obviously still sexually attracted to me, maybe even somewhat obsessed with me, after all these years. He just could not let go of me! Well, I finally relented after several cocktails.

Leo was in LSU Medical School by then and I saw him at a dive bar one night. I decided to go home with him, to a dorm room and a single bed. It was our first time and it was unprotected. I had just come off the pill due to hormone issues. Although the act only lasted minutes, the consequences lingered for several months later, as, guess what, he had planted his seed in me. Damn it! I did not take a pregnancy test until several weeks later, when I became extremely sick in the mornings. Here is the rest of the story...

After wondering why *I did not use protection*, I immediately decided I was going to have an abortion. It was an impulsive—and unilateral—decision, based on the self-centered deductions that I did not love him, I was not ready to marry him, and I did not want to have a baby, period. I never once considered the enormity of my actions.

I was an adult and did not have to tell my parents, although I discussed it with my Mother. The only advice I got from her was to pick a guy you want to marry and "tell him it is his." Well, I could not just tell a guy it was his if I was not having sex with him. In contrast to before, there was not a long line of men I was sleeping with at THIS time. I had experienced a momentary lapse with Leo. After this talk, I should have guessed that my Mother had done the same thing with my Father; but I did not uncover and confirm her secret until much later, in my sixties, after taking a DNA test with ancestry.com.

Guess what? I did not listen to her. Her rationale was stupid to me. It was the late '70s and I was in my early twenties. Abortion was not yet favored in most of the Deep South, but I had the legal right to one thanks to the Supreme Court ruling of 1973 in the case of Roe v. Wade. Nonetheless, I had to go about it delicately, in secret, but hopefully also in a safe manner.

For some reason, a relative knew how to proceed with an abortion—I do not know why and did not ask—so she helped me make the necessary arrangements. I knew I was not going to tell the biological father—I did not want him to have any say in the matter. My Mother would never help me do what I was about to do. Even so, it was my body. WHY must we make such life-changing decisions when we are so young? I was impulsive and was not yet able to consider the lasting consequences. I followed my gut intuition, more emotion than logic, which was sadly immature. I was legally an adult; so my Mother could not make me have the baby.

I soon made the appointment and went to a "doctor's" office (yes, a legitimate medical doctor performed the procedure). I learned that I did not have to go about it in secret or use a clandestine network. Today, it would have been a much more complicated decision, because I would have had more knowledge about the development of the fetus and about birth in general.

I went through with the procedure. I had bleeding and cramps afterward, but I survived. Of course, the fetus did not. I tried not to think about it at all after that day. I made the quick decision to pursue the abortion based on the information I had at the time. I would not have been so cavalier about it had I had to make that decision later, when I was older.

I will never support a law that does not give a woman the right to choose what happens to her own body. I now consider myself to be a "pro-lifer;" but at that time, at college in the '70s, we did not know the real facts of the situation. We did not know how fully a six-week-old fetus had developed—nor did we want to. My decision still haunts me today. I was asked if I wanted to know the sex of the fetus. I learned the fetus was female.

I was also feeling some regret at not involving the biological father in the decision. My immediate thought was I had to get on with my life—I was not going to let myself grovel in self-pity.

I continued going through the motions of college life, although I had radically changed within, growing into adulthood by leaps and bounds. The hormonal chemistry of my body had changed due to the pregnancy. Nonetheless, I resumed my college education, taking classes and occasionally meeting friends for drinks at the dive bars around campus. I did not see or talk to Leo again until a few years later, when I found out he had recently become engaged to marry a fellow doctor.

One night, I happened to be at one of the campus dive bars when he showed up with his friends for his bachelor party. It was the night before his wedding. Gosh, the Lord works in mysterious ways! After several cocktails, I found the nerve to go up to him while he was sitting at the bar. I vowed I was not going to get emotional. I stood as close as to him as I could and proclaimed in a deadpan voice: "I had an abortion. The baby was yours." The look of shock on his face was one for the record books. I quickly walked away. What an immature shit I was! He got married the next day as planned. I never heard from him again.

Many years later, I regret saying that to him. I wonder whether the bad things that have since happened to me may in some way have been due to these past actions (you know, karma). Back then, though, I appeared to continue my life as if nothing had happened—at least on the outside. What was done was done. Now that I know more about the pregnancy process, however, I mourn.

On occasion, I look back on the past, especially now that Leo is deceased. I wonder what my life would have been like had I made the other decision. To this day, I am still sure he was not the one for me. By the way, he divorced his first wife, then married a few more times, before meeting and marrying a beautiful woman and having several children with her. He became a renowned radiologist in California and lived a full and meaningful life.

I was still NOT considered an adult in the eyes of at least one of my parents. Even though I had gotten pregnant and undergone an abortion. I do not think my Father ever knew about the abortion. God forbid, I certainly do not think the secret ever got to my grandmother, Minnie.

Get out of Dodge

By now, I had exhausted my college manners and decided I wanted to "get the hell out of Dodge," at least for a while. I jumped at the chance to transfer from LSU to UT Austin when a couple of LSU KAT sorority sisters (who were Texans) decided to go home and, like me, lick their young adult wounds. Of course, neither of them knew I had had an abortion. It was still a secret only known to a few.

I was so excited! First, it meant greater distance from my Father and more freedom for me. Second, I could transfer my KAT membership to their thriving chapter (where future First Lady Laura Bush was also a sister). For me, it was a no-lose situation.

My search for a suitable boyfriend in Baton Rouge was moving too far away from choices that were good for me. I was ready to transmogrify, by moving on to bigger fish in a much larger pond. But I was not ready to catch any to keep—and I was certainly not ready for a serious long-term relationship. Marriage was still an unwanted choice, although the possibilities were endless... so many boys to choose from—both "frat" boys as well as independents. Richer ones, too, or ones from richer families.

We set up shop in an apartment complex on the outskirts of the campus. I met a new friend, Susu, through one of my LSU sorority sisters. I still consider her a close friend today. I started at UT in the summer semester, so I could ease into the rhythm of the much larger campus in the fall. We went to our few classes then met up each afternoon at the apartment pool, where we established the founding chapter of the "Floating Flotilla."

The "Floating Flotilla" met after classes every sunny afternoon. We had a fleet of slim multicolored air mattresses—and usually a cold drink. For me, it was always a beer. I gained several pounds that summer due to all the cold beer I drank as well as the great Tex-Mex food.

> **Playlist Song #21:**
> "Austin," by Blake Shelton.

> **Playlist Song #22:**
> "If You've Got the Money, Honey I Got the Time"
> by Willie Nelson.

Our summer and the early part of the fall semester consisted of floating on the pool, going to "redneck" bars, drinking tequila, listening to Willie Nelson, country and western line dancing, and doing the "Cotton-Eyed Joe." We toured the lakes of Hill Country looking for fun, laughter, and rich men. Austin was full of all the above—and more. Our motto became, as Willie Nelson sang, "If you've got the money, honey, we've got the time!"

"Cotton-Eyed Joe" was a popular American folk dance, dating from before the Civil War. It came to prominence again in the '80s, being featured in the popular movie *Urban Cowboy*, starring John Travolta, which resulted in country and western dancing thriving once more.[20]

The lake area around Austin—which include Lakeway and Lake Travis—is very beautiful and considered Hill Country, where leisure and outdoor fun are encouraged.

"Hippy Hollow," located on a remote section of the Lake Travis shoreline, is another iconic location. It has a steep limestone cliff that notoriously attracts naked swimmers and divers, especially hippies.[21] As well as naked swimming, there is also naked rock climbing! This part of Lake Travis was originally known as McGregor Park. Today, it is the only legally recognized clothing-optional public park in Texas. It has been administered by Travis County since 1985.

"Hippy Hollow" became popular in the '60s, due to the "cultural changes" following Woodstock. It became controversial in the '70s; however, due to the "increased skinny dipping" generating complaints from the adjacent landowners. Since 1995, the use of "Hippie Hollow" has been restricted to those over eighteen, with clothing remaining optional.

Hippie Hollow Park—illustration by Cate Lowry.[22]

One sorority sister, who I met at LSU, parents had a house on Lake Travis in the Lakeway area. We went there weekends as a getaway treat from classes. Tess was a fun and energetic friend, who was from an affluent family that owned a broadcasting company in Houston. This company operated Muzak franchises—Muzak being the creator of "elevator music."[23]

At one time, the Austin Muzak franchise was owned by Lyndon B. Johnson, who was the thirty-sixth President. I later learned that my father-in-law had piloted Air Force Two for LBJ as Vice President. What do they say about it being a small world?!

The Worm in the Tequila

Jimmy Mac—as in the 1967 song by Martha Reeves and the Vandellas—kept coming back in my life. He showed up again in Austin, where he was attending UT—I believe he was awarded a swimming or diving scholarship. It is hard to imagine him being an athlete of any kind, but there you have it. Anyway, we managed to hookup, but not in a sexual way—only as partying friends. He picked me up in his now classic Corvette and we started to get "shit-faced drunk" in Hill Country. Well, we began lightly and ended up taking shots of tequila.

Back then, tequila, or Mezcal, which is a cheap alternative, had a "worm" in the bottle. According to an article, the worm is not really a worm but a larva of a beetle or moth.[24] The article goes on to state that the agave plant ranchers "would pluck the bugs from dead or dying agave plants and place them in bottles of Mezcal." National Vinicola was the first company to add the "worm" in the 1940s. It was rendered "unnecessary" after October 13, 1977; however, when tequila was granted protected status.

Having gotten really drunk on tequila on several occasions, I could only hope I had not digested that "worm." Well, had I done so, I would have thrown it up, because I am the "throw-up" Queen, remember?! True to fashion, I proceeded to do just that on the side of the road. Thank God, Jimmy Mac had the wherewithal to get me back to my dorm safely.

Worm in tequila.

I had plans for another blind date the next day, one of my sorority sisters having set me up with a fraternity boy. I was so hungover that I was not able to lift my head, let alone converse with a stranger. I think I was still drunk when he called that morning to pick me up for skeet shooting. Good luck with that!

I would have been too dangerous with a gun and might have shot him instead of the target or plate. Looking back, I should have targeted Jimmy Mac, the "little shit" who encouraged this hangover mess.

I never set eyes on the date and cannot remember his name, although he was probably from an affluent family, his name likely having a "III" behind it. For all I know, he could have been the love of my life—unlikely, the jury is still out on that one. If you are still alive and recognize yourself in reading this book, please get in touch with me. I would love to officially meet you!

Breaking My Tailbone

The Texas KAT house brought together an intriguing group of females. I was introduced to and became friends with an affluent, beautiful Dallas girl with long and straight raven-colored hair. Her father had a ranch at least the size of the one on the popular television show *Dallas*. I met him once when I was invited to join her for a weekend there.

I was so excited and felt that we had common interests. We both liked to ride horses, and she had planned for me to ride one of the quarter horses. The one she picked happened to be "too spirited for me," as her father would later regret. I thought I had the necessary skills; but I was wrong. I was thrown, breaking my tailbone. I was sore in all sorts of other places. I went to the UT college infirmary shortly thereafter, where I was told there was no quick fix and I would have to rest. In other words, there was *no butt brace for my ass*—only time would heal it.

On the plus side, it got me out of class for a while; but the incident forever put a wedge in our friendship. I did not talk to her after that, as my day-to-day experiences led me down another path. Another lost friend—I hope one day we can reconnect and see the results of how life has blessed her.

Unexpected Special Effects

The Austin summer of 1975 was a whirlwind of fun in other ways. The movie *Jaws* was released by Universal Pictures, directed by Steven Spielberg. It was filmed off the shores of Martha's Vineyard in Massachusetts. It presented the fictional Amity Island, a small New England fishing town, as portrayed in the book by Peter Benchley.

Given that Austin is nowhere *near* the ocean or aqueous sharks, we were all excited to see the film. For the most part, I do not like scary movies. By "scary," I mean any film with any kind of horror or a supernatural theme. I was very anxious; but my friends prodded me into going. I remember shuffling into the immensely crowded theater, wet from an intense rainstorm that seemed to have gone on for days. We had our snacks in hand, intrigued to see what all the commotion was about.

As promised, the movie was "terrifying," due to the special effects involving a tiny fishing boat and a large great white shark. Much later—when I saw the original shark while touring Universal Studios in California on a family vacation—I found out it was actually a mechanical one. The theme music created by John Williams greatly added to the mounting terror; as each time it played, you knew the shark was near and impending doom loomed large.

Playlist Song #23:
"Jaws" (main theme), by John Williams.

The first scene was almost too much to endure, as we anxiously observed a lone swimmer being attacked. She became the shark's first victim—well, as far as the viewer knew. I quietly watched and thought about the time I felt a large presence underneath me as I lay floating on an air mattress in the ocean off Kauai in the Hawaiian Islands. I had fallen asleep and drifted away from the beach, ending up half a mile or so offshore. I woke up and saw the blurry figure of my Mother standing on the beach, waving frantically. Wow, I could have been THAT girl, the shark victim! That thought emphasized the reality of this film.

The combination of special effects and music had us sitting upright and on the edge of our seats from the first minute. We were so intensely wrapped up in the plot and acting that when "Jaws" leapt out of the water, we started to feel water falling down on us. I became even more terrified when I looked up and saw water raining down from the ceiling. I thought it was an actual movie special effect. In reality, the theater roof had started to leak from the large amounts of rain we had had in Austin. The manager stopped the movie so they could somewhat remedy the damage. My imagination ran wild while sitting there waiting.

I have to give the theater owner props for how quickly the problem was fixed, being able to move those in the most affected area. The management did not want to give anyone their money back, so I guess losing loads of money proved the motivation for the expedited problem solving. We were provided with free concessions as compensation and eventually got back to the storyline. Although it was a buzzkill moment for the dedicated moviegoers that day, we laughed it off later over several rounds of beers at a local dive bar.

My UT detour came to an end shortly thereafter. I knew it was time to graduate college. My Father had decided he was no longer going to pay the exorbitant University of Texas out of state tuition. I left beautiful Austin and went back to Shreveport, where I managed the junior clothing department at a local department store. After a year of working, I went back to LSU Baton Rouge, ready to study, graduate and put a bookend to the "Salad Days" of my college years.

THE REAL TEXAS RODEO RIDE

Wheel of Fortune?

graduated and received a Bachelor of Science or BS degree from
LSU in 1977. It only took me five years, after my year in Texas and
brief time working in retail in Shreveport. There was a simple call to
the Registrar's office: "Just mail me the official paper and I will go
on with my life." Not a big deal. Neither my parents nor any of my
siblings cared. After all, "BS" stands for more than "bullshit," if only
in the academic world; and I wanted the proof.

Ironically, I soon went back to Texas—to Houston. For some reason,
all my friends had migrated there, so I followed in a "sisterly" fashion.
There was a lot of opportunity in this booming city, primarily fueled
by the new money from the oil and gas industry. I soon learned it
was a home to various other ancestral fortunes, including that of
Tess's childhood boyfriend—the grandson of George Blaisdell (the

founder of Zippo, in 1932). I believe he is now the Chairman of the company, which is still thriving.

Zippo acquired W. R. Case & Sons Cutlery Co. in 1993.[25] I have never been a smoker, but I support the cutlery company, which manufactures pocket- and fixed-blade sporting knives. I believe Case was founded in 1889, twenty years after the beginning of the family hardware business, in 1869. Jeez, I wonder if my family's hardware business carried Case knives? Knowing Minnie's love of pocketknives, MOST LIKELY!

> *Playlist Song #24:*
> "It's Raining Men," by The Weather Girls.

I had thought Austin had many eligible men, but Houston in the late '70s was like spinning the wheel of fortune or winning the lottery. It was overflowing with the thirty-somethings of the "Baby Boomer" generation.

I never lacked a date for dinner, concerts, or the occasional sporting event. I was like a kid in a candy shop, meeting single men the "old-fashioned" way—either while on another date or through work or friends. It was time to reinvent myself...

"The Firm"

"The Firm," as I called it, was a prestigious law firm with a revolving door of brilliant legal minds. These minds were promising and established, male and female, and ranging in ages from young to old. It was located in a modern building of several stories in downtown Houston.

This firm was home to many important attorneys, one being James Baker, who was a partner—a close friend of George H. W. Bush and who would later become Secretary of State during Bush's eventual presidency. Bush was Director of Central Intelligence at the CIA, from 1976 to 1977, before becoming "Bush 41." This was a year prior to my employment at the firm in 1978. I was around 24 years old. George Bush regularly visited James Baker, and they would go to lunch—I remember fondly how nice he was to us "lowly" office workers.

I started my career in the paralegal world at ground level, working my way up—I was ready to learn. I began in a "girl Friday" role: filing cases, summarizing depositions, serving as a backup receptionist, answering the occasional phone call.

In all honesty, I stunk as a secretary! My typing speed (words per minute) was atrocious, so I had to use my brain—and sometimes my looks—to get ahead. I soon learned the legal terms, while observing a continuing flow of attractive first-year male attorneys, most of whom had just passed the bar. These brilliant legal minds were paid a decent salary at the time, even if they were glorified clerks. It was something of a meat market! Watching the brilliant *and* beautiful was a plus of the job and smiles abounded. It never hurts to look, right?

The mental side of law suited me, too. I wondered whether I might eventually go to law school and become an attorney like "Old Henry," my great-grandfather. I learned to write in a newly acquired legal language, gravitating toward insurance defense litigation. Of course, the attorneys with the big egos were attracted to that as well. Most of my caseload related to oil and gas litigation, so that involved a lot of learning about the extraction and transportation of natural gas and oil. It was mainly shallow drilling, not the fracking and deep wells of today. "Wildcatting" was still prevalent.

Most of the legal work was boring—doing discovery, assisting in the writing of technical papers in legalese, and filing court pleadings. This was before the age of computers, so all our work would be handwritten or dictated, for the secretarial pool to transcribe. And because copiers had not yet been invented, the resulting documents would be typed on typewriters using two to three layers of carbon paper. The research was very time-consuming, being conducted in law libraries or, if you were lucky, in a private well-stocked library belonging to the firm or to a partner.

I soon caught the eye of a balding divorced man, who started to flirt with me while I was working in the file room. I am not normally attracted to bald men, especially those with a little weight around the middle; but I formed a bond with attorney Frasier who loved to chat and was looking to fast-track my career. It was similar to my experience with Owen in high school, but without the voting machines. He told me I was too smart to be wasting my brain filing away cases. He was right, of course—but you had to start somewhere, especially a Southern woman without a law degree. Even the young female graduates from law school with brilliant legal minds started out by clerking, which basically involved spending endless hours researching cases for the partners.

In more ways than one, whatever notoriety we could obtain was earned the hard way. After all, according to the recent song "Crazy Town" by Jason Aldean, "To be a star you gotta bang, bang, bang!" I did work hard, but also received a little favoritism—such treatment did not hurt my budding career at all.

Playlist Song #25:
"Crazy Town," by Jason Aldean.

For the most part, working at the Firm was entertaining and fun, until I met another bald attorney, who took an interest in me in a totally different way. I think he watched my moves and waited for the perfect time to approach me. I did not have much communication with him, so I did not know what his agenda was; but it really creeped me out, nonetheless.

One day, leaving work late, I walked out of the building and down the street to an overflow parking lot—which I could barely afford, given my meager wages. Suddenly, a car slowed down to a crawl beside me. The right window was down and the man behind the wheel looked familiar; he smiled a wicked grin and asked me whether I would like a ride to my car. He knew I was parked down the street only a few blocks away! Something cautioned me to be wary, so I politely smiled and said "No thank you, my car is right down there," pointing to the lot. He shook his head, without making a response, then sped off. The whole encounter left me with an eerie feeling.

I tried to shake it off, but several days later I had a conversation with another female coworker who told me this same attorney had also approached her and displayed similar behavior. This was before the "Me Too" era. Thankfully, I had followed my gut and not gotten in the car with him. Who knows what could have happened? There would be other times in the future when I would encounter similar situations in a professional setting. Similar to my experience as a Girl Scout, it emphasized to me that successful individuals in all professions and from all social classes are able to mask their deviance and perversion.

Skiing on My Father's Amex Card

encountered other males at "the Firm." This time, the attorney was on the receiving end of MY drunken advances. I was on a date with Frasier. I was heading to the bathroom when I spotted a cute and intelligent blue blood, most likely with a "Junior" or "III" behind his name.

I later learned he was a single Texan who had been born into a well-respected family from Corpus Christi. He had attended a reputable prep school in Massachusetts, before going on to law school at UT, much like most of the Firm's other recruits. I had seen him walking through the halls at work with a confident stride and wearing horned-rimmed glasses. He had a deep Southern drawl and possessed a booming laugh.

He also drove a Porsche 914, which framed him and his dynamic personality well. I barged up to him, asking "Are you Mr. Wilson?" Surprised, he replied "Yes, I am." I do not know what possessed me to call him that, as he was not much older than me—unlike my date, Frasier, who was much older. The rest is history. We dated and hooked up many times thereafter; when he was not frequently traveling for a notable legal case that involved the succession of a famous and wealthy recluse.

Our office "love affair" was secret, which made it all the more exciting. There may have been an unwritten policy of no fraternizing, but we ignored it. He would call me in the afternoon, since we were in separate offices, and make plans for our next hookup. It was exciting because it happened beyond the leering eyes of Frasier and the other members of the Firm. I enjoyed every minute I spent with Mr. Wilson, and I do not regret giving him my time or my body.

We eventually planned to meet up for a winter ski trip in Aspen. He made all the arrangements. I arrived early and checked in. He flew directly from Las Vegas, much later, where he was working on the aforementioned legal case. Overall, we had a great time.

I was not much of a skier; he was an experienced skier. This was quickly remedied by my taking private lessons from a handsome instructor who looked a lot like a young "Sam Elliott." I ended up spending more of my days with "Sam" than with Mr. Wilson. We met up each night for some fun. I was hoping that "Sam" was succeeding in making Mr. Wilson a little jealous as we waved to one another from our individual ski lifts.

Unfortunately, I paid for my lessons—including tips—with the American Express card my Father had given me back in college. This card was only to be used for emergencies. I had a fun time for several weeks, until I had a call from my angry Father, who had gotten an enormous bill on his monthly statement. I was more than two hundred miles away, though, so this time he was not able to throw me over his shoulder and ground me!

Many years later, in the '80s, however; I was publicly reprimanded about this at my wedding rehearsal dinner, when my younger brother related the story of my spending on the American Express card. He received an enormous laugh at my expense—and got one up on me once again! Over the years, I have thought about getting him back for that embarrassment on the night before my wedding day. But now that both my parents are deceased, what is the point?

Voyeurism on Georgetown Street

A few years later, I moved into a house in West University Place, splitting the rent with two roommates—one being Susu. Our small brick house had three bedrooms, one bathroom, hardwood floors throughout, and even a small backyard. It was located on Georgetown Street, a quiet upper-class neighborhood near Rice University. We all got along well and, for the first time, I felt I had a quiet and safe place to return to.

Early one morning, as I was getting dressed for work, I heard a "gasp" from the front of the house. Susu came out of her bedroom and said she had seen a man looking through her window as she was dressing for work—lo and behold, there was a "Peeping Tom" in our neighborhood.

It was unheard of for such behavior to occur in West U, as we called it. Susu reported it, describing the male to the police, but the individual in question was never found. My two roommates and I later discussed it. We speculated that this person was probably out for an early morning jog and was most likely a fellow resident or a student or professor at Rice University. It may have been a serial thing or a brief lapse in judgment, when noticing a beautiful young woman in the early morning light. I wondered whether this male had a wife and family, too, like the attorney at my firm.

We soon installed very thick window shades! As I have mentioned, *there* are perverts in all social classes. We should have done so sooner...

Stand-in Bridesmaid

I had many dates, but only a few TRUE boyfriends. I do not remember how I met Jackson—a "IV" from an old money family in River Oaks, which, at the time, was the most affluent subdivision in Houston. The most exciting thing I remember about that relationship was a night of sex on a pool lounge chair. He was so impressive both publicly and privately that I introduced him to my parents over dinner when they were visiting Houston one night—something I never did!

I still saw the group of sorority sisters and girlfriends on a frequent basis. One of them, Louise, was from Houston and a good friend of Tess. She had pledged KAT at LSU, before transferring to UT with the rest of us in the summer of the "Floating Flotilla." She was tall, blond, and beautiful—the opposite of me, being petite with dark hair and blue eyes. She looked like a combination of Cheryl Tiegs and Michelle Williams.

Louise was also a good friend of Susu's, having grown up with her in Houston. She had moved back home after graduating from college. I introduced her to Jackson one night while I was on a date with him at a friendly gathering. It was spooky, but I could FEEL their attraction when they met. They ended up dating and getting engaged shortly thereafter. This did not bother me at all as I had moved on to other dating opportunities.

Months later, however, I was unexpectedly drawn back into their lives, when our paths crossed in a very big way. The night before her wedding, my roommates and I held a bachelorette party for Louise. We had planned the party for several weeks. The theme was "The Best Little Whorehouse in Texas," named for the 1982 musical comedy starring Dolly Parton and Burt Reynolds. All guests were to dress up in sleazy "whorehouse" fashion. We all had hooker names; we even hired a few male strippers, who dressed in cowboy attire with nothing under their authentic chaps. That was HOT!

It was not for the faint of heart, that was for sure, with even my most prim and proper married friends morphing into the shamefully scandalous. Come to think of it, the married ones were definitely the most shameful! (A bit like my recent fifty-year high school reunion...)

Susu, an elementary school teacher, brought home an overhead projector that displayed transparencies. We cut up pictures of Louise and Jackson, as well as other friends, sticking their heads on the naked bodies of others. We messed up when we left the window shades up on the living room windows, though. Our porn had projected upon the neighbor's house across the street and was VISIBLE to the whole neighborhood! None of the neighbors called the cops, thankfully, nor did our neighborhood "Peeping Tom" show up again. He would have REALLY enjoyed watching that show, with all the women running around in underwear!

We had a lot of fun, drinking to our heart's desire and laughing a lot. I was still asleep and nursing a hangover when the house phone (landline) rang early the following morning. It was Louise, who was also still hungover. Tess, who was going to be her bridesmaid, had driven home, but crashed on the way. She was okay, but in the hospital with a broken bone and extensive bruising. Certainly, she was in no state to perform her bridesmaid duties.

The wedding was that afternoon so Louise needed a "stand-in bridesmaid." Tess was about my height and on the thin side, so I was the most likely candidate. I did not want to get involved, due to the history between Jackson and me, but I eventually decided to be a good sport. The dress fit, although it was a little tight. I performed flawlessly "taking one for the gipper". I smiling my biggest Southern smile and pretended this was the plan all along. Thank God I did not catch the bouquet—that would have been way over the top! My roommate did, though.

The wedding went off without a hitch otherwise, with the two lovebirds marrying and going on their merry way. Jackson and Louise were a successful young couple: I believe Jackson went to Harvard Business School, to get his MBA, before moving on to a number of successful professional endeavors. When I think about Houston in the late '70s and early '80s, I think about Louise, too. Looking back, Jackson and I would never have survived anything serious—he was a little too dry and highbrow for me, anyway.

Men 2.0: More Walks of Shame

Sadly, I participated in more walks of shame in Houston, not remembering their faces a day—let alone a week—later. I did not want to remember their names. My only worry was about contracting a deadly sexually transmitted disease. I was on the pill but condoms were nowhere to be found.

The few faces I fondly remember include those belonging to two men who, ironically, had the same first name. One looked a lot like Paul McCartney, from The Beatles, while the other looked like John Denver, the American singer and songwriter. I listened to the music of both during this period. These were meaningful experiences for me, not walks of shame.

The first, my McCartney, took me away like the McCartney song "Take It Away." The other, my Denver, did not deserve the treatment I gave him, being a kind soul. Both were in creative fields: my McCartney was a film artist, who excelled with the camera, while my Denver was a print artist and graphic designer. Both were adventurous men.

My McCartney traveled extensively due to his vocation. I first met him at a friend's wedding. Since then, I have thought of him many times over the years, even when I was married and chasing a toddler in the late '80s. He was chasing his dream—one I hoped he would never give up on. We later met at an airport lounge in Shreveport to briefly catch up, while he was passing through, on his way to a shoot somewhere in Texas. Although our encounter was a friendly one, it nonetheless gave me pause, since I felt an attraction so physical I knew I could have had an extramarital affair with this man. That prompted the revelation that married life did not make me happy. I thought of his lookalike, the real Paul McCartney, and John Lennon's "supposed" last words to him: "Think of me every now and then, old friend."[26]

I had met my Denver through my current work as a marketing rep for a paper company. He rode a motorcycle, which we traveled on during our dates—it was refreshing and somewhat dangerous. I do not remember if I wore a helmet: the New Hampshire state motto— "Live Free or Die"—was our cry! Thankfully, he was responsible. The only time I had attempted to ride on a motorcycle before this did not end well. Many years earlier, I took a spin with Prothro, another very cute bad boy, who I believe is now in the music business.

One night, I was out with my Denver on his bike, when I suddenly became tired, having had an exhausting week at work. I told him to swing by my house on Georgetown Street, so I could get something. He pulled up outside; I got off the bike, walked into the house, went to my room, crawled into my bed, and promptly fell asleep. The next day, my roommates told me he politely knocked on the door about an hour later, asking for me. By that time, I could no longer use the dog as an excuse. In any case, one of my roommates told him I had gone to sleep, so he went away.

I never heard from my Denver again; I was called "insensitive" after that, with both of my roommates shaking their heads in disapproval for many weeks afterward. I guess I needed that! I do not know if my Denver is still alive, but if you are and if you are reading this, "I'm sorry for myself," as your lookalike sang in his song "I'm Sorry."

Playlist Song #26:
"One of These Days," by Paul McCartney.

Playlist Song #27:
"I'm Sorry," by John Denver.

Paper Frolics

By this time, I had changed vocations and started working as a marketing rep for a paper company, whose corporate headquarters was in Dallas. I "peddled fine paper" to a range of clientele.

These clientele created everything, from letterheads and posters to brochures and annual reports. I was a marketer and did not have the quotas of the other sales reps. Rather, I traveled locally, calling on sole proprietors as well as medium and large advertising firms, introducing our current paper options for their next project. It fueled my creative soul, while helping me get over my shyness.

I met many single men and a few married ones, although the latter were still morally off limits as far as I was concerned. Most of the artists were successful and some were extremely good-looking. I was very attracted to one who was married, though—and he to me. He wanted to photograph me in the middle of a bluebonnet field for one of his creations. He looked like Phil Collins and had the same aura of power that my Father exerted. I think he was a Capricorn. He quickly showed his *true colors* when I realized I might not be the only one. I never crossed the line. Nothing happened, but it might have had the opportunity presented itself. Our sexual tension caused many sleepless nights. I was sexually stimulated each time I called upon him.

I looked him up recently, while researching this book. "Phil" had the unique ability of being able to market himself—most artists could not do this, because their artistry got in the way of their ability to sell themselves. He still runs his own design group and remains a successful Creative Director. His business survived the pandemic, but I do not know whether his marriage did.

One of the many perks of the job was being given—or *inheriting*—a company car, an ugly brown Chevrolet, which looked like an undercover "narc" car. I did not knock it, because it saved me a lot of money. I was responsible for maintaining it. Of course, I did not have a clue how to do that! I was a Southern girl who had always depended on my Father or another man to do so for me.

My supervisor, Mr. Sullivan, was a mild-mannered man, most of the time. The following story irritated him; he could not believe my stupidity. The car would not start one day; I looked under the hood, thinking that staring at it would encourage my knowledge of the engine. When that did not work, I called my closest available male friend, who happened to be David, an attorney friend from the Firm who lived down the street.

I ultimately had it towed, since there was no oil in the car. Damn, I had forgotten to have it serviced regularly! I am sure I was the joke of all the males in the salesroom for many months after—particularly Tom Christian. To this day, I *still* do not know what I was thinking!

David agreed to loan me a car that day—an ugly green Chevrolet. I think it was a Chevrolet Impala. I was happy because I did not have to rent a car, which would have eaten into my partying allowance. David was always frugal and never had the flashiest cars, even though he could surely afford it—unlike another lawyer (at another firm) with whom I had a fleeting fling, who drove a Mercedes. Looking at some of David's cars, you would think he was ghastly poor.

I walked over to his house to borrow the car for the day. I thanked him, got in, and sat in the driver's seat, before attempting to put the seat up. I tried several times; but the seat would not move forward—it was stuck. Finally, with David's help, I managed to move it a little but was barely able to touch the pedal. Needless to say, I spent the day driving like a "Grandma"—sitting upright and peering out of the windshield as close to the steering wheel as possible.

Another laughable experience! I made it to all my appointments, which, thankfully, did not include Phil. It was the first of my many individual and collective "free rides" in life.

Cal and the Mona Lisa

Cal was a very talented artist and a very interesting character. He felt like a kindred spirit from the moment we met. He created pen-and-ink drawings and sometimes gave them to me. He would never be in my romantic wheelhouse, but I valued his friendship. I looked forward to my weekly visits to see him: he made me laugh and we had deep discussions of a spiritual nature, so it was as though I was not working.

One day, I told him I was going to participate in a past life regression session. I was just learning about them and had never participated in one before. Cal became very interested in the possibilities and decided to make an appointment, too. He called me the following week, excited to tell me about his experience.

I went to his design studio under the guise of talking about paper choices for an upcoming project. Smiling, he told me that I had showed up in his past life regression experience.

The artist in him vividly described the setting: it was in the beautiful countryside of Portugal, long ago, and I was sitting at the top of a mountain, at the head of a long line of people trailing for miles. They were waiting patiently for me to "lay my hands on" or heal their pets, primarily dogs. In other words, I was a renowned pet healer! He told me I looked very serene as I went about my task. I looked like the *Mona Lisa*. I am sure this came directly from the epicenter of his exceptionally artistic soul. I am not sure whether he participated in this scenario or was only observing it during his regression. Obviously, he knew me even then. It was very bizarre, to say the least. I later wondered if he had been on drugs during the regression, but I finally decided he was legit. We joked about it in the following months: "I need to go heal a few dogs, human and canine!"

I lost touch with Cal when I left the paper company. He was a Sagittarius, born in the middle of December. I found out he died in January 2001, at the age of 52. His memorial on ancestry.com reveals that he contributed art to be auctioned at many benefits, including the AIDS Coalition in Galveston County. At the very end, the family requested that contributions be made to the organization Citizens for Animal Protection. I take that as a message from the grave about a missed opportunity to become a pet healer or vet.

Even today, dogs (or dawgs) of all kinds are attracted to me. I was walking recently when I spotted a man with his dog ahead of me. I was about a block away when the dog saw me, laid down, then did not move. The man could not get his dog to move at all! I approached gingerly, trying not to disrupt them, then passed them by, acknowledging them. I looked back and noticed that the dog responded to his leash only when I was almost out of sight. It was like that dog knew me!

After reading the memorial, I said a silent prayer to Cal and, smiling, sadly wished my friend goodbye. I say to you, Cal, I KNOW I will see *you* in another life.

Guided by Astrology

A renowned messenger whose immense knowledge of astrology and spiritual healing deserves to be mentioned. He is John Warren Flint, aka Terran Lovewave. I had an interest in the metaphysical and wished to begin my journey of spiritual awakening, so I sought out John's wisdom and guidance. I was about 26 years old when I first showed up at his door. I believe he took on the name Terran Lovewave when he later moved to Santa Fe, as part of his own spiritual journey.

I do not remember how I discovered him; I believe he was living in Houston with his significant other. Even now, I still listen to the cassette tapes of our sessions. Some of the things he told me during our sessions, which spanned many years, went way over my head at the time but make so much sense to me now. Recurring themes in my life showed up in my chart.

One big one was my heaviness. As a child, I was overly shy and withdrawn, rarely saying a "peep," as the saying goes. It was only in my teenage years that I started having what I thought was a "normal" childhood. By now, though, you know I have never been normal. Terran confirmed this while reading my chart.

His reading reminded me of the following elementary school story. I remember doing my homework each night, staying up until after 10 p.m. to get everything perfect. I strived to always get an "A." Good grades got me attention in my family. One night I was too tired and went to sleep. And, would you believe it, that was the first time the teacher called upon me for an answer. She had almost never called on me before then! It was as though she had read my shameful mind. I was so embarrassed and almost cried, softly uttering the words "I do not know." Not knowing is a big one in my astrology chart.

During our astrological sessions, we talked about my taking responsibility for people at an early age, which caused me to forego most of my childhood. I was abandoned by my parents, not nurtured by them, becoming an adult child in my relationship with my Mother.

Terran suggested I listen to a book on tape called *Warming the Stone Child*, by Clarissa Pinkola Estés, Ph.D, about abandonment and the unmothered child. It helped a lot. From my interactions with Terran, I learned that the transiting planets would strongly influence me in clearing out my old patterns of behavior when relating to "the clan system"—a group I never felt I truly belonged to.

Remember, as a young child, I wanted to run away and be an only child. I was SO ready to release this negative energy! I wanted to learn how to "trust" and embrace "not knowing," both of which were extremely hard to do. I needed a "time-out" for my soul. This really became apparent in my late thirties and is still with me, to some degree. It seems to have emerged again in the writing of this book. Terran's knowledge of astrology and how to apply it to my "chosen path" has been a godsend in my life.

I recently read a book of his from many years ago, called *Stop the Clock: The Tao of Time and Timelessness*—a field guide for the "Cosmic Warrior" or, in my case, "Warrioress." I found the book very enlightening while listening back to our many taped sessions.

To have known him and had his guidance for fifteen years was a real gift. I am still working on balancing the mind–emotion dichotomy, balancing my sun opposite my moon. I have grown to be okay with my "know but not know" mind. I am still learning to embrace not knowing and open myself up to it with no resistance. To you Terran Lovewave, I remember you, and fondly.

Life in Houston continued to be very enlightening in many ways. I had started on a mystical journey of seeking self-transformation, as John Warren Flint would say. Ironically, I am going through another transformation in my late sixties, as I move into my seventies. Looking back, my whole life has been about remembering and passing through incarnations within incarnations. I am still transforming, but my awakening is very near. A person—or soul mate—has appeared at each juncture of my life, to help me through. These are my "angels," as I call them.

Sometimes, my dabbling in "new age" behavior got bizarre. I frequented psychic fairs with my friends. Once, I was talking to a psychic, who, out of the blue, suddenly screamed "We have a visitor!" My friend and sorority sister Mandeville was with me that day. She immediately looked across the field with a questioning expression. This psychic believed I was visiting Earth from another planet. Today, one would use the term "starseed."

Well, that certainly explains why I am so weird, if nothing else! I shrugged it off and went about my daily craziness. Every now and then I wonder "What if she was telling me the truth?" Then again, how could that psychic know? Maybe she was also a "visitor." After all, it "takes one to know one." Back then, it was considered fun and not taken seriously. I told this story to a good friend about a year ago, who responded that he, too, was a visitor! What a difference more than four decades makes!

The Fire Tragedy

I visited other psychics. I was beginning to feel there might be more to the experience than the naked eye could perceive—although I was still not completely ready to open my mind and third eye to the possibilities.

One spoke of reincarnation, telling me that I had lived in San Francisco during the Great Fire of 1851, which ended in tragedy. This reincarnation revealed that both my husband and son were killed in the fire. I escaped their fate, however, because I was in the arms of another man. I was not able to learn anything further from this psychic, but I had apparently been a lady of the night, more commonly known as a whore.

I came to realize that my betrayal had led to much shame. I do not know what happened following the night of May 4, 1851; my past life regression showed a life of darkness, so I may have gone into a deep depression or suffered from mental illness. I now wonder whether I will see my husband or son again—or whether I have already met them again in this life. All I know is I have a lot of karma to work through, which is likely to take many lifetimes to achieve... but that is a story for another book!

AI interpretation of The San Francisco fire of 1851.

The fire occurred during the period of the California gold rush which lasted from 1849 to 1851. According to an article, the fire of May 4, 1851 was the sixth of seven fires and was "by far the most damaging," burning for a period of ten hours and resulting in the destruction of between "1500 and 2000 houses" and "eighteen blocks in the main business district."[27]

The same article also included a short description of the aftermath of the fire, taken from Frank Marryat's book *Mountains and Molehills*. This information was obtained from the Municipal Record of the City and County of San Francisco:

> *At daylight you plod home, half blind, half drowned, half scorched, half stunned, and quite bewildered; and from that time on you never care to recall one-half of the horrors you have witnessed.*

Over the years, and even in childhood, I have had a strong interest in San Francisco history, especially information about the fires. I would look in awe at numerous historical photographs. I realized that I had even made a booklet about the subject in elementary school! Ironically, I spent some of my honeymoon in San Francisco, where I felt a sense of extreme sadness. This was not good for a honeymoon. There may have been other reasons for that...

I have also always had an extreme fear of fires, which was only exacerbated by my older brother Raymond dying in a fire in 1985.

Paper Company Blues

I did not completely give up my *old* ways during my time in Houston. Even so, the paper company decided that I was doing such a good job they needed to hire someone else to help me carry the load of all the new business I had created. Unfortunately, this ultimately set in motion my decision to leave.

The company hired an unconventional individual from New Mexico. We became work friends—but out of caution. She was nothing like me; she was the extreme side of *my normal*. She was a real "wild child" with very loose morals—much looser than mine. There was a limit to my wildness, but she seemed not to have a filter to hers. In fact, I would say this woman overly embraced her dark side—I felt a strange energy around her and that she was dragging me into it whenever we were together. Although we drank together, I remained wary of her, since she always got me going in a destructive direction. It felt as though we were constantly battling one another. I do not know if that was her intention from the beginning—to get me to quit so she could take over my job.

She revealed her affairs with older married men, but that is her story to tell, not mine. I suspected she had sex with my Father at my non-sister's wedding but maybe that was my overactive imagination.

At a paper conference or retreat in North Texas, things got out of hand—me with drinking and her with drinking, sex, and possible use of drugs. I expressed my disapproval of a brand of paper I felt was "cheap," throwing reams of it into the shower and soaking it with water. *Water destroys paper*. This became the talk of the conference, at least among all the salesmen. After all, I had done the unthinkable. I had disrespected the company and its product, getting myself into more trouble. That was the beginning of the end for me. Ultimately, I quit—and my workmate went on to become the marketing face of the paper company, God help them.

I soon realized I had quit without having anything else to do. I signed up for some temporary work, which was easy and allowed me to meet some interesting people, like Mercedes Man, an older salesman at Herman Miller. He introduced me to the art of fine dining. There was no intimacy—I had grown and, by this point, was reserving my sexual exploits for younger men. Temporary work, unlike full-time employment, gave me more freedom to continue taking extended family vacations during the summer, paid for by my Father.

Sex on the Beach

My favorite family vacations were those in Hawaii. At this point, we were flying everywhere. My Father had been stationed in the Pacific—in Oahu and Maui, specifically—during World War II. He had a soft spot for Hawaii and regularly kicked himself for not investing in land there at the end of the war.

One time, I brought along my good friend Leesa. My memories include an afternoon delight with an old boyfriend and a late-night hookup with a new one that ended in sex on Waikiki Beach.

The old boyfriend was a handsome college baseball player whose real passion was basketball. He played for a local Shreveport college. I met him at one of his baseball games when I was home from college for the summer. I believe he was from Illinois or Missouri—I cannot remember which, because he told me his hometown was near the border between the two.

He was now living in Honolulu, most probably for sports-related reasons. I went over to his place and saw him briefly for a quick afternoon hookup. I wanted to revisit a still active sexual attraction, but it was over in minutes and never happened again. The other male was a true one-night stand—I do not remember his name, but I will always remember his blond good looks and tall surfer body.

I met "Surfer Boy" one night while dining at a local Waikiki fish restaurant. He was our waiter; I was instantly attracted to him. I drank some more and left with him when he finished his shift, knowing nothing about him or what might happen. After all, it was the '70s. I had never done this before but made a conscious decision to follow through with it, being inebriated enough.

We left the restaurant talking about unimportant things. I do not remember asking him where he was from, but I guessed California. He knew how to get to a private section of Waikiki Beach by cutting through a wealthy residential area, having obviously done this before. We both knew what was going to happen next. This blond Adonis was hard and eager. He climaxed quickly; I did not. The sex was over in minutes. I did not have to remove my sundress and no foreplay was necessary: the thrill of being caught was enough of an aphrodisiac. At that time in my life, my firm yet nimble body could perform gymnastics, if necessary. Afterward, we sat and made small talk for a little while. We did not exchange names or numbers, nor did we make plans to see each other again. It was what it was.

He was somewhat a gentleman, though, and walked me back to my hotel. I returned to the room to my wide-eyed, frantic friend and her overactive imagination. Leesa sighed with relief: her mind had run through various scenarios—one was that I had been murdered and thrown into the ocean from Waikiki Beach, my shark-eaten body never to be found again...

Sex on the beach is exciting, but you might get sand in places you do not want. I "did it on the beach" one other time, in my late twenties, in the British Virgin Islands. This time it was with a man I knew well, thought I loved, and wanted to marry one day—a much different story.

———————————

The Story of David

Each year, on or around May 11, I check in with David, a true male friend. I have been doing this for over forty years. He acts as my personal shepherd whenever I feel lost. He is a very old soul and really gets my Aquarius moon and "untethered soul." I know I can call him, and he will remind me what everyday life should be.

He is and has been my one "true" boyfriend, with an emphasis on "friend." Even today, we are friends without benefits, never having done it—the sex act. We only came close once, when, tired from all my running around, I inadvertently fell asleep on his couch.

David was raised in Austin as an only child—something he wears like an accolade. I met his parents once and they were powerhouses. He was a disc jockey in college, where he perfected his radio voice. Every now and then, he would use this voice, which always made me laugh.

He was beginning his legal career when I met him, having graduated from Baylor and then UT law school. He eventually specialized in real estate law. I first met David when I manned the phones on the upper floor of the Firm. I was expected to do this a couple of days a week, for an hour or so. The phones were never busy in the late afternoon, so I took along a novel to read.

I always made sure I was seen reading a proper book—not the steamy sex ones hidden in my nightstand drawer. I did not get into the "one-handed" reads until much later in life. You never knew who might be watching and I was determined to move up the career ladder.

I am an avid reader, and we bonded through our shared love of books. David would make small talk about what I was reading, displaying wit by the bucketful. I am not sure whether he had read the books prior to seeing me with them or whether he hurried home to read them (or maybe just the Cliff notes) in preparation for a conversation with me the next day. I can picture him doing the latter. I will ask him to confess on the next birthday call.

David talked me into taking a yoga class, which was run by a certified yogi named Lex. Lex was very mellow. He told the story that he changed his fast-paced life when his work stress overwhelmed him. He traveled to the Himalayan mountains to learn the teachings. Many sages and teachers have attained spiritual realization in those mountains. Lex wanted to "find himself," which apparently he did, coming back to start his own yoga studio in Houston.

On one of the first nights, Lex asked us to do a meditation exercise to calm our minds. David was attuned, because he had apparently had many such experiences before. I, on the other hand, had never tried to calm my mind.

Lex asked us to focus on a white light. My thoughts were jumping around like Mexican jumping beans! He asked us to raise our hands if we could not settle our minds—I was one of the few who could not. After a few troubling moments, he responded in his most mellow voice: "That is not good!" He eventually taught me how to do so, and this has helped me over the years at times of extreme stress.

I was always better at the physical side of yoga because I was a runner and was still pretty flexible from my previous cheerleading. One night, we were instructed to do a headstand. I am short, while David is well over six foot. I performed the exercise successfully, but he had trouble with it. Finally, after several attempts, he got his feet in the air, but his posture was crooked—his body looked like the Leaning Tower of Pisa. He believed he had succeeded because he was at least in an inverted upright position! I laughed so hard I thought I would pee my pants. I only wish I had had a cell phone then!

That picture will remain vivid in my mind for the rest of my life. Many years later, I teasingly asked him whether he had ever mastered the head stand. He never really answered my question, so I can take that as a no.

I moved on to other endeavors in many geographical locations due to my innate "gypsy soul," but David found me wherever I landed. In awe, he once asked me if I was going to live in every US state? I stopped to consider his question and replied "Maybe... will that get me in the book of *Guinness World Records*?" I am still working on making that happen. Some might say I could make it in with my exploits alone.

I am glad we have never done the deed, because the sex may have ruined our platonic relationship. We probably would not be talking now. I do not know how I deserve to have such a beautiful soul in my life!

We will talk for several minutes, catching up on current affairs and laughing at life. Over the last few years, our conversations centered around COVID; he ended these by relating his desire to keep in touch more often, to "check on me." My fear is that he will perish, and I will not know, because no one will know to call me. After all, we are not young anymore.

We do not talk much about our significant others. He is happily married and once told me that his wife told him he would "make a good homeless person because he did not need much money and liked to walk everywhere." On hearing this, I thought "Good, she knows him well—and, above all, she has a sense of humor!"

———————————————

TOXIC BEHAVIOR REVISITED— GOING HOME

My Saturn Return

I felt a strong urge to go home. Why? Reality, reason, time to "pay the piper"—or perhaps all of the above... I left Texas with "no hard feelings" and Louisiana welcomed me with open arms. My parents, now in their sixties, had sold the house on Pierremont Road and built a large two-story house at the Ranch. The family business was still thriving, thanks to my Father and brothers, who had basically given up their lives to make it happen.

All my other siblings had gotten married, started families, and moved into their own houses, some of which were on the

Ranch as well. I was the only unmarried child and due for a little Louisiana lagniappe. Although I was in my late twenties, my Father immediately restarted his morning ritual of milk coffee. And, yes, I still had a curfew. My Mother was ecstatic: she finally had another adult to discuss her troubles with. I had to face my Father head-on, though, and he had not changed a bit.

I was going through a period of what astrologers call a "Saturn return." In astrology, Saturn sometimes represents your Father in your natal chart. The first Saturn return hits in your late twenties, its impact being felt into your early thirties. My Saturn return took me home to face my Father.

According to an article, a Saturn return occurs when the planet Saturn comes back to your natal Saturn, taking just under thirty years to return to its position from the time of your birth.[28] Saturn is a powerful but slow-moving planet and rules the sign of Capricorn.

A Saturn return reminds you of what is truly important and ensures you are on a path to fulfilling your highest potential, often creating a crisis that brings you face-to-face with your fears. Some "old souls" who made wise choices may find that things are solidified.

For what it is worth, I went through a second Saturn return in my sixties. Boy oh boy, has the ride been worth it! You might say I am facing my Father once again, but through this book.

I knew going back to Shreveport would not be easy, with all the hurt and unpleasantness I experienced there, but I took the plunge. Being back under my Father's thumb would be a struggle both mentally and emotionally, to say the least; but I had unfinished business to attend to.

I do not know what I was thinking. Nothing was ever going to change with my Father, especially given his attitude that women were only meant to be controlled. I moved back under the pretense of finally answering his question about whether I would come and work for the business.

I responded to that question with another question: "What is my job description?" The question hit a nerve, but he emphatically answered: "You will do whatever I tell you to do!" He stood up on his desk, shouting insults. I almost laughed, but did not wish to escalate his anger. He soon morphed into a ridiculous combination of Tarzan, Yosemite Sam, and Baby "Stewie," looming over me on his desk, pounding his chest, and raising his clenched fists.

His reaction answered nothing but said everything. In other words, I was to obey his every wish. I was to act like a "good" Southern woman who would get married, take care of her husband, raise many children, but never use her God-given brain. That was not going to happen. His ridiculous attempt at control fell flat and, for the first time, I realized the truth of the saying "actions speak louder than words." It was also when I learned about gender discrimination.

This did not apply to Minnie, however, who still commanded the business, my Father, and all those around her. My Father was now the ultimate "King Baby." He could not wait for her to retire! Minnie had destroyed any chance of a woman like me ever running the business.

Alas, there was more hurt to come! I finally found my way, but only after I had gone through one of the most self-destructive periods of my life. Yes, Saturn returns should be taken seriously. For advanced souls, though, I note that Saturn returns can encourage extreme growth, maturity, and enlightenment.

One positive thing occurred during this time. My parents had helped my siblings to buy or build their first homes. I found a small house—a complete redo—on Ockley Drive in the Broadmoor

Subdivision in Shreveport. My Father and I worked with a friend, Sheree, who had recently gotten her real estate license. My Father used his Veterans Affairs (VA) loan from the army and $50,000 in cash to help me buy my own home. The house needed a lot of work, which I was up for, being almost thirty, single, and having the energy. This VA mortgage helped me build up my credit by making a payment each month.

I had learned a lot from painting duplexes with my Mother! I did an excellent job and the house ended up looking like a French farmhouse—I later "flipped" it. I increased its value to more than triple what we paid. I started to believe I had a creative "eye" for decorating houses, but not as a vocation. To this day, I have never lost money on real estate, thanks to creative talent and a nose for buying houses with "good bones."

I had traveled back to that "red dirt road" of my past. I wanted to create a new hometown—one that would not include past traumas. I was seeing Shreveport anew, for the first time, and living the life. But what I could not foresee was I would soon experience a life-altering example of how NOT to live...

Playlist Song #28:
"Red Dirt Road," by Kix Brooks and Ronnie Dunn,
sung with Cody Johnson.

"Extreme" Love, Sex, and Drugs...

did not intend to pick up my previous dating patterns, but I was extremely lonely and looking for love. I became tired of dating around, having one-night stands that never developed into anything serious. I was not ready to settle down, by any means; but I would have welcomed a relationship with a man who treated me with respect and loved me for who I am. I did not know who I was, though, having not yet figured out that knowing that comes from going within. I now know it is all within you—you only have to search for it.

Even today, the universe has not offered up the "right man," even though I have met a few men who have had the potential. Most were unavailable to me, either physically or emotionally. I knew I was still searching for a bad boy turned good—I was still looking for the good qualities of my Father. I also knew that I still had more past trauma to work through.

Unlike the partying of my past, I was now playing much bigger games, involving a much darker side of life. Remember what I said about embracing your dark side? I took those words too literally at the time, resulting in the universe dealing me a harsh dose of self-induced *unhappiness*.

I met and started "hanging out" with Plutonian sorts. This involved extreme love, sex, and drugs—evidently, I was still vulnerable to the lure of the dark side. Going to bars with friends exposed me to guys who drank a lot, slept around, and, in many cases, did drugs.

I fell in love with one I met at a bar in Bossier City. I was with my long-time girlfriend Martha Bowdon, the daughter of Maredia Bowdon. Jack was a year older than me and had an air about him.

He was good-looking—I never dated otherwise!—with a smile that could light up a room. Oddly, we looked like we might be siblings. I quickly negated that one, although knowing my Father, it could have been a possibility.

I soon got to know Jack very well. He wined and dined me at expensive Italian restaurants, so I assumed he had money—although money has never really mattered to me. He was fast-moving and drove a black BMW, which suited him. On our first official date, after many cocktails, I had sex with him on the front passenger seat of his BMW, parked on a long dirt lane of the Ranch. He was obviously good at it because, unbeknownst to me, he was still experiencing sex with a great many women. I had mistakenly assumed he was single. I only learned the reality once I was smitten—and no turning back.

He ran a vending machine business, but I found out later that it was in fact his wife's family business. I also learned he was legally separated but not yet divorced. He had one very loyal employee, his secretary, who covered up for him when he was up to no good. I admired Jack's entrepreneurial abilities. He built the business into a profitable "cash" one. Its income came from leasing vending machines to large businesses and hotels. Most of the cash resulted from collecting numerous bags of coins from these machines.

I later learned that Jack had a son, a cute toddler, with the same smile and life force as his dad. Once the facts had been established, we spent much of our time with this little soul—I fell hopelessly in love with him, too. The custody agreement allowed Jack to see his son every other weekend, so I became the "every-other-weekend girlfriend/babysitter."

I was generous with my time and my money. I had not been schooled in the dynamics of marriage and parenthood, so it never occurred to me that my feelings and actions would make the separation worse. I had vowed to never date a married man and technically Jack was still married. Obviously, Jack had not dealt with his own feelings about it. I got along well with his family, especially his Mother, who, as mentioned earlier, called me "Miss Kitty." Jack loved his mother and she loved me.

I *did not* know that Jack was into drugs and had been for many years. I had been introduced to his light side, not his dark side. I had never done drugs before—not even marijuana. I now had a choice to make; it was not going to be an easy one, since I had come to care for this loving father. I had fallen in love with *that* side of Jack.

I chose to move forward with both Jacks. I was clearly being led by my heart, not my head. I had lost my ability to rationalize and was being blindly led by my emotions—something I had never allowed to happen before. Even my intuition told me he was not good for me and not to trust him, but I did not listen. I set aside all rationality and quickly met my own shadow side, my own personal villain who had long been hidden from others.

I could not love this man without embracing his *whole* life. He was not going to stop doing the drugs and whatever else he was doing. His addiction became obvious. Soon, my obsession with him, addiction or not, became obvious, too. I was stupid enough to think he could change. I did not yet realize that I was about to relive my childhood with Jack playing the role of my Father.

... and Betrayal

I did not live with Jack and did not know what he was doing on those weeknights I did not see him. I assumed he was working hard. At this time, other women never crossed my mind—but there were one-night stands, and his soon-to-be-ex-wife was still front and center.

I later learned he had a camp on Lake Bistineau, on the other side of the lake from my family's old camp. A red light of memory went off, bringing up many unresolved issues relating to my childhood and the actions of my parents—the never-ending deceit and unfaithfulness. I began to remember and relive some of the pain of my childhood with this man. My feelings overwhelmed me. There was something so familiar about Jack; I could not let him go.

Jack was a big fisherman. He revealed going to his camp was a source of relaxation. I had a nagging feeling that he was sleeping around while he was there. After all, my Father had used the Camp for his many affairs. I really did not know Jack very well; he smiled a little too much and I had not yet learned his "tell" signs. My intuition was on high alert.

I began having dreams in which he appeared with other women. One night, it was so difficult to sleep I got up in the middle of the night, drove into town, and waited outside his house. At that exact moment, he was heading inside with an Asian woman I had never seen before. He did not see me, as I sat in my Toyota Corolla in the dark. He was obviously drunk, maybe on drugs—who knows? It was soon after this I learned about the drug-induced nights with other women.

I sat in the car for several minutes, stunned, maybe in shock. I was not sure what I was going to do with the knowledge that he could cheat so openly. This epiphany should have been a sign to exit quickly, but my investigative mind wanted to know *why* before making a decision. I thought of Terran Lovewave and "not knowing."

I tried to work out the hurt and extreme betrayal rationally. I had still not learned it is okay to show emotion and cry. I needed to cry—but I could not. This was clearly a big deal, but I had no one to talk to. My own personal nightmare was becoming REAL. Was I going to be my Mother?

Memories and the scars from my childhood flooded in. My adult thinking included the choices of leaving him and running away as fast as I could, confronting him to hear his side and possibly forgiving him, or keeping everything inside as if it never happened. The last option was not viable. After all, I had witnessed his behavior with my own eyes. Did the why really matter? I was never one to run away from any confrontation, but this was much bigger than a love triangle.

I *could* leave this crazy relationship behind before things went any deeper. It would not be easy, but I could do it. Would I? I had countless back-and-forth conversations with myself, trying to find my Libra balance. At the other end of the spectrum, my emotional mind was telling me I loved him and did not want to leave.

Jack and I were not married, we did not have children together; and I did not owe him anything further. I needed a strong lesson in emotional strength and self-respect, neither of which I had at the time, having not bothered to develop them.

And then I thought of something even more irrational: "I could make him love me enough so that he would not need other women, if only I was strong enough!" Totally absurd. It was now ME who was trying to control him!

I eventually gave in to the physical longing. It was a choice—but the *worst* choice I have ever made. Matters only got worse. The hurt and mistrust would only grow deeper and deeper. There were always going to be women willing to accommodate the sexual needs of a supposedly rich and handsome man. I had seen this as a child. Now, as an adult, I had to realize the truth of it.

Was I going to experience this hurt repeatedly? Apparently so. Maybe I was on a path that did not involve faithful love? I eventually said goodbye to Jack, but only for a while, as I decided to step back and put some distance between us. I became less available. I longed to do something constructive with my life that did not include infidelity and betrayal.

Growing a Mail Order Business

My never-ending quest for knowledge had not waned and my idealistic mind wanted more from life. I took several post-college courses in subjects like psychology, which challenged my reason for being and my somewhat archaic ways of thinking. I was not going to let myself become stagnant in a fast-paced and ever-changing world.

To my chagrin, I also learned that betrayal could come in many forms. My increasing emotional hurt fueled my creative juices and writing became my creative outlet when I needed to "let go" of destructive thoughts and patterns. Indeed, my creativity flows when I am with certain men.

By this point, I knew I was not meant to run the restaurant supply business, but I thought about creating my own business within the existing one. After all, the hardware business was in my veins. I began doing some of the business' advertising on a part-time basis. This included printing mailers to promote new products and the sales of them.

I formalized a business plan and approached my Father with my idea of selling restaurant supply products directly to consumers via mail order. At the time, the business was still selling primarily to restaurants and school cafeterias. I wanted to deliver goods directly to the home consumer under the name of the business. There was no competition: the market would primarily be home chefs and others who loved cooking but wanted restaurant-quality home kitchens. Such sales of small goods were the bread and butter of the existing business. I thought it was a win–win situation.

My Father must have thought so too, because I got the go-ahead to try out my new plan. Was this a sign that he was starting to look at me differently, with new eyes? I was still looking for his approval. I worked on the startup day and night, while exercising like a madwoman and losing a lot of weight. I called the new business Weekend Gourmet.

I had the knowledge and experience to produce a catalog from beginning to end, having worked with many artists on these types of projects while in the paper business. I hired Tangney, a talented Creative Director and friend from the advertising world, to put the catalog together.

The photos would show the products in indoor and outdoor settings, including the Ranch. I was on the cover, wearing an apron reading "Weekend Gourmet" over my business attire. I was about to step through a revolving door. This was meant to show a busy independent woman juggling business and creative home cooking. The shot was taken in downtown Houston.

Weekend Gourmet catalog cover.

I used the connections my Father had developed in the food service equipment industry to order the products. This enabled me to buy in bulk at a discounted price. I could also get products directly from the manufacturer to ship to a customer's home, if necessary. I had ordered enough product samples for the catalog, which was going to show a combination of commercial and household cookware, utensils, and storage that a busy working woman could use to prepare a gourmet meal at home. I had everything I needed!

I hired a college student to man the phones during the day. I took up the slack otherwise. We mailed the catalogs in bulk to customer names compiled from numerous lists in the tristate area. I had access to an extensive list in Houston. We set up payment facilities at the bank, taking credit cards by phone or checks by mail.

The business had a slow start, which I think was due to the mail service and the time it took customers to go through the catalog and decide on purchasing products. We started getting business, though. The phone started ringing and the mail started coming in. We were not overwhelmed, but I felt it was a success as long as we were not losing a lot of money.

My idea was a good one, although I soon realized that one catalog mailing was not going to make the business grow. I would have to send out more, at least one a quarter. When the sales did not increase quickly enough, I learned in no uncertain terms that my progressive idea was a little ahead of its time. An iron fist was starting to emerge, too, as the office politics occurring behind closed doors decided against continuing to put money into my new business. The old establishment of my family's restaurant supply business was not ready for my progressive ideas.

I had hoped my grandmother would support a woman in the business. I now saw a little of what my Father must have gone through in the early '60s, when he had to persuade my grandparents to let him start a new restaurant supply business. He had had a brilliant and progressive idea. Although he was successful, this did not happen overnight, but his true business genius became clear over time. I believe he would have given me more time to produce more catalogs, but Minnie still held the purse strings. She dominated the financial side of the business and she, like some of my siblings, was never a big fan of the idea. They probably placed bets on it failing! It did, but it was now evident I was not meant to run ANY part of the family business.

A few years later, my Father went into semi-retirement, following a bout with breast cancer. On learning of the diagnosis, my Mother nastily proclaimed that "Maybe now he knows what it feels like to be a woman!" These harsh words stung even me. It was a low blow, even after everything he had put her through over the years.

I guess that is when my Father decided to sell the business to my three younger brothers, although one of them was not working in it at the time. My Father kept running things, but he was now my brothers' problem. I did not receive any compensation for being part of the business or a part of the family, for that matter. My younger brothers were not the only ones who gave up something of themselves for the business, though; we were all thrown into adverse circumstances and had to deal with them in our own individual ways.

Disappearing in the British Virgin Islands

There were still some orders coming in from the catalogs, but these eventually dwindled, so I closed the business. The strong wind of change pushed me away from my family. At first, I was outwardly angry, but to no avail. Consequently, I turned my anger inward and became depressed, considering what had happened as the ultimate family betrayal.

I needed a distraction from the pain, which I found in Jack, once again. He had seen my Weekend Gourmet catalog and suddenly appeared in my life again. We began to travel together. At first, we spent seemingly harmless weekends in Hot Springs, Arkansas, and at a friend's beach condominium in Gulf Shores, Alabama. We took the baths at the renowned Arlington Hotel. We relaxed with laughter and sex, sharing easy conversation as we drove for hours in his BMW through the countryside of Arkansas, Mississippi, and Alabama.

We stopped to take pictures with our cameras in front of railroad cars, old buildings, and anything else of interest. One old hotel he posed before had an old sign that read "Fox Hotel." We experienced life to the fullest and found humor in the small things. I needed balance, but it was still hard to find with Jack. Spending time with him was easy, but the time away from him was difficult.

I ultimately dove headfirst into his life, including the drug-induced jaunts. Ironically, the first was a late-night trip to Houston in his roommate's van—we slept in the back, while his roommate, hyped up by cocaine, drove. The most significant was a whirlwind trip to the Virgin Islands. In between, Jack and I would party at Lake Bistineau. One night, we took some pills—I did not know what they were, but I blindly (and stupidly) followed his lead and swallowed them. More than a day later, I remember waking up, a couple of his friends standing over the bed with worried expressions. They later admitted they thought we had overdosed. Once again, I experienced a "knock on heaven's door" (as in the Bob Dylan song of the same name).

Each jaunt took me away from the inner pain I was experiencing, as well as my sense of responsibility, since I told no one where I was. As far as I was concerned, they had abandoned me! I am sure Minnie never had a sleepless night worrying about my whereabouts. She was a businesswoman and liked routine, showing up each day to sign the checks and "lady it," not "lord it," over the business. She viewed my disappearances as laziness. Lord knows, had she known what was really going on she would have expired at the thought!

The extreme moment—to my mind, the "icing on the cake"—was when we decided to escape on a "vacation" to the Caribbean. Jack and I flew to St. Thomas in the US Virgin Islands in *February* 1983, when I was twenty-nine. We soon got bored with the tourist traps and decided we needed to be more adventurous. We explored the neighboring islands, including St. John, and several owned by the British, which are more commonly known as the British Virgin Islands.

With reckless abandon, we bought two one-way tickets to "paradise" and island-hopped on a small propeller seaplane. The flight itself was quite an adventure, as the pilot showed us the beauty of the area, flying low across the pristine waters. I was in awe of what we were about to encounter in Virgin Gorda. Unfortunately, I was ill for the first few days (probably due to drinking some water), which put a damper on things; but I soon recovered and was ready to snorkel in the beautiful turquoise waters and ride around the island by Jeep. Jack bought me a skimpy bikini to show off my lean body. I was officially an island girl! And falling head over heels in love with this man...

Playlist Song #29:
"Two Tickets to Paradise," by Eddie Money.

We stayed at the Bitter End Yacht Club in Spanish Town on Prickly Pear Bay. It was beautiful—I had never seen anything like it, not even on my many vacations to Hawaii. We went snorkeling in the surrounding bay and visited "The Baths," as they are officially called—natural tidal pools with boulders up to forty feet long, featuring caves, tunnels, arches, and scenic grottoes that open onto the sea.[29]

Sidney Kate in "The Baths," Virgin Gorda, British Virgin Islands.

We met an interesting man whose last name was Angel; he lived on the island, peddling timeshares. These new condominiums were being built on the cliffs along the bay. He also had ties to Shreveport. Who would not trust a guy with the name Angel?

We quickly adapted to Virgin Gorda life with Angel as our guide, moving into one of his furnished condos on the premise of trying it out before a potential purchase. Small developments rich with investors were popping up all over the island and his company was taking advantage of that movement. He escorted us on many of our adventures, having local knowledge of the island and things off the tourist path.

We visited the beautiful Rockefeller Resort in Little Dix Bay for dinner and drinks one night. I enjoyed their Pelican Smash— created in 1964—a combination of different types of rum, whiskey, bourbon, pineapple, orange, and guava berry.[30] I was enamored by this luxurious resort, which felt at one with the surrounding landscape. As I often do, I vowed to return one day—but never did.

An article states that this resort is a "tropical playground for the well to do."[31] It was originally developed by Laurance Rockefeller, who "happened upon a half mile of pristine beach on the island of Virgin Gorda while sailing the waters of the Caribbean" in 1958. He subsequently opened the resort in January 1964. It later became a property of the Rosewood Hotel Group, in 1993, many years after my visit.

Like the Bitter End Yacht Club, this beautiful resort was destroyed by Hurricane Irma in 2017. Both properties have since been rebuilt, Rosewood Little Dix Bay in 2020 and Bitter End Yacht Club in 2022. Let us hope the extreme storms of the future will miss these beautiful properties for many years to come.

Playlist Song #30:
"Caribbean Queen (No More Love on the Run),"
by Billy Ocean.

Playlist Song #31:
"Hot-Hot-Hot," by Arrow.

The Angel and the Devil

Angel and the boat driver (a new Rastafarian friend) later took Jack and I on a day trip to Tortola, a nearby remote island. According to another article, Tortola is "home to some of the most beautiful beaches in the world," having been the site of many classic film adaptations, including *The Old Man and the Sea* (1990), from the Ernest Hemingway novel.[32]

Jack and I ditched Angel and his friend, before meandering through a mangrove forest and finding a beautiful beach. A certain thrill accompanies having one all to yourself. One thing led to another, and we soon found ourselves nude and hot for each other. It was a beautiful encounter, except for the coarse sand—getting this everywhere can be unpleasant, but we quickly remedied that by jumping in the ocean.

I had already met an Angel; but I was soon to meet a Devil, too, who showed up late that night at the foot of my bed. The British Virgin Islands were known to be an early home for pirates. Jack and I were asleep in our condo when a famous pirate paid me a visit—he might have seen me naked on the Tortola beach earlier and wanted some of the action.

But there he was, in full dress, with his flowing black hair and beard framing his face. I sat up and looked directly into his very evil eyes. He motioned for me to follow him. I tried to scream "Get out!" but could not. It felt dreamlike but was more like seeing an apparition. I shut my eyes and willed him to go away, which he finally did. Looking back, I think he was trying to show or tell me something very important. I wish I had gone with him, if only in my mind. I realize that sounds crazy, because I might have disappeared forever.

When Jack and I eventually returned to the real world from our dream vacation, we were even more in love. We would have gotten married in the British Virgin Islands had Jack been single. His divorce took several more months to finalize—but by that time, he was back to his old ways of living. I finally realized that even though what we had was special, I would never be able to trust this man. I woke up from the dream and walked away.

Many months later, the details of the encounter with the pirate were still etched into my mind. I could still picture his face, physique, dress, and manner. I decided to do some research using the encyclopedias at the local library. I discovered that the pirate standing at the foot of the bed was indeed Blackbeard![33] The mental picture still haunts me! He was a very scary man, although he had not set his hair or beard on fire, as he was known to do. I later imagined I might have been bound up with "Blackbeard's Curse," as his soul was damned.

Although Jack and I were over, I was still moving in a very destructive way. It would take major rehab to get over Jack and detox from the drugs and pirate apparitions. I grew during this time, although my shadow side was still very heavy and dark.

For the Love of the Bowdons

Had I fallen as far as I could? The failure of my business and getting away from Jack and the many nights of cocaine abuse and other excesses had been traumatizing. I realized I needed to cleanse my mind and body by purging it all, so I made a life-altering decision to change direction. This would take several months. I could not do it at home, because being under the thumb of my Father—who was still the central source of my pain—would only make matters worse. I could not afford expensive clinical restoration.

The eventual answer did not cost me a penny. I ran away to the home of two loving individuals—Maredia and Jim Bowdon—who nursed me back to mental as well as physical health. Their daughter and son had both moved out. I think they missed having younger people around them, so they welcomed me with open arms, hugs, and genuine caring. I learned that being hugged was a good thing. And, for the first time in my life, I felt truly loved in an unconditional way.

Maredia went off to teach Journalism at my old high school, while Jim, semi-retired, cooked me three meals a day. I gained weight and welcomed the pounds, which I badly needed, since I was literally skin and bones after all the drug use. He made great coffee, and I particularly liked his full breakfasts.

I felt special and was entertained like royalty. We had many intellectual conversations, talking about anything and everything. They had an extensive library so I did a lot of reading and resting. Their positive energy was just what I needed. I slept well at night and healed my soul. I wished that these two beautiful souls were my real parents. I would not have had my blue eyes, but I would have had beautiful red hair and a gorgeous smile, which would have been totally fine. From that day on, though, they adopted me as their daughter, becoming my surrogate parents. Their love gave me the courage to move on with my life. I still feel they are watching over me, particularly Maredia.

Those few months with the Bowdons cured me. I will always remember their generosity as a blessing that could only have come from above. My friendship with these two individuals lasted well over fifty years. Maredia, Jim, and Martha, their daughter and my friend, have all passed now: Jim in 1996, Martha in 2002, and Maredia on June 13, 2022, at the age of 94.

I spent many hours with Maredia in the months before she died. We talked about her life and she actively listened to mine, knowing I was writing this book. She would ask the full names of the men in my life, then recite them aloud to see whether they were good ones. Like my Father, she had many sayings, one in particular being "Worry is like a rocking chair. It keeps you busy but gets you nowhere."

If you ask anyone about the Bowdon family, you will spark warm feelings of affection. I dedicate this book to Maredia because without her caring and motherly love I do not know how I would have survived the many hardships that came my way. Her positive spirit still boosts my soul. Anyone who is interested can read her obituary, which was written in her honor by a male friend of mine—a great writer and former love, Dude.[34]

Marriage on Valentine's Day

With the strength I gained from the Bowdons' love, I started a new life. I had completed my Saturn return and was in my early thirties. I left behind my old "druggy" friends and made new ones, although I still drank alcohol.

Soon after, I met another younger man who was, as they say, an "Air Force brat." His father, nicknamed "Buzz" was an Air Force pilot who had served in Vietnam and flown Air Force Two under Vice President Lyndon Johnson. Many vets today come home with stories to tell. I believe that to be a good thing. I am sure Buzz had stories to tell from both, but he never did.

Playlist Song #32:
"Stories That They Tell," by Scotty Hasting.

Robbie was born in California and was living in Shreveport when we met. He was four years younger than me and had graduated from Tulane University. We fell into a comfortable relationship and enjoyed each other's company. It all happened so fast! I was ready to commit and procreate, so I moved into his tiny two-bedroom home.

We became even closer when my older brother Raymond passed away in a tragic fire. I had not been close to Raymond, as he traveled extensively—and secretly—with the military. Raymond had married his childhood sweetheart when he was young and they had two children, before he moved back to Shreveport and settled down with his current wife, following several failed marriages. Like me, Raymond was a damaged soul and had a hard time with relationships. He was also my Mother's confidant. He was my older half-blood brother, but legally adopted by my Father after being abandoned by his birth father.

I did not see it at the time, but he was probably also a victim of my Father's abuse. He became a heavy smoker and drinker. The tragic fire that killed him was a direct result of him falling asleep with a lit cigarette burning. Raymond was living at the "hunting camp" on the Ranch at the time. He died alone on September 24, 1985, a month before his forty-third birthday.

Robbie was good to me, and I immediately said "Yes" when he asked the important question during the 1985 Christmas holiday. Robbie was twenty-six; I was now over thirty. He was somewhat old-fashioned; he thought the right thing to do was to sit down with my Father and obtain his permission to marry me. Who cares what my Mother thought, right? It was now the '80s and I was way over the legal age, but it was the South, where manners were *still* important.

Before my father reluctantly said yes, there was a long moment of silence, as he stared directly at Robbie and asked him "So, who is going to wear the pants in the family?" Robbie paused for a moment and then thoughtfully said: "I am going to let her think she does!" They both laughed. It was the first time I saw my soon-to-be groom display intelligence. He had successfully passed the test! All the while, I was sitting there, seething with anger at being treated like a possession to be bartered away. Little did Robbie know that my Father would actually wear the pants and that he was about to be controlled as well.

A wedding date was set for February 1986. "What God has joined together let no man put asunder"—Matthew 19:6, Mark 10:9. The wedding went off without a hitch, except I saw my Father cry for the first time. I am not sure whether he was sad at losing his daughter to marriage or whether he thought I was making a mistake by marrying the wrong man. Ironically, we honeymooned in San Francisco and Hawaii. My parents paid for some of it. Married life was good. Life finally settled down and seemed "safe" for me; but my nature soon got restless and had to find a way to placate my energies and boredom.

With Every Death There Is a Birth

Minnie passed away in September 1986 at the age of 94. Before this, she was still sneaking out in the car for weekly trips to the library. My Father had a "buddy" at the local Department of Motor Vehicles who issued a license allowing Minnie to drive until she was at least in her late '80s. When this stopped, though, she managed to find an extra key.

I would regularly see her driving past my house at about five miles an hour. I never told my Father, because I felt these jaunts were harmless—she loved her independence and going to the library. One day, though, she was creeping along and rear-ended a garbage truck! She was okay but was caught red-handed. As a result, her driving privileges were taken away forever, meaning she no longer had freedom or the independence. It was a celebratory day for my Father, who, finally, for the first time in his life, had complete control over Minnie.

Shortly thereafter, I became pregnant with my son—and this time the pregnancy was wanted. I found this out after a weekend of drinking bourbon at an LSU football game. I soon immersed myself in self-care books and started taking care of myself for the baby's health, taking the necessary prenatal vitamins. I stopped drinking, aside from an occasional wine at dinner. The excess iron made my stomach churn, but I endured it for the growing soul within me. As my due date of July 25 slowly approached, I started to feel nervous at the thought of the pain I would have to endure. My imagination was in overdrive! I thought about my Mother and all her births, knowing I could get through this as she had.

On July 11, I woke up and told Robbie I did not feel the baby. This scared me, so I immediately called my obstetrician gynecologist, who I quickly found out had taken a vacation. The doctor on call promptly instructed me to come to the hospital, where I was put on a fetal monitor. Everything happened very quickly from there—my son had decided it was time to emerge into the world two weeks early.

I was rolled into the delivery room, where the on-call doctor, nurses, and anesthesiologist were patiently waiting. I smiled at the scene and heard music blaring in my ears. I will never forget that song—"Total Eclipse of the Heart," by Bonnie Tyler! The lyrics are all about "darkness, the power of darkness, and love's place in the dark," according to the song's writer, Jim Steinman.[35] I should have known the lyrics of this song would foresee my future. I had a cesarean section: the doctor cut me open and rearranged my insides, moving my bladder and intestines aside, before pulling E. from my uterus.

I began to cry, mostly from happiness and awareness that my son was *okay*—too early to determine if he would be NORMAL! At least he appeared that way on the outside, having all the necessary fingers and toes. Boy, was I relieved! With all my past transgressions, I did not know what would come out of me. Robbie was present at the birth. I am sure he got an eyeful of my innards, which could not have been pretty. My son was a "preemie" and a little jaundiced, but his Apgar score—which is given to newborns after birth to confirm heart rate, muscle tone, and other signs—was within a normal range, so he was whisked away to be cleaned up.

I was still drugged, so did not feel the pain of the incision until much later. As my friend Sheree would later say, I performed the "C-section Shuffle"—because it was hard to stand up straight following the fresh incision—and for many days afterward. She, too, experienced a similar procedure about a week later. We both examined our very dirty floors as we shuffled along all bent over.

My son was delivered to my room soon after in a clear bassinet. He was tiny! The most remarkable thing happened when, hearing my voice, he *pushed* himself up on his arms and looked around at me. Even the doctor was amazed! To this day, E. is a very strong athletic male. He inherited these traits from his father *and* my Father.

Playlist Song #33:
"Total Eclipse of the Heart," by Bonnie Tyler.

Tornados Do Skip and the No-Nap Kid

Life with another soul depending completely on me was a new experience altogether. E. and I faced our first tornado alone, as my husband was selfishly playing tennis at a nearby gym. I knew there was a big chance of the tornado coming when I saw the darkest clouds I had ever witnessed. I was scared. I feared tornados more than hurricanes because their direction was so unpredictable. At LSU, we had "Hurricane Parties" when the threat of one was imminent. We were happy we did not have to attend classes. Hurricanes were not normally a threat to Shreveport, which was in the northern part of the state.

My fear further scared my baby son. As instructed, I found a place at the center of the house with no windows. I chose the hall running along the back of our one-story Ranch residence—a house we had bought once we were married. I climbed under the flimsy mattress of E.'s baby bed, taking E. with me, somehow thinking this would save us.

After a few minutes, E. started screaming his head off, trying to get away. Suddenly, we heard what sounded like a very loud train heading toward us. I knew whatever was going to happen would be over in minutes. Then, all of a sudden, there was no noise. I finally crawled from under the mattress and looked out of the window: nothing was damaged.

I later found out that the tornado had jumped over all of the neighborhood, before touching down in Bossier City, Louisiana, miles away. It was a strong one and there had been damage, but thankfully we had been spared. About an hour later, my husband waltzed in, still in his tennis gear, as though nothing had happened. What a jerk!

As E. grew by leaps and bounds, I was determined to do everything RIGHT in order to stop the cycle of dysfunction and abuse that I had experienced as a child. I was going to be the best Mother I could possibly be. I would not skimp on affection or love and I would ensure he had everything necessary to succeed. I did not once consider that I was exhibiting a form of control.

This little boy tested me at every turn—I was exhausted before he turned two! He was extremely active, continuously questioning, and never slept. My husband traveled each week so I was basically a single mom. The long weeks of his traveling and the lack of any financial assistance started to wear on me mentally as well as physically. Also, my mother-in-law made matters worse, since I felt she was reluctant to let go of her son. Now she was hyper-focused on her grandson.

On occasion, I took E. to "Mother's Day Out" at a local church, so I could have some time for myself and transition back to part-time work. He was very active, and his caregivers called him "the no-nap kid". He would stand in his baby bed, peering at all the other kids, making noises, so none of them would sleep. It was hell for the babysitters, who just wanted an hour of peace and quiet during the day. You can imagine what being his Mother was like! I lost so much weight I thought I might have a deadly disease.

I also never slept, even less than when I was on cocaine many years before. My muscles hurt like hell most of the time because I was not getting to the REM stage of sleep. As a result, I was in a bitchy mood every day, which was exacerbated by the constant intrusions of my mother-in-law, who was always showing up unannounced.

Many years later, I finally realized this was her way of reaching out to help—she just did not know how. Her relationship with her son was really at the heart of my discomfort, but I only addressed that problem a few years later. I could have used her help, rather than turning her away; I was very stubborn and thought I had to do it all myself. I was going to be the perfect mother, unlike my own Mother.

I went to a specialist because I thought I might have developed rheumatoid arthritis. RA is an autoimmune and inflammatory disease that causes your immune system to mistakenly attack healthy cells, resulting in painful swelling in the affected parts. After many tests, ruling out all diseases known to man, I was finally diagnosed with fibromyalgia, a soft tissue condition. Not much was known about it at the time.

According to the Mayo Clinic, this disorder is characterized by "widespread musculoskeletal pain accompanied by fatigue, sleep, memory and mood issues."[36] Researchers further believe that fibromyalgia amplifies painful sensations, by affecting the ways your brain and spinal cord process painful and non-painful signals. Many people with fibromyalgia also have tension headaches, irritable bowel syndrome, anxiety, and depression. A check to all! In my case, the depression may also have been postpartum.

More pain and trauma! As if I had not had years of it already. I finally realized I needed to reduce my psychological stress, by exercising and TRYING to relax, which the latter was very difficult for me to accomplish, as a "Type A" personality. I had long forgotten the meditation that Yogi Lex had taught me.

Even though I was struggling, my little boy was quickly growing, and his intelligence was developing. I read him endless books and gave him the best educational toys. This was thanks to my side work selling "Discovery Toys" through home parties—like Tupperware. Recently, I was saddened to hear Tupperware had filed for bankruptcy. This company first began selling its products in 1946. Still in business today, Discovery Toys prioritizes the "play experience," which they believe develops the fundamental skills of curiosity and passion. This is thought to lead to a child's early learning success.

E. was sometimes too smart for his own good, reminding me of myself. He was very active, and I was still very tired most of the time. I now had something else to blame for my exhaustion, because I had started to work full time again.

As E. grew older, I started to feel uneasy in my marriage. I was not happy and certainly not fulfilled. I wanted more excitement and needed more from life. I would soon realize that I would never find it living married in Shreveport.

Divorce on April Fool's Day

We moved to Houston, so my husband could get a more stable job—he started working for an oil and gas company. I also thought it would be good for us to distance ourselves from our parents. My husband was enjoying his new life, but I was not. Houston was not fun for me *this time*, unfortunately.

E. went to kindergarten at a local church school, where he seemed to be thriving. I loved his teacher, who laughed at his Southern sayings, such as "I am fixin' to do it." She asked jokingly "Is 'fixin' ' a word?" She was the first teacher to suggest that E. might have a learning disability, specifically attention deficit hyperactivity disorder (ADHD). My Southern response would have been "I have never heard of such a thing!" Growing up with my Father, I believed hyperactivity and "out of the box" behaviors to be "normal."

Meanwhile, I was trying to make my marriage work. I was *not* physically attracted to my husband at all. Counseling did not help, because, according to my spouse, "there was nothing wrong" with our relationship or him, for that matter. The psychologist soon diagnosed his narcissistic behavior; however, he did not confront my husband with this at the time. I was not familiar with the label of narcissism then and did not care to find out. I had finally had enough and was ready to go. I filed for legal separation and moved back to Shreveport, leaving my soon-to-be-ex-husband in the dust.

My decision only fueled his hatred for me. Everything was my fault in his narcissistic mind. How dare I leave him? Well, I did, with E. in tow. Our fates were decided by the legal system. Joint custody was difficult, having to shuffle my son back and forth to drop-offs in distant parking lots every other weekend. There were heightened tempers, and a legal restraining order was even threatened. It was very hard on my son who did not understand. Ironically, my wedding (on Valentine's Day) was dissolved on April Fool's Day. The marriage was over—I started making plans for a new life and, hopefully, new love as well. As Maredia Bowdon would say: "Been there, got the t-shirt!" I was moving on.

Many years later, I look back and see that the period of rebuilding my life after Jack and then marriage and divorce to Robbie was tougher than I initially realized. I had to dig deep to uncover any feelings of romantic love as a divorced single mom living with my parents at the Ranch. The only thing I do not regret is being a mom to my only child. I knew one thing for sure: I still wanted the best for him. I was determined to provide for him. No matter what the world threw at us, I thought we could conquer anything together. I never once considered how I would do it or how difficult it was going to be.

Living at home with my parents and joint custody every other weekend was not working out. I longed to "get away," emotionally as well as physically. I still harbored thoughts of moving. I decided I would never be happy living in Louisiana, since I wanted to see more of the world and experience other cultures. It was time to begin my journey of wanderlust, which still pushes me onward today.

Playlist Song #34:
"Tracks of My Tears," by Linda Ronstadt.

I also wanted my young son to experience the diversity of the culture within the Deep South and beyond. I began planning road trips for this purpose: we traveled to the Gulf beach town of Biloxi, Mississippi, and to the small town of Foley, Alabama, to eat at Lambert's Café, the "home of the throwed rolls." I relished my partial freedom and decided that, like Bob Dylan, I "had stayed too long." I was now approaching my late thirties. I wanted "more" from life. I decided I was going to leave my hometown for the last time; but the planning of it was going to take some time.

Playlist Song #35:
"Mississippi," by Bob Dylan.

Lambert's Café, Alabama—"Home of the Throwed Rolls."

The Order of Things in Dog Years

My plans to leave were moving much too slow. Even so, living at home was good. E. thrived in the country air and my parents loved and cherished him very much.

My Mother was happy not only because she could spend time with E. and me on a daily basis, but also because she had a drinking buddy in me. She used to allow E. to sit on her lap and steer her Continental up and down the long dirt lane leading to the "big" house.

My Father refrained from "acting up" in front of E. He often played baseball with him. Even so, my son was acquiring some habits from my Father—who seemed to get crazier with age—most of which I did not want him to develop. I wanted to move on from the past.

My Father still had a soft spot for his animals, but the canine "caste" system of hierarchy persisted. The grocery shopping was mostly dog food, as my Mother dragged large bags home each week to feed the mouths of the many dogs. My young son saw the injustice of this "caste" system and its hierarchy, especially when it came to food discrimination. Feeling the need to balance it out, he stole some delicious morsels of "inside" food and slipped it to his favorite "outside" dog, Pearl. I laughed in wholehearted agreement with my son: I was proud of him for standing up for the less fortunate. I knew then he had a kind heart and a sensitive soul.

My son—E. with Pearl and Annie.

Bronco Firefighting

The Christmas holidays were approaching. It would be my first single Christmas with my parents since my early thirties. My Father loved Christmas. He seemed to smile more during the holidays as though he was a young child again. He loved fireworks and spent a lot of money purchasing boxes of the "good" ones, including endless firecrackers, roman candles, fountains, and, best of all, the large and colorful "aerial" ones that shot into the sky and lasted for several minutes.

I have always been somewhat scared of fireworks. Mainly because of my Father, who would showcase his courage and daring personality by lighting the bundle and waiting until they almost went off in his hands. It was frightening to me! This year, though, he did not need to light fireworks to show off...

A close relative—who shall remain anonymous—did it for him. This person decided to shoot roman candles from the "big" house into the nearby field. He thought it was safe; but it had been a dry month and the grass in the nearby field was dead, at best. The nightmare of all nightmares occurred: E. and I watched from the living room window as the whole pasture burst into flames, like the burning of Atlanta in *Gone with the Wind*. Thankfully, there were no cattle in this pasture.

The relative started freaking out and was no help when it came to remedying the problem. My Father, knowing he did not have time to get the tractor and bush hog, jumped into his Ford Bronco. He had the "brilliant" idea that he would put the fire out by driving directly over the flames. I am not sure if he picked a favorite dog to ride with him. If he did, and if they were going to catch on fire, he would have his best friend alongside him.

I quickly pulled my young son away from the window and the scary scene unfolding before us. I watched my Father—backlit by the bright flames of the background—in amazement. I feared he would spontaneously combust as he proceeded to drive back and forth across the flames, as though he was cutting grass. Eventually, thankfully, the fire was extinguished and, once again, my Father had pulled off another daredevil stunt—like that time he drove through the floodwater.

I thought of these two powerful elements. Fire and water will destroy one another: water will extinguish a flame, while fire will boil water to nothing. We did not have the necessary water that night, but my Father must have had an angel looking out for him—or was it the devil? In any event, my close relative was in big trouble.

There would certainly be other times when my Father needed an angel. His temper got shorter with age. There was a "road rage" incident or "shoot 'em up" with another man. This man was chasing him down the country roads, shooting at him from his truck. My Father was contributing to the gunfight. He fired back with his World War II pistol, which he always carried in the glove compartment of his car. I assume he had a license to carry, being the Keatchie Voluntary Sheriff. The man had gained distance on him, so my Father was firing backward, while still looking forward to drive. He did not hit his mark, thankfully—something that surprised me, as he was a very good shot. My Father finally got away by rapidly disappearing behind the remote-controlled Ranch gate.

What Is Mine Is Mine

I had rented out the marriage house while I lived at the Ranch waiting for the divorce to be finalized. The joint custody agreement was still in effect, so I had every other weekend and time during the summer to myself.

I had invested my "separate" funds from the sale of my first house into this marriage house. I had also sunk my personal funds into its redo. I had good memories of the house and my son's first birthday there, but it was ultimately just a house. I was not attached to it and did not want to live there. The marriage was soon over, and the divorce had been finalized, so it was time to sell it. I made money from the sale, as usually happens with my real estate investments. My husband was upset that he would not receive any money from the sale. Too bad!

E. and I then moved from the Ranch to an apartment in Shreveport. I was now working full time for a local law firm, which allowed me the financial freedom to buy another house. This new three-bedroom house was located on a quiet street at 225 Atlantic Avenue in the same neighborhood as my first house. Did this street name anticipate my love of the Northeast?

Several years later, I found out that Jeff, my high school boyfriend, had grown up down the street. I had never known this. It is a small world, as one would say!

This quiet neighborhood was full of families and young children. By this time, my son was in elementary school. He was ecstatic! He finally had a large backyard of his own. I was very surprised when my Father, in one of his generous moods, showed up at my door with the Porters in tow, to build my son a large treehouse—the Father I loved from my childhood still existed.

Given my past and my experiences with my Father, I never thought I would ever pursue a married man. At least not another one who was not legally separated—but I did! I had had a crush on a handsome one for many years, going back to our college days. We had first met at a local bar during the summer break from our separate colleges. I had initially learned of him and his family through my hometown circles and was surprised I had not yet met him. When I did, I was instantly attracted to him. That was also the case when seeing him again.

We had a brief affair... with a lot of guilt on my part. I do not know about him, because we never got deep enough into a relationship to discuss it. Looking back, I was vulnerable and, as Johnny Lee sang, "Lookin' for love in all the wrong places." There I was again, doing things I should not be doing with men in committed relationships. Boy, was I going to get negative karma for that! And I did, eventually.

Like most shallow sexual relationships, this one also faded away. I do not name him here; as far as I know, he is still married to his wife after all these years. She was very nice to me when we had dinner together and she did not let on whether she knew. Surely, there must have been others! I do not know why she put up with his Peter Pan behavior. Like my Father, he was perpetually unfaithful and definitely refused to grow up.

Playlist Song #36:
"Lookin' for Love," by Johnny Lee.

Back in the Legal Saddle

I had advanced my legal education by completing paralegal school and obtaining my Certified Legal Assistant (CLA) certification from a national organization. I fleetingly considered law school when I re-entered the legal field with my new professional status.

I was working from dawn to night throughout the week and was too exhausted on the weekends to even consider dating. My jobs at varied law firms followed my earlier experience in insurance defense. I first worked for two attorneys who both had brilliant legal minds. Drake and Pam were great people to work for and I finally felt as though I was using my God-given brain. My organizational skills had also improved thanks to a previous part-time position with attorney Roland on a large document case.

I enjoyed researching for hours by myself and discovered I loved legal investigation. There was a large insurance case about a man who had mysteriously died at a respected hotel in Dallas. We represented the insurance company, which had been sued for the payment of the policy. Suicide or murder, that was the question!

I was asked to take a "kitchen sink" approach and create a witness list of anybody who could be a potential witness to the cause of death—anything to prevent the insurance company from paying out the exorbitant amount due under the policy. The attorneys were amazed at the creativity of my mind and got more than they bargained for, to say the least. I finally felt as though I had developed a skill with merit! I worked for them until I felt I needed more responsibility, moving to a smaller firm that offered me just that—as well as more take-home money for my young son.

I later moved on to two more law firms to earn more money. At the first one, I worked for Brian—an attorney who was a friend and valedictorian of our high school class. He was a partner in the firm and understood my position as a single mom, needing money to pay for necessities to care for a small child. Brian was easy to work with; he was kind and considerate.

We collaborated on a large automobile product liability case with lawyers who had flown in from Chicago. I worked day and night researching and organizing many documents with their paralegal to prepare for trial. I had to hire a sitter to watch E. so I could work until well after midnight. I logged numerous hours but was denied payment. It had been determined I was considered a professional so did not qualify for overtime. This was unfair, especially since I had had to hire a sitter to take care of my young son in order to work.

In the end, Brian took out his wallet and wrote a personal check to cover the overtime money I should have received. I will never forget his kindness! The greediness of the partners at this firm left me with a bitter taste that I could not ignore. I decided to move on to another small law firm, where I was treated with respect and my needs as a single mother were understood. I continued to use my creative mind, within the limits of legal parameters, diversifying my learning and challenging some of the younger lawyers along the way.

Once, I was preparing a witness list for a trial in which a payout of several thousand dollars was at stake. The case related to a fatal automobile accident with no obvious witnesses. A young blind man had been walking along the road, close to the accident. The insurance company had not bothered to question him, but I put him down as a potential witness.

Perplexed, the lead attorney questioned me: "You know this witness is blind, right? He could not have seen the accident. Why would you list him as a witness?" I looked him in the eye and responded:

"Studies have shown that when an individual has a deficit in one sense, their other senses are enhanced, such as hearing, touch. and smell." In other words, this blind man may have heard something, due to a heightened sense of hearing, leading to conclusions that may otherwise never have been considered. The attorney shook his head and walked away. I still think it was a good argument: my creative mind will never stop questioning things.

At this time, I was also receiving offers from other law firms, offering greater responsibility, higher salaries, and more benefits. Apparently, there was a shortage of talented paralegals. I felt as though I was moving up some invisible ladder—but to what end? Should I consider attending law school and become a lawyer? I decided I could not. My time was not my own. I had a child to support. I could not spend endless hours physically researching cases in a library (at a time before online legal learning). I was by this time the primary parent in my son's life—and he needed me more than I needed a law degree.

Dealing with a Diagnosis

I enrolled my very active son in sports. He needed an outlet for his endless energy. It started with baseball. My Father was happy about this, because he had been a catcher in college. Truthfully, however, E. soon became bored with it. He was put in an outfield position, where he would pick grass and stare at the sky. God forbid a plane should fly overhead—the game would be over! My love for baseball did not wane, though: I still support my "Yankees" and revel in the talent of the "Louisiana Lightning." Being from

Louisiana, I am still a big fan of Ron Guidry, who played as a pitcher for the Yankees from 1975 to 1989.

By the early '90s, E. had moved on to—and excelled at—soccer (or football), which was fast paced and kept his attention. The Shreveport city league had a competitive youth league. His practices were after school, in the afternoon, down the street from our house. It was hard juggling work as well as my son's sports activities, but I managed to do it.

My son played in this soccer league for a few seasons. His team won many games and championships. He learned a lot about playing soccer and still loves watching the sport. I enjoyed meeting and becoming friends with the parents, who encouraged all the players. My friend Jerry—who I had gone to high school with and was the younger brother of Perry, who I once dated during a summer home from college—had a son on the team.

E. had previously attended a nice "Baptist" kindergarten while I was married to Robbie. His class was taught by a great teacher, Mrs. J. One day, she told me that my son had a problem identifying colors. She would place the primary colors before him, then ask him to tell her what each color was. E. responded that he did not know, yet he could pick out "brown"—a combination of the three primary colors: red, blue, and yellow.

At the time, I, too, was puzzled by this and wondered why he did not know the primary color red, yet he knew the color brown. I knew that his two favorite books were *Where Does the Brown Bear Go?* by Nicki Weiss and *The Little Mouse, the Red Ripe Strawberry, and the Big Hungry Bear*, by Don and Audrey Wood.

It would make sense for him to know the color brown from the first book and the color red from the second. I read the latter one day, also finding it a very good story—but the bear never appeared in the book, even though the full title included *The Big Hungry*

Bear. Some of my son's behaviors never made sense, even to me. Go figure...

I soon began to see that my child learned differently. This was the introduction to my discovery of my child's artistic mind. His favorite sitter was an Education major at Centenary College. One day, she told me he would bring out *Where Does the Brown Bear Go?* whenever she asked him what book he wanted her to read him. When she started to read the first page, though, he already knew the lines and would recite them, word for word. He had memorized the sentences on each page, but did not like to read the words. This dislike of reading has remained with him to this day. I believe it was because his first attempts at reading were failures. He will be listening to the audio version of this book.

As I grew to know him better, the more I learned about his mind, soon realizing he was a visual learner. It was no surprise that I immediately knew which "self-portrait" was his when Robbie and I attended his first "parents' night" at kindergarten.

Both Mrs. N., his preschool teacher in Houston, and then Mrs. J., his kindergarten teacher at First Baptist Church School in Shreveport, suggested he might have a learning difference. He needed special attention. I later became a struggling single mother attempting to pay for the best private education I could afford.

I subsequently enrolled E. in the local Montessori school. I soon found out that although E. was definitely smart enough, that type of learning gave my son *too much freedom*, when he needed a more structure learning. The teachers at the Montessori school, like the others, believed he might have attention deficit disorder (ADD) or ADHD, and sent him for testing.

ADD was the popular label given to most hyperactive children at the time. Several young children received such a diagnosis. During this time, the learning procedure in most schools in Louisiana was as follows: do not try to figure out the source but medicate the child—so he or she will sit quietly, like a robot, allowing the teacher to teach the class. Most schools jumped on this label whenever a child was easily distractible and had behavior issues.

I did not blame the teachers by any measure, since they were paid to teach and not to play disciplinarian. Rather, I blame the system for not trying to find alternative teaching methods which did not label a child who learned differently as lazy or stupid, as commonly occurred. After all, many of these children are neither but extremely intelligent. Each child is unique, right?

There were alternatives to medicating children who did not have extreme behavior problems, such as behavior modification for those different forms of learning. However, this would have involved teachers and parents working together and taking time away from teaching in order to understand the balance necessary for the individual child.

There were no psychologists or psychiatrists within the school system; those professionals were in private practice or, in extreme cases, in institutional settings, where they were paid handsomely for their time. Most parents did not want to take the time, nor did they have the money. Health insurance had yet to address this learning problem. I was determined to learn how to address my son's "misunderstood" mind.

My long working hours made things difficult. I knew my son needed help after a male teacher found a pencil drawing of a man with a big stomach and stars surrounding his head. The person in the drawing looked disturbed. The teacher insisted my son had drawn this picture. I asked my young son who it was in the picture. He never directly identified the person, only saying he drew a picture of a man and thought it was funny. Still, something looked vaguely familiar about the person. Perhaps this was all a figment of his imagination, but the details of it seemed real to me. I had a creepy feeling about it.

The drawing bothered me so much I proceeded to ruminate over it for days. Was I too busy to see that something was clearly wrong? Had I missed signs of abuse? A few months later, my ex-husband and I hired a psychiatrist to investigate the issue. After many conversations totaling many professional hours (and costing lots of money), it was determined that there were no signs of abuse.

I had to let it go at the time, but the image remained at the back of my mind and continued to bother me for many years as I watched my son grow into a man. Although I could not prove it, my intuition told me there was more to it and something was being withheld from me. I became a little paranoid imagining I was not being told the whole truth. After all, "what is normal in a not so normal world?"

Both my ex-husband and I were given questionnaires to fill out; it seemed to me he did not know his son at all. From prior medical observations and our answers to these questionnaires, the doctor soon diagnosed E. with ADHD and obsessive-compulsive disorder, otherwise known as obsessive-compulsive personality disorder.

I was determined to discontinue the psychiatric sessions soon after this, when the psychiatrist could not find the right medication to treat E. At the time, Ritalin was the drug of choice for ADHD, but after a trial it became clear that it did not help my son with his symptoms. Was this an indication that he did not in fact have ADHD? My question remained ignored. The psychiatrist then put him on Dexedrine, commonly known as "speed." It broke my heart to see my son walk around the house like a zombie, as if all the life force had been taken from him.

The good that came out of the many sessions was E. learned to think strategically; he also learned to play chess, which offers lifelong lessons in and of itself. Looking back, I am not so sure the

WAY BEYOND THE GRITS | SIDNEY KATE

psychiatrist was not an oddity as well. He was one of a few doctors who had been okayed for repayment from my ex's medical plan. Perhaps we should not have trusted this psychiatrist with our child's gifted mind. Even now, I still wonder whether we should have gotten a second opinion.

The Montessori adventure ended soon thereafter—but another door opened to another adventure, one that continues to this day. I read all that was available on the subject of learning disabilities, determined to find a way to get my son the educational help he needed.

I knew I was not going to find it in Louisiana, whose educational systems seemed lightyears behind the times. I ultimately found a private school in Florida that worked alongside the medical profession and specialized in educating gifted children with various learning disabilities, primarily ADD and ADHD.

I immediately started packing my bags. I decided to postpone my personal dreams. I had found the excuse I wanted to move away. Any considerations of attending law school were discarded for good when I put the house on Atlantic Avenue on the market and handed my resignation to my employer at the law firm. It was a good sign when my house sold in one day—and, once again, I made a profit!

When it came to my child's future, I would settle for nothing less than the best. I have spent many years proving this; it being a lifelong mission. I started the journey thinking there might be an "easy fix," but that has NEVER been the case. At that time, though, I was convinced and determined my young son would achieve a successful outcome from the cultural stigma of this sometimes devastating and highly diagnosed mental disorder.

My parents supported our move, although my ex-husband did not. He was clueless as to what E. needed, fighting me tooth and nail.

He argued that E.'s needs could be met in Louisiana, which was not the case—at least not in the drugless way I hoped to try. When this did not convince him, he argued that the additional miles added hardship to his custody agreement. His narcissistic mind prevented him from considering the best interests of our son and he eventually lost this battle. E. needed more than the Louisiana public schools could offer.

PERSONAL LIFE UPROOTED— FLORIDA IN MY FORTIES

Changes in Latitudes, Changes in Attitudes

Moving to Florida was easy, but living there was hard. Yes, there were many beautiful beaches as well as outdoor restaurants, bars, and free outdoor activities. It was costly to live there, though, and my son's school was very expensive. My parents were helping me out with what I was not able to afford.

I started working as a CLA at a law firm in West Palm Beach that specialized in insurance defense work. I was excited about my new adventure, which was going smoothly—until, one day, everything was disrupted by office politics.

I was minding my own business and doing the work I had been given. One of the secretaries, through office gossip, found out what my salary was—more than hers. This person then went to one of the partners and threatened to quit; petty jealousy was evident. One of the lawyers I worked for was not so nice either. He was married to the daughter of a partner, so he had a definite "in," giving him some power. Most of which he did not earn. I thought of him as a rat—he also shared a name with a legendary mouse.

It was a grind to drive to Boca Raton each morning to drop my son off at his new school, *and* then drive back to West Palm Beach for work. This tiring daily routine was augmented by the constant pressures and demands of the new job. I was stressed, to say the least. The writing was on the wall; these various challenges finally took their toll, and I soon started looking for other employment.

I said goodbye to law once again after performing some temporary work dealing with legal contracts at a national corporation. Looking back, the positive experiences outweighed the negative. The single good thing that came out of it all was that I acquired the necessary skills to foster my love of writing.

Playlist Song #37:
"Changes in Latitudes, Changes in Attitudes,"
by Jimmy Buffett.

A Crossroads in Life—So Many Different Children in the World

The new school in Boca Raton, named Crossroads, specialized in educating children with diverse learning disabilities. This school changed E.'s life. It was started by a family from South Africa. It was there that we were introduced to Mrs. C. She had taught for many years in New Jersey, then moved to Florida with her husband in semi-retirement. She had worked with gifted children for several years. I knew she was going to be important for my son. Mrs. C believed in my desire to help E. achieve without the aid of medication.

My son excelled during his "one-on-one" education with Mrs. C. The school manager, Daryl, was a retired soccer (or football) player from South Africa. He had been a very good one. He taught my son many soccer moves. I think he might have had ADHD as well, because at times his behavior was similar to that of the children he taught. I believe this is why he started the school with his parents.

One day, late in the afternoon, the fire alarm accidentally went off. Daryl could not figure out how to stop it and was becoming impatient with the ongoing sound. He stuffed tissue in his ears.

When I arrived at the school around 5:30 p.m., Daryl was standing on a ladder trying to figure out how to disconnect the "hardwired" fixture. My son was standing at the foot of the ladder instructing him how to do it. I then realized that despite the labels E. had been given; he had a much different gift. Daryl finally figured out how to turn the alarm off that day with the help of my son. Many times since my son has been asked to "fix" mechanical and technical problems that others his age could not.

The important thing during this period was that E. was allowed to be E. Mrs. C. was very pleased with his rapid progress. He was learning about three grades above his current one. He still had his "quirks"—one being that he loved to vacuum. He was allowed to vacuum the classroom if he desired, even when it was clearly an inappropriate time to do so. In allowing this, Mrs. C. gave him some control over his environment.

I laughed when I saw the smile on her face as she watched him vacuum her classroom. It occurred to me that he would make a woman very happy one day! Well, that has not happened—not yet, at least. He is both left-brained and right-brained, being both mechanical and artistic. Today, E. still delights in finding innovative products that make life easier. His latest find is—you guessed it—a streamlined vacuum cleaner! It is cordless and bagless, as he demonstrated to me, and is manufactured by a UK company.

At Crossroads, I was introduced to a whole world of brilliant children with learning disabilities of all kinds. I was amazed when I told one child savant my birthdate. He immediately told me what day it fell upon! I also met each child's parents who, at times, were even more interesting than their children. I have made some lifelong friends as a result, especially in another single mother and her son. He was a classic ADHD child whose mouth was always getting him into trouble. All these people made my life more exciting, to say the least.

Finding Hockey at a Birthday Party

Once he had settled into school, I enrolled E. in the Southern Florida soccer league. He excelled, thanks to the moves Daryl had taught him. He quickly became known to his teammates as "Fast Eddie."

One day, his coach told me he thought he had talent and suggested I enroll him in a focused program for soccer, which would involve extensive training. Being a single mom, I was uneasy at the prospect of allowing him to move away and work with people who I did not know and, frankly, did not trust. I had heard horror stories of children sold into slavery on the premise of obtaining elite sport training.

I knew that his learning was most important. He was finally on the right track. I was not going to let him throw away a specialized education for an uncertain path in sports. I struggled with the decision for a number of weeks, but eventually politely refused this training.

Soon after, my son discovered a passion for hockey at a friend's birthday party. The father of the friend was a professional hockey player, a goalie. E. returned from the party with a big smile on his face—one I had not seen for some while. He was excited to play hockey, having tried on the goalie pads, taken shots from the other attendees, and been encouraged that he might have some skill at it.

I did not know much about hockey but soon learned there were two kinds: roller and ice hockey. The former was the less expensive. I enrolled my son in a league at the Atlantis Roller Rink in Lake Worth, run by Jacques, a former professional Canadian hockey player. E. was placed on a team named the Whalers, after the NHL Hartford Whalers, who played professionally in the NHL from 1979 to 1997.

He wanted to try out for the goaltending position. His first pads were made by Cooper. Most goaltending pads were made of horsehair then, so they became very heavy when they were wet. I had to laugh when, at his first tryout, he managed to stop the shots even though his pads were on the wrong way. He had the outside edge inward. Finally, one of the officials politely showed him how they should be.

E. started playing in a competitive roller hockey travel league on a team named the Vipers. This team was composed of some very talented boys whose parents were nice, for the most part, except for one single father who I called "the fanny pack from hell"—because he always wore tennis shoes, shorts, and a fanny pack around his waist. I am only kidding, of course, since Marrone, an outspoken Italian from New York, frequently kept all the parents (and the kids) in check.

I liked him, although I acted as though I did not, just to mess with him. Marrone was the one to bluntly point out the first day of tryouts—and later tell the officials—that my son had his goalie pads on incorrectly. He quickly followed up with the snide remark: "You sure he wants to play goal?" He laughed to himself, as though my son was not good enough!

Many puck stops later, though, I was laughing louder! He was a good man and helped out by bringing a fertilizer pump of water to spray the children (and the parents he wished to shut up) when the extreme heat got too much at outdoor tournaments. At times, he even fed the crew fried chicken. His heart was in the right place.

All the parents were excited about the team's potential. They won—A LOT! I cannot be sure, but I suspected many of the other children had been diagnosed with ADHD or a variant. This did not seem to affect their play, except sometimes a few became very focused on a single play, losing track of the bigger picture. I suspected some of the parents were ADHD as well, but that was not talked about. I wondered how many of the players were on Ritalin.

One mother in particular became a lasting close friend. She and her family still offer me an unparalleled source of support. Their story involves an interracial marriage and the raising of two beautiful and intelligent children who have "survived" what I would definitely call an exceptional life.

Nancy, a special education teacher, is originally from Omaha, Nebraska. She is now retired after teaching children with extreme disabilities at a state-sponsored school in Palm Beach County. Her upbringing was very unlike mine; she came from a loving Midwestern family. We nonetheless had much in common; she, like me, has experienced some difficult hardships as an adult. She is an overcomer—always displaying a beautiful smile and a positive attitude.

Her work and personal caring for others has offered beautiful gifts to those blessed enough to cross her path. She gives her whole soul to others. She teaches "peace and love." I value her friendship above all others. She always maintains a positive attitude, from one crisis to another. She has "talked" me through many years of dysfunction.

This one enduring friendship, combined with the love of the Bowdons, has helped me through the roughest periods of my life. Who needs therapy when you have such caring souls around you? I laugh, but the truth is she and I have always been there for one another over the years and still are. Yes, friendship is a two-way path. Nancy is a true "soul" sister.

Playlist Song #38:
"That's What Friends Are For," by Dionne Warwick.

E. continued to attend Crossroads and had another group of friends from the school, who were very bright children but not athletic.

Here is one story that still makes me laugh. My son tried to teach a friend how to rollerblade—prompted by a request from his mother. She wanted to lure him away from his excessive playing of video games. That was quite amusing, since she binge-watched the shopping channel. The family had a beautiful house in Boca Raton.

I drove up one day to see my son skating circles around Jason on the front sidewalk. The latter had airline pillows corded to his body, so he looked like the "Michelin Man" on rollerblades. His mother, another outspoken Italian from New Jersey, was scared her son would fall and break a bone; so she wrapped him up so tightly he could not move, much less skate. I do not know why she was so worried; his father was a successful ER doctor and could have fixed him up in no time. He managed about a yard of skating before going back to his stationary video games. I wonder what happened to him in his later years. He was a brilliant kid with an overprotective helicopter mom, who I loved dearly. It takes one to know one, right?

The Crazy Path of Ice Hockey

Having distinguished himself on the roller hockey team, E. eventually turned to competitive ice hockey. I had promised him that if he did well in the former, he could move on to the latter. What I did not know is that it would add several thousand dollars to the already taxing amount of money I was spending on his sporting activities. Paying for ice time was not cheap. My bank account dwindled further with each advancement, but I look back on those times without any regrets.

E. progressed in both school and in hockey, as did my friendship with Nancy and her family. Our sons played together for the Vipers and both then switched to ice hockey, playing together in a local league and then for rival teams.

Youth sports are interesting both on and off the ice. Many deals are made behind the scenes, which do not necessarily involve the talent of the child. Money is a great motivator—and it talks. I have a slew of personal stories about this negative side of hockey. Parents who want their child to succeed can be overtaken by greed and desperation, ultimately driving them hockey-crazy. To be fair, this happens in every sport where competition for positions and playing time can make or break a child's spirit. It also happens in education, especially college, where the race to achieve can be similarly overwhelming.

The involvement of parents can sometimes become extreme, especially in ice hockey, given the tremendous costs to play. Not only did we have to consider ice time, but we also had to buy expensive equipment. Being able to afford the best equipment was its own competition, with goaltending being the most expensive by far. Needless to say, all of the local hockey stores knew my son's name! Whenever he grew an inch, he needed bigger pads, gloves, and sticks. Helmets became expensive, too, since he wanted his to be painted with a design reflecting his team.

My son's first ice hockey rink league game was at Gold Coast Ice Arena in Pompano Beach. The teams were divided up by the rink officials. My son lucked out and once again was put on a well-rounded team called the Lightning, named after the NHL Tampa Bay Lightning. Some of the players, like my son, had come over from roller hockey. The coaches consisted of former hockey players who happened to have children on the team. These boys and their parents were awesome—we all got along and there was an amazing team spirit.

E. had practices and games early on Saturday mornings. He was not a morning person. This was always hard for me, because I had to get him up before dawn in order to give him time to get fully dressed. His uniform consisted of many layers. At times, he slept in his gear the night before, so all I had to do was walk him to the car so he could sleep all the way to the rink. We also had to cross the train tracks before the 5 a.m. train came. It was a long train. You would be about fifteen minutes later if you did make it over the tracks before it passed through. It was fifteen minutes my son could not afford.

As he got older, he walked into the rink wearing skates with blade guards and finished getting dressed in the locker room. I did not go into the boy's locker room, so one of the fathers would help E. tighten and tie his skate laces. He wanted these to be extra tight because he had a sensory thing going on with his feet. Socks with seams bothered him. I had to hunt for a particular sock. He was also very particular about anything tight around his neck.

My son had a *structured* dressing plan which he did not deviate from during the many years he played hockey. Some of it was due to superstition, as was the case for many hockey players, especially goalies.

The team had a special bond and went to Denny's after most Saturday morning practices and games. One of the boys, Ryan, the coach's son, always ordered "Moons Over My Hammy"—scrambled eggs with ham and cheese on grilled sourdough bread with hash browns. It is still on the Denny's menu! Ryan was a very bright and interesting child, and I often wonder what vocation he chose.

The Lightning were winning most of their games in the late winter and early spring of 1998, making their way to the championship game. All the parents and many grandparents were in attendance. My Father and Mother flew in to see E. play hockey. As my father had excelled as a catcher in baseball, he was keen to cheer for his grandson playing hockey. The similarities in equipment, especially the goalie helmet, were apparent.

The kids were keyed up and ready to play. Everyone was in fine spirits. We took our places on the bleachers, ready to cheer the team on. My Father, who was sitting at the end got so excited he fell off the bleachers. He was very fortunate not to get badly hurt. Luckily, an orthopedic surgeon, who was also the father of a player, was in attendance. He checked my Father out and found he was good to go.

Nonetheless, my Father was in rare form, handing out dollar bills to each player after they won the game. I smiled as all the players lined up with their hands out eagerly awaiting my Father's generosity.

A father of one of the players stood at the end of the line holding out his hand. He was an extremely tall former basketball player. He looked out of place holding out his large hand. My Father, who was very short, laughed as he handed him his winnings. The two men, one black and one white, smiled at each other with a look of understanding. I reflect on the scene and think about the history of racial relationships and today's suggestion of *reparations*.

Much more fun and laughter was had when we all went to Pizza Hut, where Big Nic, the Italian grandfather of Little Nicky, another Lightning player, paid for pizza for our diverse group.

Getting Much Crazier...

For most of the boys on the team, the next step was to try out and join a *travel* ice hockey program. By this time, E. was training at goalie camps in Canada in the summer months of the offseason.

One of these elite camps was in Scarborough, a town near Toronto, in Ontario. The school was run by a famous Russian goaltender. Many of the goaltenders attending the camp were currently playing in the NHL. During the season, though, E. trained with local goaltenders, many of whom were older and had played at a higher level. I was meeting all kinds of interesting families whose sons were gifted goaltenders.

During this time, many talented players started to lose interest in playing hockey, due to the politics of money and power creeping into the mix. Several gave it up completely, which was unfortunate, because some of them were extremely talented. Some went on to excel in other sports, while others chose negative behavior and eventually got into trouble with drugs. Playing hockey took a lot of time and energy. It was good for my son; it held his attention. I believe it most probably prevented him from getting into trouble and going down a negative path.

I realized the level of jealousy toward him, especially from other goalies, was increasing. Some of the remaining parents negotiated positions for their children behind closed doors. I was first exposed to this behavior when E. was a Squirt—Squirt hockey being for kids ten years of age and under.

In youth hockey, only one goaltender can play, so it is the most competitive position. The judgment of a goalie's skills is not always objective, especially at the lower levels. A goaltender could appear to be very talented if he played in front of a good defense. I have also seen many goaltenders be credited for a shot that missed the net. This type of padded stat boosts the goaltender's save percentage and makes him appear more talented on paper than he really is.

Having a talented offense was of course important, but winning championships came down to having good defense. Unfortunately, at the Squirt level, the children were only focused on scoring goals, not defending them. They had yet to learn how important defense was or how to be a true team player—after all, a goaltender depends heavily on his players.

I had much experience observing professional goaltenders train at hockey camps. I knew when a goaltender should take responsibility for a goal—a bad goal, which he should have stopped—or when the team needs to take responsibility. Many goals, for instance, have been scored following a deflection off one's own player. As they used to say, a goaltender is either the hero or the goat...

E. tried out for but did not make the Squirt travel hockey team at Gold Coast. To stay competitive, he started playing at a higher level, with the Peewees—for kids twelve years of age or under—in the rink hockey league. His disappointment was evident, but he continued to learn, train hard, and compete at this higher level, getting as much ice time as possible.

A month or two after the season began, I received a call from a goaltender's mom who had seen E. compete at a goalie camp the previous summer. Her elder son was a goaltender in a higher age bracket, playing travel hockey at Incredible Ice, a rink in Coral Springs. Her younger son was playing defense on their Squirt travel team, which was called the Coral Springs Coyotes, named for the NHL Phoenix Coyotes.

She told me her son's Squirt team goaltender had been injured and would be out for most of the season. The team desperately needed a goalkeeper. The rink tryouts were over, and most goalies had already been placed on rival teams. The Coyotes needed a high-level replacement because this was one of the best travel teams in the area.

E. and I were told the date and time to head over to the rink to "work out" with the team. It was really a disguised tryout, but he was excited about the opportunity. We showed up on time. He went into the locker room to get dressed. I anxiously awaited the practice to start. It seemed like forever, but the team finally emerged onto the ice to warm up.

I noticed a small child sitting on the sidelines with a cast on his arm and immediately knew he was the injured goalie. The practice proceeded without incident. I was never prouder of my son, as he stopped almost all the shots from each player. His many hours of private training had paid off. I had to remind myself to breathe!

When the practice was over, the children slowly skated off the ice. One by one, the parents came up to me and introduced themselves, welcoming E. to the team. I was given a schedule and asked to fill out some forms and pay the team fee. Afterward, alone and waiting for my son, I sat there stunned, thinking that sometimes life's blessings come from nowhere. I looked up and once again thanked my higher being for my child's amazing gift.

I waited a while for E. to come out of the locker room. He was very quiet as we walked out of the rink together. His coach, who had played defense on the Michigan State Division One hockey team, later revealed why. He prefaced the story by praising my son's maturity, stating "I could not have handled the situation as well when I was his age." Apparently, some of the players on the team had told E. to "go home," because he "was not wanted." Yet, despite these nasty comments, E. went out on the ice and competed to the best of his ability. The assistant coach was very supportive of my son thereafter.

Much later, I found out these stinging words were fueled by the injured goalie's jealousy. Up to this point, there had been only one goalie and now there were two, my son having earned the starter position. Once the other goalie's injury had healed, he began to prevent my son from warming up and practicing before a big game. Indeed, he once got in the net and would not get out during the warmups before a championship game in Canada! My son had to literally push him out. The coach should have remedied the situation but did not do so.

I learned later that one of the defensemen—who was a talented player—and the injured goalie had come to the team as a "package deal." The goalie, not the team, got the better deal. Some of the other kids were from prominent families; one had the same last name as a Florida governor, while the injured goalie was the son of a prominent surgeon. Always money and power...

Lone parents would often make derogatory comments about my son's play. I once publicly told off a father when I became fed up with his unpleasant remarks. I felt he did not know what he was talking about, so I made my thoughts evident.

The team eventually gelled and went on to win games and some championships, so the whole experience was more positive than negative. After all, it was *only* youth travel hockey.

Wishful Drinking

During this time, the stresses of work and hockey resulted in me doing a lot of "wishful drinking," which consisted of consuming many glasses of chardonnay to relax. I spent many nights at local restaurants helping my son finish his homework after a long day at work and his hockey practice.

One favorite was Tony Roma's, which specialized in baby back ribs, while another was Tom's Place BBQ, whose ribs, collard greens, and barbeque beans were the best I have ever eaten. E. loved ribs and still does.

We became fast friends with a nice bartender, Harvey, who took a "fatherly" interest in building up my son's confidence. Many nights, we talked to Harvey for hours about the progress E. was making in school and hockey. Though Harvey has since passed, I believe Tom's Place is still in business, having moved from Boca Raton to Boynton Beach, after its original restaurateur, Tom Wright, suffered a stroke.[37]

Playlist Song #39:
"Wishful Drinking," by Ingrid Andress and Sam Hunt.

My social life was NONEXISTENT during this time. I needed adult stimulation away from my son, but I could never find a suitable sitter and did not "trust" just anyone.

I could have been disciplined by more than child services one particular night. I had gotten two tickets to a Davy Jones concert but had not been able to find a sitter. Davy Jones had been a member of The Monkees, a popular band from the '60s. The concert was great; I was drinking my usual white wine, but soon became intoxicated as I had not eaten. I do not know what I was thinking, as my drinking and driving could have endangered both of our lives.

I got lost and pulled off the interstate to look at a map, which was very blurry. Thankfully, E. was an excellent map reader, and we got safely home without incident. It was very much a wakeup call, though. Not only did I learn a valuable lesson, but my son saved me that night. I was very thankful I had raised a good son.

Specialized Learning for All

Money became a big factor in school choice and whether my son could continue to play hockey. After much thought, he was transitioned into a public school, Manatee Elementary. Mrs. C. assisted me in securing an Individualized Education Program (IEP) to help him manage his special needs, given his time and organization issues.

IEPs were introduced under the Individuals with Disabilities Education Act, in 1990, which amended the original Education of

Handicapped Children Act from 1975, to ensure equal access to education for all children with a disability "identified under the law."[38] The document basically sets out an individual's special education program on paper.

My son's learning disability qualified him for educational assistance under this law. He needed individual help with organization as well as extra time on tests and assignments. Mrs. C. had taught him how to adjust, in accordance with his "learning and processing," and she continued to help him transition to public school under a 504 Plan, which provided "an elementary or secondary education of accommodations that ensure academic success and access to a (successful) learning environment."[39] Nonetheless, success required a team approach, with parents, teachers, and school officials working together. I was all in.

His homework increased significantly, which I blamed on the higher teacher-to-student ratio in public as opposed to private schools. Obviously, due to the increasing student load and the many distractions in the classroom; teachers had to give more homework. I learned a lot about a range of subjects while assisting my son with his homework. He was also still being tutored by Mrs. C. who made life a lot easier for me.

Radio Silence—Are You in the FBI or the CIA?

By this time, I had finally landed the job of my dreams (or so I thought), which not only required my legal experience and research skills, but also my talent for writing. I was hired by the State of Florida's Department of Health, where I worked in the investigative branch of Health Quality Assurance at the Agency for Health Care Administration. This agency investigates unlicensed healthcare activity and was established to shield Floridians by providing "oversight of health care providers."[40]

My work life changed dramatically, being thrown into an unfamiliar yet exciting world of identifying, preventing, and halting unorthodox and sometimes criminal medical behaviors. The hours were the same, but the workload was intense. Dividing my time between E. and my cases was exhausting.

Once again, I had a stable job with a decent salary with health and retirement benefits. I was an ideal candidate for purchasing a home and ended up buying a house with three bedrooms and two bathrooms in Lake Charleston in Lake Worth—a family neighborhood near my son's elementary school. E. was happy walking or cycling to his friend's house and living a somewhat "normal" life. We both felt more safe and secure.

I had also gotten an unlisted phone number for safety reasons. Sheree, my close friend, finally reached me by phone one day after trying for months. She asked "Are you working for the FBI or the CIA?" I could have easily been working for an undercover agency! Working for the agency could be a cloak-and-dagger job at times. I often kept to myself, writing reports for endless hours on end. I can see how some might think I was hiding something.

Some of the ways we discovered unlicensed activity and, ultimately, criminal behavior were quite dangerous. My fellow investigators were involved in a few cases that made the newspapers. Most of the very extreme cases were investigated by men who had previously been involved in law enforcement and knew how to use a gun if necessary.

I especially enjoyed working with Phil, who had retired from the New York Police Department (NYPD). He had been working at the agency for several years. He was a kind man, who I could not picture as a police officer. I am sure he was a good one. He focused on investigating malpractice cases, especially those relating to cardiac patients who had died under questionable circumstances.

A case would be opened after a complaint had been filed at the State Agency in Tallahassee. It would then be sent to the nearest office, where the supervisor would dole out the cases to the agents. Phil was overwhelmed with cases at one point, so he gave me my first medical malpractice case.

I reviewed all the relevant medical records and researched the matter thoroughly, before completing my investigation and submitting my report to him for review. Phil told me later that, "it was the best report he had ever read!" We then submitted the report and accompanying documentation, which consisted of medical records and related statements, to the legal department in Tallahassee for further review. I later learned the medical doctor was cleared of any wrongdoing thanks to my diligence.

Each agent's caseload varied, due to our diverse backgrounds. My cases were mostly legal in nature, based on complaints relating to violations of standard of medical care and medical malpractice. Some were clearly without merit, being complaints about a doctor's "bedside manner" and, ultimately, cries for attention. Others were unwanted diagnoses from medical professionals that the patient believed their doctor was "insensitive".

Malpractice was found in some instances and could be extreme enough for a doctor's license to be revoked. There might have been a surgical mistake, with a foreign object being left within a patient's body during surgery; or in rare cases, where the wrong appendage was mistakenly removed. We investigated all levels of medical-related positions—there were complaints against nurses and pharmacists, mainly for drug abuse. I also investigated a few hospitals as well.

My supervisor began to give me some extreme cases relating to dangerous unlicensed activity. One of the more interesting ones involved a woman from South America, who claimed she was a doctor. She hung her fake licenses on the wall of her house/clinic in Hollywood, Florida.

The truth was that she was not a licensed medical doctor, but a licensed cosmetologist. Statements from legitimate sources revealed she was injecting all sorts of foreign substances into her patients, who were seeking to look younger by any means. Several models sought her services for lip enhancement, while one "patient" claimed she had injected "fillers" into her chest muscles, becoming very ill as a result. In some cases, this injected "filler" might be unintentionally injected into the bloodstream. However, little information was available to the public in the '90s. These lay individuals who were seeking to look years younger would not have known of the dangers involved.

The FDA now cautions that "You seek a licensed health care provider with *experience in the fields of dermatology or plastic surgery*."[41] Of course, this woman was neither. In addition, she was practicing in an unsanitary environment, with cats roaming in the examining room. This was before the regulation of these conditions and the creation of sterile surgical centers. All sorts of "unlicensed" dermatological and plastic surgery procedures were being performed in homes and even hotel rooms, on occasion.

According to an article, botox (otherwise known as Botulinum toxin type A) has been approved since 1989 for treating a variety of medical conditions involving muscular spasms.[42] Ophthalmologists originally used it on humans in the 1970s for the treatment of crossed eyes and, later, for the treatment of migraines. Botox was only approved as a "filler" for wrinkles or moderate to severe frown lines in April 2002.[43]

I completed my investigation of this woman, and due to her criminal activity, the corresponding report with accompanying documentation was turned over to law enforcement investigators in the State of Florida as well as the Attorney General and District Attorney (DA) offices. She was subsequently arrested and fully prosecuted under the law. Thereafter, I worked on several cases with investigators from the DA's office—intense yet fulfilling work. I was satisfied for the most part until I became disillusioned with the hostile work environment within the agency itself.

Discrimination and Sexual Harassment Prior to "Me Too"

I kept to myself, researching case report after case report. In some extreme cases, the interviewees of a case would get aggressive and start arguing with me, extreme enough that I sought protection. Sometimes I felt I needed protection from my own coworkers.

At times, I was forced to listen to and *expected to laugh at* dirty sex jokes making fun of women. A few other female coworkers did not laugh—but did not say a word about the behavior. Some comments were made in other languages, particularly Spanish; the male in question thought I did not know what he was saying.

At the time, there was little recourse to report such behavior. I am sure this behavior never reached Tallahassee. It went on for weeks and months. When I was interviewed for a higher-level position, I felt as though I was being attacked; I was alone in a room with two men, whose questions were harsh and intimidating.

I was competing for this job against a woman who laughed at their sexually offensive jokes and played games on her computer when she was supposed to be working. She got the job. I learned the latter tidbit about the computer from my son, when he accompanied me on "take your child to work day." I had given him some money to get some water and a snack. He saw her playing games on her computer during work hours and reported back to me, asking "Mom, why is that blond lady playing games on her computer? Will you play games on the computer with me?"

Creating a PVC Pipe Dream

Life continued to throw things at me. I had thought my prayers had been answered by this job. It soon became evident I was in a rapidly changing hostile work environment that I had no recourse against and could no longer endure. I decided I needed to get away from it.

I put in my resignation; although I, once again, had no plans for the future. I clearly stated my reasons for leaving and spoke about the sexual harassment and discrimination in my exit interview, which was only a standard written form. There was no human interaction. Who knows if my exit interview ever reached the head of the agency? Most probably not...

I sold my house in Lake Worth, making another profit—although my Father soon demanded much of it back. He had sold the business to my brothers several years earlier and was now looking for money in his strictly budgeted retirement. His health was also starting to deteriorate, although I did not know that at the time, as he did not share these details with me.

I was determined to give South Florida another shot, so E. and I went as far west as we could go, traveling the "Alligator Alley" highway to Fort Myers and Cape Coral. We found a small apartment in the latter. I was on the Gulf again; the Gulf which I had enjoyed in my childhood. Unlike my childhood, though, I was exposed to a wide range of people and their different cultures, the South Florida of the late '90s being ideal for that.

After we moved, to my chagrin, I learned that my son, being a quiet person, hated the very change I thrived on. I had grown up in a protected environment; so I craved adventure and novelty, the wanderlust of being exposed to new cultures and meeting new people. As in the words of the Mama Cass song, I was driven to "make my own kind of music, even if nobody else was singing along." I did not once look around to see my son *not* singing along.

Upon reflection, I may have pushed a little too hard. Looking back, even though it was clearly unplanned, the constant moving forced E. to become accustomed to different lifestyles. The modern Florida included a diversity of people and a greater need for communication and understanding. At the time, I thought if he could succeed in different places, then I probably did what was best for him in the long run. I now know I made a lot of mistakes.

On occasion, I thought about running away from everyone and everything—and I sometimes *still try to*, but for much different reasons. A lot of my desire to escape then was due to my deep-seated need to distance myself and my son from any abusive environment. I had hoped to protect him completely, which I now know was never going to happen. I certainly wanted to distance myself from the traumas of my childhood.

I decided to homeschool my son instead of enrolling him at yet another public school. E. was still playing competitive hockey, so homeschooling gave him time to travel to tournaments. Otherwise, he would have missed a lot of school. He thrived under my teaching; I bought books and tapes on subjects that were age-appropriate. We went on numerous field trips, after which he would write reports. I was following the Florida educational guidelines closely and all was moving along nicely.

Things became more demanding when I discovered that E., unbeknownst to me, was playing songs to the neighborhood via a radio transmitting station he had built. I was petrified the Federal Communications Commission would storm the house to confiscate the equipment and impose criminal penalties for unlicensed activity.

Yes, my son is very bright, but he is basically an introvert. He spent hours on the computer by himself, mainly gaming—but who knows what else? Having an investigative mind, I worried that he was being exposed to predators online.

He loved electronics and he loved music, so it was inevitable he would create a way to incorporate both into his life. Much later, when he was in college, he created a patent that was published in Europe in 2013, allowing an internet user to interact with a station to broadcast the user's selection of media. His idea created a vote based method and system. Sound familiar?

He had a hard time getting anywhere with it. His age and the prohibitive costs of hiring an attorney to assist in completing and submitting the required papers to procure the actual patent deterred its development. Sadly, it was eventually abandoned.

A Different Perspective on Hockey

I wanted my son to be happy and I wanted him to succeed: I did everything I could to make that happen. My son enjoyed playing hockey; it made him feel good about himself. He was rapidly advancing in terms of his skills and was ready for a higher level of competition at Coral Springs.

There were two travel teams that year; he chose to try out for the second, because it offered him more play time, he thought the Head Coach was exceptional, and the Assistant Coach was the understanding coach from his Squirt team. This second team ended up succeeding and playing against the first team in the state playoffs!

The Athletic Director of the Junior Everblades had seen E. play in these state hockey playoffs and heard about him when he was on this Coral Springs Squirt team. Our move to Cape Coral put him within proximity of the Everblades Arena near Fort Myers in Estero, Florida. This arena was named for the professional Florida Everblades, an East Coast Hockey League (ECHL) team. It is now called Hertz Arena.

Accordingly, E. tried out for and made the travel team of the Junior Everblades. He was, once again, the "new kid on the block" and forced to adjust to a new team and new players. One of his good friends, a very talented Canadian player from Quebec, decided he wanted to play with E. on the Everblades as well. Mags, one of his favorite goalie instructors and mentors, was the starting goaltender for the Everblades ECHL team.

I was anxious to see what difference living on the Gulf of Mexico—as opposed to the Atlantic Ocean—made. The children and their parents were in fact quite different. I initially thought it odd that I was asked to be the honored "Team Mom," who liaised between the parents and the coach. I later found out no one else wanted to do it. As a result, I had numerous organizational responsibilities which caused my stress levels to soar tremendously. One of my responsibilities involved reporting stats, which I took a little too seriously. The defensive stats were always hard.

I knew a lot about saves and save percentages from the many hours I had spent intently watching professional goaltenders at the camp in Toronto each summer. Both my son and I were exposed to several NHL and professional goaltenders, including Mags, who also trained at this facility.

The goaltender training was intense in Canada each summer. I witnessed many unbelievable saves by professionals and older students from around the world. My son learned many valuable lessons—including an intense work ethic—from training with a famous Russian goaltender who some students called "The Russian Bear."

In short, I knew what a "missed net" was! There were many times when a shot by a forward or, in some cases, a defenseman on the other team missed the net. The player should not be credited for a shot on goal, nor should the goalie be credited for a save. Well, the lines could get blurry here. This initial burden became something of a nightmare when certain parents would regularly come to me insisting that their son's stats were wrong.

These stats were very important for all players when attempting to get the attention of scouts looking for talented players. After all, all these dedicated players dreamed of making it into professional hockey, ultimately the NHL. Many wanted to play one day for the local ECHL team, the Florida Everblades, or the new expansion team, the Florida Panthers. I began recording all the games with my large video recorder in order to legitimately document and justify the shots and saves, but it did not seem to matter.

There were also some incidents of unrest and infighting among a handful of children who wanted the same jersey number. It was hard to make everyone happy! I thought I had finally placated most of them, only for my son to tell me that one of the children on the team had spit on him. That behavior was unacceptable—I became upset and reported it to the Athletic Director.

I soon found out the child in question was the son of the Athletic Director's secretary—he had not only spit on my son, but also trashed him to other players. It was obvious her son had behavior issues, and he had apparently gotten into disciplinary trouble on many occasions. Of course she took his side, smugly imposing her "rink power". She outright lied for him.

The Athletic Director believed her and not my son, taking her side. I knew my son was telling me the truth—why would he make up such a story? We were strongly encouraged to forget it; but my son could not let it go, nor could the other boy and his mother. I have mentioned before that, after some previous intense altercations with parents, I had learned to reign in my own thoughts and shut my mouth.

I finally let it go, but the child and his mother continued to be bitter, if not vindictive. It had a detrimental effect on the team's play. The mother continued to "bad-mouth" me behind my back. My son steered clear of the other boy altogether or as far as he could possibly get. I was proud of him for taking the higher road and pushing it aside for the greater good. The team ended up excelling that year, only losing in the state playoffs.

After that last playoff game, E. decided he was done with the Junior Everblades and decided to MOVE ON MENTALLY AND PHYSICALLY. The petty politics of the parents ended up getting so bad the coach eventually quit. I was still the "Team Mom," so I asked the coach why. He said he was not able to coach the team anymore as the parents complained about everything he did. He also told me in so many words that he was not paid enough to babysit the parents.

For the most part, my son brought positive change to each team he played for; he also helped elevate the play, which was a blessing as well as a curse. Wherever he went, there would be jealousy and competition for playing time from other goalies (or players speaking for other goalies). This was because the team did not come first.

There is a saying in all competitive team sports that "there is no 'I' in team." This can be hard for young players to comprehend.

Sadly, there was a lot of fighting for positions, ice time or better stats, rather than just playing the game. This behavior was worse among the goalies, because only one goalie could play a game. It was never-ending, all the way through the levels of junior hockey and up to Division I at the college level.

Team Florida—an elite hockey team that was picked to compete against other teams across the country—was more of the same. This was high-level competition but also VERY political. A lot of negotiating and exchanging of money was also happening behind closed doors. The best players did not always get a chance to compete.

Quebec Conundrum

During this time, my son got the chance to try out for another prestigious team that was being formed to compete at the Quebec International Pee-Wee Hockey Tournament. This tournament has been in existence since 1960. It is considered the most prestigious of the minor hockey tournaments, hosting a hundred teams from all over the world.

I was still homeschooling E., making lesson plans, planning field trips, and diligently following the Florida educational requirements. E. was learning quickly. He decided he was going to document the tournament for one of his special projects. He only made the team because one of the other goalies could not make it, but it was still an honor he was not going to refuse. At the same time, unbeknownst to others, including me, the parents of another chosen goalie were conducting some serious business behind the scenes.

After the tournament was over, I found out this other goalie's parents had paid several thousand dollars to ensure he started the first game. They wanted their son to be showcased—but that backfired when he started throwing up before the game due to an intense fear of the high-level competition. The first game was against a team from Pittsburgh; the father of one of their players had played for the NHL Pittsburgh Penguins and was in attendance. That team was highly talented and went on to win the division.

Our team was extremely handicapped, especially with this goalie. The team's lines and play were also severely disrupted when a player who we had never been seen before showed up at the last minute. This boy's father was wealthy and very important. He was originally from New York but now owned a massive home in South Florida. The scuttlebutt was that he once considered buying the Ottawa Senators and had built an ice rink on his property.

This boy showed up for the first game. It was all very secretive! He was nice enough and my son immediately liked him, seeming to have a lot in common; but most of the team did not like him. I could sense a certain loneliness in this child. It would have helped the cohesiveness of the forward lines had he practiced with the team a few times before the game. I felt other players had been sacrificed for this one player, whose father's money was more important than the best interests of the team.

He also had a personal bodyguard—a former goalie who had played high-level hockey, accompanying him everywhere. This bodyguard immediately saw the injustice relating to the goalies on the team. The Pittsburg team ran all over us, racking up goals right and left. My son waited patiently for the coach to pull the starting goalie, but that only happened when he had let in more than ten goals.

The coach finally put E. in the game when there were less than two minutes left in the game. The TWO MINUTE WARNING HAD BEEN CALLED! He was introduced on the loudspeaker; our last name was mispronounced. Oh well... In any case, by this time, the deficit was so great my son could not help the team. The competition was over. All the players were exhausted and ready for the game to end.

We were immediately placed in another bracket and played other games. My son was asked to start the next game against another team from Pennsylvania, which we won. The other goalie started one of the following games, a game that was sponsored by Snapple.

The team had a great time in Quebec City even though they did not win their division. Each team that participated in the tournament had a custom pin created so they could exchange pins with other teams. E. was able to purchase pins of a few famous Canadian NHL players who attended earlier tournaments while they were Peewees.

On the positive side, this tournament cemented team play and taught my son how to be a team player. He met and competed against hockey players from around the world, which built up his confidence in his ability to play among athletes who were the best of the best. This experience has stuck with him and helped him to be strong in all aspects of life.

I, too, learned much in Florida, connecting with and finding friends for life. We both came to understand that our experiences during this period of our lives taught us lessons we would fall back on much later.

I realized that I had learned all I needed to learn here. I knew that Florida was only meant to be a stepping stone to further growth for both of us. I felt that the specialized education in Florida had provided E. with the help he needed and the tools to begin achieving his educational goals. He had found a sport he loved and would continue to play—and hopefully he would have some fun with it along the way.

Florida had presented an array of eclectic individuals, most of whom were looking for something they would never find. My gypsy soul began to tug me forward; it called me to other places. I realized I had made many mistakes which I *would* eventually learn from. I focused intently on the goals I perceived to be best for the both of us. I wanted for the present to move quickly into the future.

I ultimately realized some of the struggles E. was facing were direct consequences of my own judgments, choices, and actions. I began to question my motivations. I was making my own mournful music and making him sing along, too. I needed to take a hard look at where I was going with my own life, alongside continuing to meet my son's needs. I decided to step back from the stress and pain of the past. I hoped it had taught me things that I could build on in a positive way.

An opportunity soon presented itself: I received and gladly accepted a job offer in Vermont. I saw Vermont as a peaceful answer to our frantic, troubled life. I was headed to the Northeast, where I felt I would be able to find better employment and enroll my son in an excellent school. He would be able to continue playing competitive hockey. The perk of being able to drive to tournaments, rather than having to spend a fortune flying everywhere, was an added benefit.

I asked my Mother if she could help with the airfare and some of the expenses relating to moving. I began getting ready for the big move; hoping to positively change my trajectory.

At the same time, I did not realize that a higher power had other plans. I did not realize resentment was brewing among my siblings—for better or worse, I may have willed what happened next into existence...

Finding Out Family Secrets

Does every family have secrets? Well, my family certainly did— and many! I only learned some of them as an older adult. Both of my parents had chosen to hide the truth from some of us, but not others; and, more sadly, certain siblings had also chosen to hide the truth from one another. My middle brother bore the burden of one huge secret alone.

I continued my preparation and was readying for the move to Vermont when my Father passed away in August 2001. He was eighty-five. His death was emotionally hard, since we had been at odds. I had been so caught up in "my" own life—a life that prevented me from going home when I found out he was sick. I had my own struggles, financial or otherwise, so was not empathetic to his battle. I was only able to go to his funeral because my Mother sent me some money to drive to Louisiana. My son and I traveled there in a rental car.

I was estranged from most of my siblings during this time as well. I spent several hours consoling my Mother, while my siblings discussed "the secret" in a meeting. I only learned about this secret a few years later when I received the estate papers—including the will—in the mail. I found out that I had another sister who I knew nothing about. My Father had met and had an affair with a nurse during World War II while he was married to his first wife.

My Father had told my middle brother several years before, swearing him to secrecy. He was afraid my Mother would find out and finally decide to leave him. I do not know whether that would have happened, but for him it must have seemed a real possibility. I believe my Father should have been honest with her—after all, it happened before he met her. I later learned he only found out about this other child years after he had married my Mother. My Mother never found out, though, so his secret remained safe.

Although this was the biggest secret, it was not the only one. I was consoling my Mother at the kitchen table when my non-sister burst in. She was in the sibling meeting that I was not invited to. She loudly asked "Is Daddy my real father?" My Mother looked startled. I was shocked—the thought had never crossed my mind! I thought "Here she is making everything about herself and ignoring my Mother's grieving." But now the question had been asked, it hung in the air around us.

I was in my late forties, but I had never once considered this. Now, though, the cat was out of the bag. My inquisitive mind revved up, starting to put two and two together. I had always wondered why she was not named after dead ancestors, like the rest of us, and she did not really look like the rest of us. Many more thoughts about the past came to mind, some being very unpleasant. Until this point, my Mother had remained silent. She then calmly answered the question, saying "Yes," but nothing else. They stared at each other for a long while. Of course, it was not technically a lie, because my Father had raised her as his own, so he was legally her father.

This was my Mother's chance to tell her story—and for some healing to begin. I watched her closely, looking for an indication, but she said nothing more about it. I only learned the truth in my sixties, long after her passing. My Mother would take all of her life secrets to the grave—for what reason, I will never know.

A Question of Power

The children were left to work out the details of our Father's estate. I was deliberately held at arm's length and not involved in *any* decisions about my Mother's care. They made their plan without me. The judge and jury of my siblings had spoken—I was to have no say in what occurred next.

No one was interested in hearing my side of the story. Years later, I found out a few believed I was *taking* extreme amounts of money from my parents. That rumor may have been started by one particularly vindictive sibling. The truth was my Father and Mother had helped me out financially, BUT they had also helped out my other siblings when needed, too. I believe they had tried to be more than fair with *each of us*, helping us all out during times of hardship. This truth had not yet come out, however. I finally got to tell my side of the story many years later after all the damage had been done.

My siblings decided to legally interdict my Mother. She would be given a stipend to live on, to cover any medical expenses, but nothing else. The estate money would be tied up in an ugly bow. I learned about the impending meeting at the lawyer's office from my Mother, who wanted me to attend on her behalf. I agreed. When I arrived, I walked into the biggest ambush I have ever witnessed. All the responsible parties were sitting around a large conference table—those who had orchestrated it and those who had innocently gone along with it.

I stood up and told the group I thought it was a big mistake. I wanted to fight for my Mother and help her take back some of her power. Was there an alternative that would allow her some power over her own life? I knew that taking all her rights away—especially her ability to make minor financial choices—would destroy her.

What is more, the interdiction documents were a matter of public record, erroneously telling the world that my Mother was mentally incapable of living the rest of her life as she saw fit. This bothered me the most. What had happened to the respect Minnie was afforded later in life? My Mother should have been treated in the same way.

I do not believe *any of my brothers* intended to cause my Mother harm; I now know some of them had their individual reasons for going along with the proceedings at the time. It was strongly implied they were looking to protect their eventual inheritance. Whatever money was left in the estate would be distributed to the children following my Mother's death. I had learned this procedure in a class on estate law in paralegal school. I wanted at least one of my siblings to come forward and explain their reasoning to me, but that did not happen. I felt my Mother was being imprisoned.

In any event, the judgment was rendered and the proceedings were over. I *want* to believe that all my siblings thought they were doing the right thing for her, to give her an easier life until her passing. But I still believe legally interdicting my Mother in this way indirectly hampered her will to live.

For centuries, women, especially Southern women, have found it hard to express their individual identity and exercise their individual power. I felt this decision was a huge step back, not only for my Mother, but also for all women who had gone through something similar. I vowed that I would NEVER allow anyone to do anything like that to me. I will always stand up for the individual rights of women like I did as a young girl in a pencil skirt and pillbox hat. Susan B. Anthony still exists within this much older girl.

Little did I know that her legal interdiction would also take away my power as well. I was deliberately not sent a copy of the interdiction. I went to the clerk's office to purchase a copy to read the truth as my siblings saw it. I could not believe what I saw: their words sharply stung my soul and I felt attacked. There was my name, in black and white; it was erroneously believed my Mother needed to be protected from me!

It was a blatant power move. I had no way of defending myself, other than suing my siblings for defamation. That was something I could not find the heart to do; not even to the ones I believed rightly deserved it. Besides, I had no money to do so. I was the reason for the interdiction—the public scapegoat! It hurt me immensely, but I chose to move forward.

At first, the interdiction prohibited me from seeing or talking to my Mother. My younger brother called me and told me what was going on after I had repeatedly called my Mother without her answering. I was only living in Vermont, but I could have been on Mars, being so isolated from her and the rest of my family.

After many months of uncertainty; however, I was finally allowed to call her and tell her I loved her. Following this, I frequently mailed her cards, although I am sure such communication was strictly monitored by her "wardens" or hired sitters, who had no familial ties. I sometimes thought these women had more power than me. I do not know if my Mother even realized what was going on.

For the next few years, I believe my *middle and youngest* brothers, who lived nearby, were sincerely trying to attend to my Mother's day-to-day needs. They both communicated with her regularly. My non-sister, who lived many miles away, was not required to ask permission to visit my Mother; she could see her anytime she wanted.

Even so, my Mother was eventually set aside and isolated from life. In my opinion, all the years of abuse she endured from my Father paled in comparison to these later years. Numerous sitters were hired to care for and run her life. They were being paid a fortune! Some of this money could have been given back to my Mother, if only so she could briefly hold it in her hands or hide it in her clothes pockets, as she had frequently done earlier in her life. I believe some of these caregivers may have even stolen things from her. I only trusted one of them; I had no power to fire any of them.

I was eventually given permission to visit my Mother, but only when the powers that be had tied all her money up legally, so only a few could disperse it. E. was in his early teens by then. I asked my Mother what she wanted to do while I was there, to give her the power to choose. I drove her to the hairdresser and ran other errands with her, but always with a sitter accompanying us. I guess I was still not completely trusted. Did they think I would abduct her and disappear into the night?

That day, we also visited the cemetery where my Father was buried. I was surprised when my Mother excitedly proclaimed "Look, there is John—he's waving to us!" I was shocked by the statement, but I later learned that sometimes people see their dead spouses when they themselves are close to it.

The next day, my son asked permission to interview his "grandmommy," as he called her. He had told me he wanted her to talk about her life to help her to feel special, so I brought along a handheld recorder. I had used it for one of my many paralegal jobs. I was hoping she would tell him some secrets no one else knew. The sitters did not bother monitoring him. After all, he was considered a child. What damage could he do? Well, as it turns out, plenty!

The major secret my Mother told him was that one of the sitters had hit her, among other things. He played it for me, proud of his accomplishment. I was livid and became extremely concerned for my Mother's safety, although I had no power—legally or medically—to help her. There and then, I decided I was going to take back some of my power and, in doing so, some of hers, NO MATTER THE COST. I had evidence now and told one or more of my siblings about the recording, in the hope they would do something about it.

My Mother was being abused; not by my Father, but by one or more of her sitters. To this day, I am saddened by and have such empathy for any woman who is made a victim and cannot get out of an ongoing situation. My Mother was not able to do anything about her circumstances; but I knew I could save myself from a similar fate. She was a VICTIM until the day she died, which, sadly, was less than four years later.

FURTHER BEYOND THE GRITS

The Vermont Turnaround

There is a driving turn in Vermont known as the "Vermont Turnaround," which you have to perform in order to obtain your driver's license. According to one online description, it is done in the following way:[44]

Signal.
Turn and look.
Stop within 18" of the curb.
Put into reverse, turn and look 360 degrees to make sure there are no cars.

Back up until you can see the edge of pavement in triangle or back door window.

When you can see the edge of pavement in the back window start to turn, turning the wheel all the way, looking where you are going.

Keep turning until you are straight, then straighten the wheel, looking where you are going. Use the passenger side mirror to make sure you remain on the pavement. Stop behind the legal stop.

Put in drive, signal left, look and go.

To me, this language seems verbose. Basically, you back up and then drive forward in order to change direction. I compare this turnaround to my previous life, my current life, and my future life (which has yet to happen).

I had dreamed of living in Vermont since childhood, envisioning the old-fashioned Christmas cards with horse-driven sleds heading through snowy pastures. It is unlike anything in the South, with its beautiful Green Mountains, peaceful countryside, and sugar shacks producing maple syrup. I like the snowy winters and prefer the cold to the heat. Vermont has a spiritual element; it is my spiritual place. My great-great-grandmother Eliza was from Vermont.

After the interdiction of my Mother, my son and I flew from Florida to Boston with a hurricane barreling close behind us. The landing was difficult, but we got there safely. This was late in August 2001, only a few days before 9/11.

I rented a car in Boston. We drove to Burlington, Vermont, seeing the most beautiful double rainbow on the way. This added to the surreal feeling of positive new beginnings. I had never experienced this feeling before. The new environment gave me hope that I would eventually find renewal.

The fall weather was upon us. The Green Mountains were so beautiful; the leaves were changing to bright autumn colors. The mountain looked like several patchwork quilts. I pressed a few autumn leaves—one orange and one red—to mail to my Mother. I missed her so much; I missed seeing her, talking to her, laughing with her, and, occasionally, eating Chinese food with her.

E. and I dove into life in Burlington. E. entered Tuttle Middle School in South Burlington. His 504 plan was put in place by the school's special educator, but he was only allowed extra time on *tests*—nothing more. Sadly, I no longer had Mrs. C. to advocate for any further accommodations. None of his new school and hockey friends knew he had a learning disability. Back then, kids (and their parents) did not talk openly about learning disabilities.

At the time, the Vermont public schools were believed to be some of the best in the country. I hoped he would excel with his few accommodations. I also hoped the teachers would cooperate and his transition would be as effortless as possible.

I still had my ongoing financial problems. I immediately started working at the University of Vermont in the Benefits Department located in the Waterman Building on campus. The pay was not good, but I finally had decent benefits. Later, though, I questioned my decision to work for so little pay, as benefits do not put food on the table.

At the time, I did not understand why the University of Vermont was also known as UVM. According to the university website, it was chartered as the fifth college in New England in 1791, the same year that Vermont became the fourteenth state in the union. Its legal title is the University of Vermont and State Agricultural College, but UVM derives from its Latin name, *Universitäs Viridis Montis*, which means University of the Green Mountains.

The wider damage caused by 9/11 was stingingly real. Vermont borders upstate New York, which is not far from New York City. We felt uncomfortably close to ground zero. I was at work in the Waterman Building when a coworker and I heard the news and turned on a small television in his office. Other coworkers joined us; we watched in astonishment at what the rest of the world was also seeing. I felt an overwhelming sense of fear that no one could ever be truly safe. At that time, the pettiness of previous family hurts seemed small. I had a staggering urge to immediately get in touch with my son.

My son's class was also watching some of the 9/11 events. I could not imagine how a young teen mind would perceive such a moment. I am sure it had a traumatic impact on some of them, as the fear of nuclear attacks had affected me in the early '60s—although my worries of the unknown as a seven-year-old paled in comparison to the reality of this disaster.

Our lives returned to something approaching normality soon after, though—well, *whatever* normality we could attempt. For the most part, living in South Burlington was a period of happiness and growth. I learned a lot about the Vermont way from true Vermonters.

They welcomed my Southern spirit with open arms, even though they blatantly and repeatedly pointed out "You are NOT from Vermont!" Most of the inhabitants had Anglo heritage, in contrast to the diversity of South Florida and the racially diverse environment I had experienced when growing up in the South. Today, though, Vermont has changed and become more racially diverse—for that, I am glad.

E. tried out for and made the youth travel hockey team at Cairns Arena, a beautiful hockey rink located down the street from his school. His team was the Cairns South Burlington or CSB Hawks. We needed to fit in. At first, I thought that might not happen.

After the tryouts had been completed, the coaches looked to the bleachers and asked "Where are E.'s parents?" I slowly raised my hand. All the coaches and parents looked at me puzzled as to why a male was nowhere in sight.

I was in the minority as a single parent, but the parents were very nice and our children were having fun. These families had dual incomes. Most of the parents had their own businesses; some were the budding entrepreneurs behind Burton snowboards and Rhino Foods, the latter being a specialty ice cream manufacturer founded in 1981. These parents provided each player with a "Chipwich"—or chocolate chip ice cream sandwich. Both these companies have survived today.

Their homes were dispersed throughout South Burlington, Shelburne, and Charlotte. I rented a townhouse at Stonehedge, minutes away from my work, E.'s school, and the hockey rink. Everything was looking up! Was this meant to be?! There were still daily financial worries, though, and one or more of my checks to the hockey team bounced. I was continually trying to work this out. I desperately wanted E. to continue playing the hockey he loved and seemed to excel at.

The expenses for the rental car I drove during our first four months were starting to add up. I needed to purchase a car that I could drive in all weather—one with all-wheel drive—but I had to wait until I had been gainfully employed for a period of time. I eventually purchased a Jeep Cherokee Grand Wagoneer several months into my employment. Prior to that, Joyce, a fellow employee, noticed our struggle and helped me out by donating her deceased mother's station wagon. I was so thankful for her very kind gesture!

I am not sure what year this car was, but it had very low mileage. It was worth less than $800, so I did not have to pay taxes on its license. It was yellow; I promptly named it the "Mellow Yellow," after the song by Donovan. I was somewhat embarrassed when I drove

WAY BEYOND THE GRITS | SIDNEY KATE

to the rink, parking next to all the elite cars. I think E. was equally embarrassed. He later revealed to me that Bobby, his friend, told him no one in Vermont cared about nice cars. That was true *at that time*, to a point, unlike materialistic Florida. The Mellow Yellow not only sufficed; it also gave us many months of driving pleasure.

I worked at UVM for the next few years. I continued to raise E. by myself and struggled to make ends meet. I had no help from anyone in my family. Travel hockey was still expensive. It was expensive to stay in hotels for a few nights, but we were sometimes able to save on gas by driving with other families to games. We drove to tournaments in the neighboring states of New York and New Hampshire. We also played a few games in Montreal, Canada.

"Please Help Me!"

It soon became clear that I would not be able to support our lives on my current salary, so I left UVM for one reason alone—the need to make more money. I knew I would miss my UVM coworkers. I went back to law. I started working as a paralegal / investigator for a plaintiff attorney in Burlington. There were only a few employees at this firm.

In addition, I took on a series of second jobs, too. One was selling VHS videos from a call center at night and on the weekends. Most of the VHS videos were from PBS and WGBH, which rebranded to GBH in 2020 and now streams television broadcasts of NPR. Many British television dramas like *As Time Goes By* and comedies like *Are You Being Served?* were also included in the sales packages.

Eventually, cable streaming services almost completely replaced the sale of VHS videos and DVDs.

Another job I had was delivering phone books. Most phone companies stopped delivering phone books for economic and environmental reasons. Also, the introduction of online options allowed individuals to get telephone numbers in other ways.

Even so, I could no longer afford the rent at Stonehedge, so we ended up continually moving around. My son, who was now in his high school years, bounced around from school to school. Each school welcomed him—and his hockey talent—but it quickly became very embarrassing. It may have looked to others as though our continued moves enabled him to further his hockey, when that was far from the case. The real reason was too humiliating to admit to those who were economically advantaged. I wanted him to continue playing at all costs.

I finally thought we had found the right fit at a private school, where we did not have to worry about school districts. E. had been asked by one of his CSB teammates to come and play; his father also went to bat for us, having seen E. play many times in the past. I was excited at the prospect, but unfortunately everything fell apart when the available scholarships had already been awarded. E. was not awarded a financial scholarship; I could not afford the higher tuition.

During this period, I started renting a condo in Williston, until I could no longer afford to pay the rent there, as well. Our absentee landlord was empathetic but could not justify giving us a few months until I could recover. I tried to borrow some money from friends. Some friends offered help but not enough to survive on.

I sold everything I could to raise money—including the Mellow Yellow—in a yard sale in front of my Williston residence. I wish I still had this car, which was definitely a classic. I never saw another one like it. I would have sold my body had anyone been interested. I had a teenage son in high school and two cats to support. I quickly learned I would have to swallow my pride: I needed help and had to find an alternative—any alternative.

Finding help ended up becoming a full-time job. I went to every church, charity, state, and government organization looking for assistance. I called several local officials as well as the offices of senators, congressmen and congresswomen. I stood in line at food banks, local churches, and the Salvation Army—hoping for a miracle. I was not too proud to ask for handouts of toilet paper. I even called the office of Bernie Sanders and talked to an assistant who helped me with healthcare assistance. This caused me to revise my opinion of Bernie Sanders—he did care about the people of Vermont.

This seemingly endless search was exhausting. I felt bad all the time. I knew something was wrong with me. I had been pushed into survival mode—my son and I needed the basic necessities of water, food, and shelter in order to live. I had never encountered such an extreme situation.

I had heard stories about welfare assistance, but I had never been forced to ask for it. The few dollars I received were not enough and I was not able to find any further answers. We were on the verge of being homeless and desperate to find a place to live. I ultimately ended up in a hospital, but not by my choosing.

I sensed there was something medically wrong with me. This turned out to be a fact. Dr T., my gynecologist, put me through the usual tests and discovered a suspicious area. He was very understanding about my circumstances and hardships. I did not have enough money to pay for his services. I did not have health insurance. He and his office manager found a way to continue treating me out of the goodness of their hearts. I was cleared for a procedure to investigate further. He believed I might have cancer—I feared the worst.

That night, I sat crying on the staircase of my empty condo on the verge of eviction, crying out to God and not knowing if he would listen: "Please help me!" I was so fearful about what might happen to my son should it be cancer. Until that point, my faith had not been strong; but now I was at my wit's end. I was desperate for any help. I needed more than financial help. I needed a *true* miracle.

I remembered a dream told to me by my Father in which he saw my son and I driving around—a U-Haul trailer behind the car—with nowhere to go. That dream had become a reality. What hurt the most was my own family had deserted me.

My ex-husband also turned his back on us. He flew into Boston for business, drove up, stomped around the condo, then left without offering a dime! I did not care what he thought of me, but how could he desert his own son? I knew why: I had taken full responsibility for E., so he felt he was off the hook.

Holly, who was still in my life and a good friend, drove from Boston to help me. She and John, her husband, gave us financial support. I am forever grateful to her for this gesture. I vowed there and then I would do something special for her one day—another soul sister and blessing from living in Florida.

———————————————————

Faith, Hope, and Earth Angels

God did answer my prayers, but in his own time. I thought I had been abandoned by those closest to me; but the following experience revealed I had never been alone.

The time had come to uncover the truth of my illness, but I could not afford *not* to work during this time. Dr. T. was going to perform an outpatient procedure. I was given anesthesia to put me "under". I began to enter a very real—not dreamlike—state.

Dr. T. was accompanied by a handsome young doctor, with wavy golden hair, who greeted me: "I am Dr. Faith." He politely asked if he could observe my case. This was not an unusual question at a teaching hospital, so I quickly consented. I felt a calming affinity with Dr. Faith.

I watched Dr. T. perform the procedure from an angle above. I felt a little pain—I told them and they gave me some more anesthesia. The procedure was soon over. I watched Dr. T. leave to clean up, while Dr. Faith remained by my bed. He leaned over me and quietly said, almost in a whisper, "I have observed your case and you are going to be all right."

All I remember afterward is waking up, looking around, and asking Dr. T. where Dr. Faith was? Dr. T. was a religious man (which I had not known before) and he proceeded to calmly say, "There is no Dr. Faith—you may have seen an Angel!"

Time flew after this. I went through two more major surgeries—a radical hysterectomy and a later procedure to determine whether the cancer had spread. I experienced a roller coaster of emotions worrying that my eventual diagnosis of squamous cell carcinoma had spread to my lymph nodes and beyond.

The two surgeries were performed in the summer of 2003, over two months. Looking back, that was very quick. The second surgery should have been a minimally invasive laparoscopic procedure, but the extensive scar tissue from the previous surgeries caused my bladder to inadvertently be cut—necessitating repair, the insertion of a tube, and the wearing of a temporary bag while my bladder healed. I also lost a lot of blood and had to have a blood transfusion. This second surgery took a lot out of me, causing me to become very weak.

I later found out my non-sister had called the doctor *during* the surgery, demanding to know what was going on. I will never know for sure, but she may have played a part in the surgeon cutting my bladder.

I remember spending hours alone in my hospital bed looking out of the window and reviewing my life. I did not realize it at the time, but a man, another old soul, was working outside on the other side of the window. He was doing hospital renovation and would later become a good friend, one of my Northern Stars. I did not *officially* meet him until I moved back to the Northeast, almost twenty years after my surgery. I share so much past karma and many lifetimes with another Northern Star who I am yet to meet.

Playlist Song #40:
"A Thousand Years," by Christina Perri.

It was not an easy road to recovery. E. stayed with a generous hockey family—one of the few we remained friends with—during my surgeries. We were still officially homeless at that stage, having been evicted from the Williston residence. We had lost everything, so we (E., me, and our two cats) had no place to go.

We were offered a room in the Burlington Hope Lodge—a hospital facility for cancer patients and their family members—but when E. learned we would have to give away our pets, he emphatically stated he would sleep in the car. This would not do.

With the help of my younger brother's church—and, unknown to me, a donation from my youngest brother—I got together enough money to lodge at a local extended residence hotel. I wore the bag for several weeks, due to the cut bladder, and my surgical dressings were changed regularly by a visiting registered nurse. Holly and her son drove up from Boston with several casseroles of food, helping me through my recovery. It was much longer than expected.

Playlist Song #41:
"Somewhere," by Barbra Streisand
(from the musical West Side Story).

Playlist Song #42:
"Another Day in Paradise," by Phil Collins.

Dr. Faith's hopeful words were still fresh in my memory. A few *Earth Angels*, people I did not know before, appeared out of nowhere, offering the sanctuary of kindness and restoring my faith in others. The help they provided enabled me to make it to the next stage of my journey, one filled with hope, faith, and love.

Playlist Song #43:
"True Colors," by Phil Collins.

The residence hotel allowed E. and I to survive the hardest part of my recovery. I became stronger by the day and started scouring the newspaper for inexpensive rentals, but there were none. Homelessness was a serious concern for many in Vermont at that time.

I eventually found a way through a subsidized housing program, Section 8. I qualified and was given a Housing Choice Voucher, finding a condo rental in South Burlington. According to this plan, I paid a percentage of the rent, and the voucher covered the rest. It was not easily accomplished, but I finally negotiated and signed an agreement.

E. was now set to go to South Burlington High School. He had somehow managed—without any money—to continue his training over the summer and continue with his hockey. The South Burlington Rebels welcomed him with open arms.

I was now even more hopeful. I had survived and was positive we were moving toward a better future! My son later captured my emotions in a painting I call "Sunflowers in the Darkness"—a charcoal painting of my favorite flower, the sunflower, illuminated by moonlight on a very dark night. The painting represents my personal feelings of hopefulness following extreme darkness.

The world outside continued as "normal" as I battled through the remaining dark shadows of my present.

Playlist Song #44:
"I Am Not Okay," by Jelly Roll.

My Mother's Passing

E and I were living in the townhouse in South Burlington as my Mother's health began to quickly deteriorate. My middle brother, together with the accountant, sent me money to travel back to Shreveport. It was bittersweet; she was in the hospital but wished to return home for hospice care. I remained silent, although I was still upset with my non-sister for her intervention in my recent surgery. She did not ask me how I was doing.

I knew my Mother was not going to live much longer, so I wanted to be with her as much as possible. We decided to have a slumber party in her hospital room, involving all the sitters, my non-sister, and me. We slept on pallets on the hospital floor. I woke briefly in the night to see my non-sister whisper something in my Mother's ear. I went back to sleep because I could not do anything to stop whatever it was.

My Mother eventually returned home and passed away peacefully, surrounded by us all, in August 2004. It was a few days after my fiftieth birthday. The lawyers got busy with the help of my middle brother and the estate of both my parents was finally settled.

I was still very weak from the cancer surgeries. With the help of a few loyal sitters, I sorted out, as best I could, the items in my parent's house that clearly belonged to my brothers. My non-sister had already left taking all that she wanted. My middle brother, on the other hand, had previously overseen the division of the furniture. It was fairly done, with consideration for all involved.

Not long after, I returned with E. to Vermont. He had spent some valuable time with his other grandparents while in Shreveport, which made him happy.

Becoming a Messenger with an Unclear Message

I was now fifty. My Vermont Turnaround was still in progress. I continued healing from the surgeries. I had survived and had a fresh chance at life. I was ready to go from idling to driving—to moving forward! I knew I had a strong message for others, but I did not know how to relay it.

I was determined to "live my best life," as Joel Osteen would say. I started going to church on Sundays and told my story to anyone who would listen. I knew I was being led into new situations, even though I was not sure of the why or what or where. Would I even bother rewinding the mantle clock? It would continue moving forward in time regardless.

I was strong enough to begin working again. I took on temporary employment through a local service. I had some interesting jobs, including answering phones and working for a few powerful professionals.

E. was heading into his senior year. Several of his hockey friends had previously gone on to prep schools. We had not been able to consider that possibility, as we had been in survival mode. Most of our hockey connections knew his prospects had been put on hold; he was still playing as much as we could afford, which was next to nothing.

Prep schools were created to further a student's education as well as their sports careers. A goaltending coach who we knew from earlier approached him with the possibility of attending a known prep school in Yarmouth, Maine. The admittance requirements were strict, and the cost was very expensive. Financial aid was available, however, so I applied right away. North Yarmouth Academy or NYA had been founded in 1814 and was known for its preparation for Ivy league schools, especially Harvard. Although education was the primary purpose, I was optimistic about the opportunities this school could provide in terms of education as well as hockey.

NYA was home to Travis Roy Arena, built in 1975, which honored a hometown hero—Travis Roy. He was born in Yarmouth, attended NYA, and went on to play hockey for Boston University. At the age of twenty, he was injured during a game, became paralyzed from the neck down, then spent the rest of his life in a wheelchair. He subsequently created the Travis Roy Foundation, which is dedicated to researching and assisting with spinal injury cases. He wrote the book *Eleven Seconds* about his tragic experience. He used his own personal tragedy to create a positive future for others. He devoted the rest of his life to telling his story about the power of love and hope for the future.

I chose to adopt this philosophy for myself: my own message had now become clear.

The Beginnings of Taking Back my Power

After my Mother's death, I not only remained geographically removed from my siblings, but some of our communications also stiffened—especially after I dropped a bomb that spread like wildfire among the rest of the family. At the time, I was sincerely trying to let go of past hurts and move forward.

I was riding in the back of a limousine to the graveside ceremony following my Mother's funeral. Several cars had been rented for our family; I rode with my youngest brother, who I felt had been good to me. I was comfortable talking with him. I did not know he and his wife had donated the money enabling me to live in the residence hotel. The ride started amiably, as we discussed our lives and how our children were doing. All our children were riding in the last limousine.

I saw one of the housekeepers get into one of the following limos. Hurtful memories of the past swiftly came to mind and—not meaning to—I said "I do not know how she can show her face at our Mother's funeral." My youngest brother looked at me questioningly. I relayed the story, explaining who I was referring to and that she was the one who, according to my son's recording of my mother, had been "hitting her." I continued to explain I could not be around her, as I knew she had also had "sexual relations" with my Father.

I still felt I needed to speak up on behalf of my Mother, even after her passing. Indeed, I was going to speak my truth and be my authentic self. I knew this individual had had "sexual relations" with our Father, but I was not sure what else had been going on. I did not know if he was giving her money, as he had done with some of his other mistresses.

I could only speculate that there was likely more to it. I thought this woman was deceptive and had great audacity to attend the funeral, riding in a limo alongside the family members. I think I truly shocked my youngest brother, who clearly showed it, but did not say another word. After that day, I do not believe anything else could have shocked him about our Father.

It later became clear that someone in the family—not my youngest brother—did not agree with or want to believe the truth of my statement. After all, I was still seen as someone with no power in the family, although that was about to change.

An Economic Miracle

My Mother's estate was settled quickly, as everything was already in place. The wills of both my parents were finally probated and we received our individual portions of the inheritance. The checks were distributed by the executors, primarily my middle brother. I was thankful to receive my smaller portion. I was paid the same inheritance as the others, minus the amount the "powers that be" decided I owed prior to my Mother's interdiction. I had previously been asked to sign a legal document to state I would repay the money—that had originally been given to help me—when the estates were settled.

According to the will, the primary portion of the estate included the Ranch, as well as several properties inherited by my Father through Minnie and Dump. Some of it had been purchased by my Father and Mother from my Father's sisters while they were alive.

There were also existing mineral rights—which are inheritable in Louisiana—accompanying the land my Father had inherited. Our ancestors had acquired some wealth from these rights over the years, especially from oil wells. Some of them go back to the time of my paternal great-grandfather, Old Henry, when he purchased land during the Depression. Others were inherited from Minnie's side. The first oil well had been drilled in the early 1900s, when oil refineries had their beginnings.

The massive acreage of the Ranch was divided into sections, to be split among the siblings. It was performed by the same attorney who performed the interdiction—not the estate attorneys—which I found odd. My siblings quickly chose their individual pieces of property, with my youngest brother and I receiving the last two sections, 12 and 13. My choice was also limited by my youngest brother having already built a house on part of Section 13, but we worked everything out amiably.

To this day, I believe our land was not chosen by the other siblings because they did not believe it was of much value. No oil or gas wells had been drilled in Section 13 for a long time. My youngest brother later told me he originally chose it because thirteen was his lucky number in sports, which he always wore when playing basketball. Thirteen has always been my lucky number, too, due to the fact I was born on Friday the 13th.

As life goes, what started out as unfair turned into an ongoing blessing—and the number thirteen ended up being very lucky for both of us! Soon after, an unimaginable blessing emerged from nowhere—I do not know how or why it happened, but it did. My younger brother, the minister, later said that our family was so blessed because of my various hardships. I only know it started less than a year after my Mother's death...

Living in Two Places

Out of nowhere, energy development started booming in the South, especially in Louisiana and Texas. This was primarily due to the area's unique geological features and the availability of pipelines for transportation. The first natural gas pipeline in Louisiana was laid in 1908.

In 2005, our family was contacted by numerous oil and gas companies, who were hoping to obtain leases to drill wells on our lands, especially the Ranch. Leases were accordingly executed for the future production of natural gas wells at all levels. The future drilling was to be from 10,000 to 14,000 feet below the earth's surface, including horizontal drilling. There would eventually be fracking.

I started to see some income from these leases. This income enabled me to get off of Section 8 and purchase the condo I had been renting on Hayes Avenue. I was able to send E. to the prep school in Maine. NYA did not have a dormitory for students. E. was supposed to live with a family in the North Yarmouth area. This fell through at the last moment so I rented a small apartment. It was close to the school. I later found out it was across the street from where Travis Roy had grown up!

I now had two residences—one in Vermont and one in Maine. E. was still a minor and not able to live on his own, so I lived with him until he graduated from NYA in the spring of 2006. It was quite a juggle, but my health had improved and I was up for it.

Once school began, everything moved quickly. E. made new friends, including some international students from Sweden and the Czech Republic who were hockey players. I met their very nice parents later in the year. That year was another memorable experience, with much ongoing politics around the goalie position.

E. continued to play hockey and, after prep school, competed in a US Junior League in Cleveland, Ohio. He eventually moved up to Division I college hockey (never to be confused with hockey college) in Denver, Colorado.

I was now financially able to support E. with his hockey. He attended specialized training sessions in the summer—in Toronto, Canada, with Vladislav Tretiak, a famous goaltender, and in Massachusetts with Joe Bertagna, a legendary goaltender and coach.

E. learned much about life from both of these great men, as well as from Ed Walsh, another phenomenal goaltender coach. He had also offered his services to Dartmouth, UMass, and Northeastern University. My son spent many weekends in Salem, New Hampshire, practicing with Walsh or Walshie, as everyone called him. Ed and Joanne, his wife, are caring individuals who helped me tremendously in the period following my cancer surgeries. All of these honored goaltenders were beneficial contributors to E.'s training and development.

I continued to learn from other coaches as well, sometimes having to hold my emotions—and tongue—in check. This was especially the case with the overly egotistical coaches, who hated spending even a minute conversing with the MOM of a hockey player or, in my case, a "Goalie Mom"!

This strained communication continued through college. Communications with the National Collegiate Athletic Association (NCAA), the Dean, his secretary, a female Athletic Director, and a coach who eventually got fired were all included in my experience as the mom of a hockey player in high-level competitive college hockey.

I think some of these individuals actually learned something. Some things never change... I wish the only difference between a pit bull and a hockey mom was lipstick, because my bite is much worse! The good news is that all of my meaningful endeavors did help other goaltenders in some way.

In 2008, my increased income from oil and gas enabled me to buy an investment property near the University of Denver (DU) campus, which I rented out to several American players on the hockey team and my son, during his time there. I made sure their rent was affordable. They had not gotten the full athletic scholarships some of the Canadian players had received. I consider that *my* financial donation to the Pioneers and DU. I eventually sold the property in 2016.

I will only say that as E. advanced in his hockey career, things were just as eventful and even more colorful. But that is his story to tell one day, if he wishes to do so.

My son was a talented goaltender, but the higher the level, the greater the politics. Some of his teammates made it to the NHL and he was happy for them. As for the rest, they "rode the bus" in Europe until they finally gave up on their dream.

With a few continuing educational accommodations, E. successfully graduated from DU with a BS, before continuing to Vancouver Film School. He is now in his thirties and lives in Atlanta, Georgia, where he is building a professional life as a very creative cinematographer. He has recently finished shooting a documentary with a film crew in Normandy, France, commemorating the 80th Anniversary of D-Day and the Battle of Normandy.

The Smell of Lifebuoy Soap

Over the next few years, my life continued without incident. I had decided that Vermont was my home and, for once, my monthly income—or "mailbox money," as I call it—meant I did not have to worry about my next meal. I relaxed for the first time, not having to make any decisions about my life.

As an empty nester, I enjoyed getting to know my neighbors, a divorced single mother about my age on one side and a genuine younger couple on the other, all of whom became trusted friends. My two cats, Sunshine (Florida) and Maple (Vermont), were great company. I know my Father would have insisted on me having a pet for a best friend.

I suddenly started to smell the scent of Lifebuoy Soap, which my Father had always used. The smell became more and more noticeable, especially at night, when I was trying to sleep. My Father had been dead since 2001. Weird, right? Eventually it waned...

During this time, my neighbor, who worked in ticket sales at the Flynn Theater, got me tickets to a special event—a renowned psychic whose name escapes me now. I had never been there before and was excited by the prospect. This beautiful theater opened its doors in November 1930, having an art deco style, as was common in the era.[45]

The big event finally arrived. In excited anticipation, I got there early and took my seat in one of the front rows. The medium started the show and proceeded to walk among the audience, randomly picking up on "spirits." About midway through, she called out "Does anyone know John and Mary?" Common names—everyone knows one or two, right? I did not think anything of it, except my Father's name was John...

Many people raised their hands. The medium went from person to person, patiently discounting their connection. As she did so, she continued to relate that John was getting irritated and was screaming at her. I perked up and quickly thought "that sounds like my Father!" I then finally realized that "Mary" was also very close to my Mother's name, "Marie."

Looking around, I feared my Father would direct her to me. I decided I was not going to raise my hand, no matter what. The medium really did not like my Father's continued yelling. She became very annoyed. Now I was ashamed of him. She then started to describe what he looked like, pleading "Will the rightful son or daughter please step forward?"

She described his appearance and mentioned he was hooked up to a breathing machine. I would have raised my hand if she had described him as having white hair and blue eyes. My intuition told me it could be him... but I continued to sit in silence, listening and watching. The medium never did find John and Mary's family member that day...

I enjoyed the rest of the show, which was very entertaining. At the end, as I got up to leave, I realized the young boy and his father who had been sitting next to me were related to the medium. She approached them and hugged them. Great, I had been sitting next to her family the whole show! That was creepy and I felt bad about not raising my hand.

That incident troubled me for months—and I still question it. I planned to visit her and tell her it was me she was looking for. I wanted to find out what she had to say in private, not in front of a large group. Had my Father and Mother been trying to communicate something important to me? I never did meet with the medium to find out.

Some years later, I was having a conversation with my younger brother about my Father's death. I asked him to describe what the end of my Father's life was like, since I was not able to see him before he died. What he told me was very eerie.

He told me our Father died on a ventilator. The respiratory doctor and the primary doctor were at odds over how to proceed—whether to leave him on or take him off. The respiratory doctor believed my Father had already gone, but the primary doctor thought there was a possibility of survival.

My Father had not set up a medical directive allowing him to naturally pass. It was then I realized my Father had died on a ventilator or breathing machine. The medium was definitely in contact with my Father and Mother and they did have a message for me! I moved on from this revelation, questioning whether I would ever find out what they wanted to tell me. Later, though, I would learn this as well...

Feeling Different, Feeling Incomplete

As I mentioned at the beginning, I have always known I was different. These feelings increased especially after my cancer in 2003. Those surgeries as well as the radiation treatments I endured ultimately changed my physical anatomy, leaving me with outward as well as inward scars.

My vivid imagination had pictured the surgical destruction wreaking havoc on my female organs. I felt less desirable—as though I was not a whole woman anymore. I did not want to expose my outward scars to any man, plus I was very sensitive about putting anything inside my body.

I later read I was experiencing sexual dysfunction. The combination of surgeries and radiation affected the chemicals in my system, creating hormonal imbalances. These imbalances disturbed my physical, mental, and emotional wellbeing. I was not warned about this by any doctor.

The above explains my life after 2003, but not before. I realized I had become the person I was as a result of several life experiences. I term this my "cave period," which started in Florida, in 1995, and ended in 2021—a little over twenty-five years, from my early forties until my late sixties. Being in Vermont brought the intensity of this time to light and I learned a lot about myself.

In Florida, in 1995, I had been so engrossed in raising a child and working to get ahead that I almost forgot I was a desirable woman with my own needs. I had not bothered to interact with, go on a date with, or have sexual relations with anyone. I was attracted to men, but did not have the time or the energy to act on it.

That pattern only continued following the ravages of my surgeries. I knew I was not bisexual, asexual, gray sexual, fray sexual, demisexual, or any of the other sexuals. Had I gone to a therapist at the time, they would have had a field day diagnosing me!

In any case, I had already weathered marriage and divorce, raised a child into adulthood, and overcome sickness and homelessness. I was comfortable in my economic situation. I seemed to have it all, at least outwardly. I had survived and was healthy. I put on a "good face" to reinforce those beliefs, but inside I felt incomplete, that my life was a mess. No one could see this but me. I wanted and needed to get my act together! Did I need a relationship with a man to fulfill me?

My cave period was not entirely solitary, however. I frequently traveled to Vancouver to see E., who lived in a high-rise apartment during film school; and to Louisiana to visit family members and friends. I had special times with both traveling all over the United States. I eventually made it to Europe, too. I had a full life—or so I thought—with many friends, despite losing a few to death.

I ended up spending more than fifteen years in Vermont. I made memories I will forever cherish and some very good friends. Two of those friends are the owners of Pulcinella's, an Italian restaurant on Shelburne Road. They have created something very special, with the best Italian food I have ever tasted. The meatball recipe is a family one and a personal favorite, along with the marinara sauce.

I cherish these memories and those I made with two other authentic people: my young friend Kelly and her husband, Josh. I met Kelly when I rented a storage unit to house my many possessions. I still have that storage unit today. I guess part of me does not want to ever leave Vermont.

Even so, my "Vermont Turnaround" had come to completion...

Trying the South on for Size

I sold the houses in Vermont and Colorado in 2016. I experienced another difficult time in relation to a lawsuit over mineral rights that went back to the '50s. This lawsuit had started in 2012 and continued until 2016. It was a big hardship for all of my siblings, but we weathered it. I was almost financially devastated by it, though.

I had to make a choice about where I was going to live. I wanted to stay in the South, but living in Louisiana was not for me, so I looked at areas around the beaches of the Gulf of Mexico—Gulfport and Bay St. Louis in Mississippi and Fairhope in Alabama. These were all beautiful places I would be happy to call home. I was eventually drawn back to the Atlantic Ocean and ended up settling on the beloved Southern state of South Carolina. I started my journey in Beaufort, a small town between Charleston and Hilton Head.

Still in my cave period, I wanted to stay a loner, but I realized I needed to head out into the world. I rented a bright turquoise beach house on Ebb Tide Court in Harbor Island. I remained there for about a year while looking for a potential place to buy. I loved the island's privacy but quickly decided I was more of a "townie," as many of the locals would term it. I was also looking for a smaller house—the few available ones were way overpriced.

I then moved to Seabrook Island, southwest of Charleston, where I rented a house on a golf course. I wanted to be sociable once again. I frequently drove to Folly Beach, to revel in its unconventional atmosphere. I visited a local restaurant, Loggerhead's, in the hope of spotting Bill Murray, the actor, who occasionally showed up there. I also spent time at Low Life, a restaurant with very good food.

Good food was important again and I was grateful to be back in my element in grits country. Indeed, the South Carolina shrimp and grits were the best! I went out to bars and restaurants alone, talking to many people and making many new friends. These individuals called themselves South Carolinians, whether they were originally from there or not. My Louisiana drawl did not compare to the buttery language spoken by many of these people.

The South Carolina terrain was called the "lowlands" for a reason. For one thing, it was very swampy, especially around Charleston. The land and surrounding water were conducive to growing rice and shrimping—but it also housed all sorts of animals, birds, bugs, and alligators. You would think I would have been familiar with these creatures, having grown up in Louisiana. I was not. I had been raised in Northern Louisiana; the alligators were predominantly seen in the swamps of Southern Louisiana.

Eventually, the heat and bugs got the best of me, so I decided to return to the Northeast, where the winters were cold and the bugs were few. This time, though, I was in my sixties. In 2019, I headed to New Hampshire, a no-tax state.

I spent the COVID years in New Hampshire, isolated. That period caused many to think about who and what was important. E. had little work due to the difficulties relating to the required distances between individuals on film sets. He moved in with me. This gave me comfort. I did not have to live through this period alone. We were unable to physically connect with others, not even siblings, and the future was very uncertain.

I learned much about myself during that time. I went inward to examine what was *really* important. I hoped I could eventually achieve self-love.

The forced alienation came to an end in 2021. E. moved back to Atlanta, Georgia. I remained in New Hampshire. We were hungry to get on with our lives. My sexuality had been awakened once again, miracle of miracles—I later wondered if the period after COVID or the COVID vaccines in particular had spurred its resurgence. In any case, I had joyfully exited my cave period and started moving into a whole new world.

Playlist Song #45:
"You Make Loving Fun," by Fleetwood Mac.

Coming Full Circle

often wonder whether life will ever come full circle or whether I will only gaze upon parts of an arc that never fully develops. A beautiful rainbow does exist. Its vibrant colors encourage me to dream of experiences chasing its beauty, even though I know I will never find its end. There can only be an illusion of an end.

My Southern story is by no means over, though! I have turned my many moments of sorrow into dancing. Joel Osteen, the evangelical minister, once said "God saw sacrifice and turned lack into abundance."

The financial miracles and abundance of blessings that have come from my suffering give me hope. This is how I feel as I write this chapter. I am happy with my life in New England. The natives still comment on my Southern voice, which they remember, and I certainly stand out wherever I go. At the time of writing this book, they have yet to hear my life story, though.

There are still many stories within me, some of which may be written as fiction. They continue to accompany my everyday life. I will tell a few more here, because they are important for my ongoing growth and learning. I like to think the following stories are about connecting with others on a personal level while cultivating my own culture.

Here's Johnny!

In 2021 and 2022, people were coming out of COVID-19 hiding and starting to travel more. I visited friends and relatives in the South. My travel took me through Atlanta airport. I stopped for lunch at an airport restaurant with Southern seafood on the menu. I sat quietly at the bar with a beer, waiting for my flight to be called.

I noticed a pleasant bartender smiling and talking to his fellow workers. For some reason, I felt I needed to talk to this man; so I waited a few minutes while he finished conversing with a few other customers. I started out by mentioning my age, as I could not tell his, revealing I grew up in the '50s and '60s. That got a huge smile! We were both the same age, and we struck up what turned out to be a very meaningful conversation—a "meant to be" conversation.

This man—whose name happened to be the same as my oldest brother's nickname—cast light on his unique life experience in those few short moments. I listened to his story; I was immensely entertained by learning we had so much in common.

In particular, we discussed separate entrances and forced busing. He talked about his personal experience with the "balcony," as I call it. I mentioned my experience with separate entrances as a young child. He revealed that sitting in the balcony was not in fact sad, but fun. He enjoyed watching movies with his friends and family. He told me that he had a few white friends who asked to sit with him there. They said it looked "so much more fun" than sitting below.

Johnny also told me he was a high school athlete—a football player. He further revealed that the forced busing issue had greatly affected his athletic path. He and his fellow football players had been prevented from playing at a school with a coach he admired due to racial segregation. He emphasized he felt he *did* have a "choice," even though many today would have falsely viewed that as no choice.

We revealed to each other our thoughts about watching our opposite lives through young eyes. I listened in awe as he told me stories that clearly mirrored mine. He put a positive spin on things. I *did not* expect this reaction to issues that are viewed so negatively today.

I thought about my childhood dreams—how I had never considered my own path not being *my own* choice but one shaped by others. Of course, as I got older, I realized that gender did indeed play a big part in my life's decisions. What I thought I wanted—such as the opportunity to run the family business—had not been available to me.

I suddenly thought about my grandmother, who, in the South, was an exception to the rule. I also thought about Julia and Ruby, about

Rev and the Porters. I left the restaurant that day after saying a pleasant goodbye to a kindred soul I would certainly call my friend, any day.

Five Kindred Souls

I recently came across four special kindred souls: Delores, Willie, "Q" Fanning—which is short for "Quo Vadis"—and Bobbie are just a few of the many Southern people who have given me hope. I have their numbers in my cell phone. These individuals, whether they were born to it or whether they learned it, represent the authentic goodness of the South.

Delores ran the breakfast bar at a Marriott hotel in Bossier City, Louisiana, near the Louisiana Downs racetrack. Willie and Q greeted me at breakfast at a Marriott in Decatur, Georgia. And Bobbie is a genuine *soul sister*, who I met recently at Ralph and Kacoo's in Bossier City. I met all of them while traveling in the South after the pandemic. Delores, Willie, and Q went to work at 5 a.m. each morning. I do not think Delores had a day a week off work; I am not sure about Willie and Q.

I was staying in Bossier in the spring 2021, in the aftermath of COVID. I was doing some writing. I woke up early each day, at 4 a.m., and there was Delores, with a ready smile and a genuine heart. She was a friendly face in a crazy world.

She served breakfast to the many construction workers, who traveled during the week to earn money to feed their families.

There has been a great need for such traveling workers recently, much more than in the past. Delores knew most of their names; her smile and kind words brightened their breakfasts as they started their days. For some of these workers, this hotel was their way of life every day of the year.

Delores and I discussed life. I learned about her struggles caring for her aging mother, who lived with her. This seems to be a recurrent theme in black Southern families—several generations living together. I think it is admirable. We laughed about life, bright and early each morning.

I had similar relationships with Willie and Q, although they worked in Decatur. I took a picture of Willie, a native of Buffalo, New York, in his United States Army Buffalo Soldiers jacket. He told me about his army days with the Buffalo Rough Riders, who were established in 1866. I later learned he has struggled with and overcome his own demons over the years. Q had a heartbreaking yet positive story of survival after debilitating illness. I hugged and waved goodbye to them, hoping I would see them again, which I did.

I met Bobbie while dining at a restaurant in Bossier City. She sat down next to me at the bar, so I struck up a conversation with her. A single mom, she was not without her personal struggles—but, like the others, it was obvious to me she has maintained a positive outlook on life. Boy, is she wise for her fifty-something years!

We talked about our current situations—had you seen us, you would have thought we had always been friends. I left with much "food for thought" and a word of advice from a powerful independent woman I will never forget. She told me these wise words that go something like this, "YOU pick who you let sit under the shade tree with you." I thought about my past relationships and the times that I felt I had no power to choose. I promised her I would always be good to myself.

A more recent encounter with a fifth kindred soul is also worth noting here. This story is more conceptual in nature; its central theme is oddly Southern, even though it did not occur in the South. It is about a man—whose name I still do not know—praying out loud.

I was in the gym, alone, at another Marriott hotel in Burlington, Vermont, trying to "exercise off my emotions." It had been a trying week, both mentally and emotionally. A young man was talking on his cell phone next to me. I first thought he was talking to his girlfriend or wife, then soon realized the conversation was in fact with his minister. I am old-school and do not wear earbuds; neither did he. I overheard his conversation, which I found very intriguing. He continued to tell this minister how much a recent sermon had affected him.

It seemed he had done something requiring forgiveness. He then began to say a prayer into the phone—probably the most beautiful prayer to God I have ever heard. It was a long enough prayer for me to finish my round of cycling. I felt a sense of renewed hope with each word he uttered; I wanted to speak to him as I walked out, but thought better of it, because it was such an intense personal moment.

As life (and God) would have it, I saw him the next evening at the restaurant, where he was talking to the manager. I soon learned he had been the breakfast chef on the morning of the encounter (an excellent one, by the way). I told him his prayer had touched me at a time when I was struggling to understand my direction. I told him it was the "most beautiful prayer" I had ever heard and thanked him for blessing my life in a good way. To say the least, he was amazed by what I had said to him.

As he walked out, he looked back—a sign he had understood. Maybe in some small way I had blessed his life, too. If life has taught me anything, it is that you can learn from anyone of any race or age at any time, so do not be afraid to speak to the people around you, even if they appear different to you. I believe you can find at least one thing in common with any person. It does not take *six degrees* to connect with another and you may learn a lot about yourself by doing so. I *will* remember Johnny, Delores, Willie, Q, Bobbie, and... the unknown prayer chef.

Unexpected Grief

The month of February always seems to bring happiness and pain. In February 2023, I felt that emotional pain as my middle brother battled for his life in a hospital bed in Louisiana. He had been in the hospital for weeks, the updates seesawing between good and bad. My siblings and I were once again reunited, bound together by our feelings of love for our brother.

Emotional reactions to family crises are too real to ignore. As I have stated from the beginning, I choose to confront the past in order to move into the future. Moving into the future does not mean ignoring or forgetting my past, though. I wish to remember my past experiences, both joyful and painful, without going through that same anguish again. I WANT to let go of those memories of past secrets and the hurt caused by them.

What I have learned from my past has helped me prepare for the blessings of abundance and prosperity I now receive. I remain on my life's path, attempting to work through the strong feelings within. During this time of grief, my siblings and I bonded with laughter over stories about our childhood—many of which you now know.

We all joked that when my middle brother woke up, we would finally ask him for the truth—"Were you the one who put sand in the gas tank?" I believed it was my middle brother, while my younger brother (the Professor) claimed he did it. I suspect it was a combination of the two. My younger brother most probably gave my middle brother the idea.

My younger brother still wants to say (jokingly) he was given away to the Indians, so he can justify his rightful ownership of the Indian blanket. I then watched this same younger brother put his cell phone to his arm to check his sugar levels—a reminder we are all older and need to take care of our health.

Our laughter was an effort to cover up the turmoil we were all feeling deep inside. For me, the truth was the pain of the past *still* existed just below the laughter. The question we all had—"If I had only known, could I have been there for him?"—resonated around the room. We could not have, though, as my middle brother had not let us in; he was the chosen one, the bearer of family secrets. He had many of his own secrets hidden deep inside.

I could have chosen to say my childhood was easy and written only about family stories that raised laughter—but that would have made me a liar. We all have "traveled a broken road." We all need to know we are loved, no matter our mistakes. We all need to remember we are blessed—something that became clear to me given the uncertainty about my middle brother's future.

The events of those days brought back all my childhood experiences and accompanying emotions in vivid color. Seeing my middle brother—with an appearance similar to mine as well as that of my Father—hooked up to a ventilator for weeks on end drew me back to the past.

It is not fair, I thought. He is a good person, with a wife and two grown children who need him. I also needed my brother to heal and to live, for my own sanity. Each day, I continued to search deep within my being and cry out to Jesus to will his healing, so he could recover and waken from his sleep after the heart surgery. I know now that was God's plan. I prayed for the healing of our family's broken road—and for my own, for that matter.

Playlist Song #46:
"Bless the Broken Road," by Rascal Flatts.

Please Tell Her I Am Sorry

In 2023, I got up the nerve to visit another medium, for a private session. I sat down at a table in a small room and very quickly noticed Nova was young and adorably cute. I immediately sensed her to be a kind soul, beautiful inside and out. I had barely sat down when my son called me on my cell phone—I had told him not to call me at this time, although I did not say why. As usual, he did not listen.

I quickly pushed the "record" button on my cell phone. The second timer started spinning rapidly and wildly. I asked Nova whether this was normal. She began by saying an elderly man was coming through, speaking in the same voice as mine. I assumed she meant Southern. She described him as having white hair and I immediately knew it was my Father. She depicted him as looking much like me, with the same facial structure and the same eyes. She told me he was sad. He repeatedly said "he was sorry."

I suddenly pictured him at a younger age, long ago, when he would be quiet, perhaps even depressed. I only saw him cry once—at my wedding. She went on to describe him, pointing to her eyes and letting her fingers flow down her cheeks, to signal tears.

She told me there were many women. Yes, I knew there were many women. Had he learned his lesson? He continued to talk through Nova, to say he was "sorry." I felt it was genuine and not an act, like his apologies to my Mother during my childhood. He now seemed to be remorseful about his role in his children's development. He said he should have gotten professional help.

Next, Nova told me she saw a house—white, two stories, with flowers in the yard. I believe this was his childhood home. My Father relayed "I did not have a mother." I thought about the coldness of Minnie; he might have felt unloved and abandoned as a child as well.

Strangely, all of what he was saying through Nova made so much sense now. He asked whether I would forgive him. It seemed my Father had been trying to speak to me for twenty-two years to ask me this question. I decided I would forgive him. I would write him a letter, which I did shortly after our session.

After that, my middle brother, who had recently passed, came through. Most of it was harmless friendly banter, talking about the cat. But then he got serious, talking about his son and wishing he had been more attentive to his sensitivity. My Father and middle brother were talking simultaneously. Nova told me they were teasing each other.

I could easily imagine this, as they were so alike in that way. She then switched screens and started to describe a man my Father said he had picked for me, who would be good for me. Nova told me he repeatedly stated "You definitely have a type!" Well, this is very true! (MY TYPE is a version of you, Dad!) My Father, through Nova, described this man. I knew for sure when "big" hands were mentioned. I remembered the many times I had commented on those hands during my conversations with this man. This was my Father's way of confirming who he was talking about. It shocked me almost out of my chair! Great, now my Father and this man were both ghosting me!

I told Nova I had recently said goodbye to this man, since I thought we were over. But I proceeded to have second thoughts. Amazingly, this man texted me out of the blue early the following morning.

There were many other descriptions of many other people, some of which were very playful. And then Nova described a woman with a raised wine glass, asking me to "sit with her out on the veranda." At first, I thought it was my Mother. Now, though, I think it was my "Other Mother," Maredia, to whom I dedicate this book. Indeed, it would be especially fitting for Maredia Bowdon to offer me cheers on finally completing my book! I had read several pages to her when she had lost most of her eyesight at the end of her life. This made much sense to me.

Upon her passing, Maredia probably had a little "talk" with my Father about my book—about his treatment of my Mother and his other ugly behavior. I could "see" her enlightening him as to how his actions had strongly affected my life. Maredia knew a lot about him from our many talks.

My Father told Nova he wanted me to tell the family story—that it was time for the truth. I jokingly told Nova to tell him I wanted the Indian blanket he had traded me for as a young child, which my non-sister had somehow gotten her hands on. I am still laughing away the sadness, right?

As with life, the one-hour reading was filled with laughter as well as sadness. I remember thinking "Wow, my life has come full circle. Life is definitely stranger than fiction!" The reading concluded with a series of images of people; some of these gave me much food for thought, as I tried to figure out who they were and whether they were dead or alive. One image was of a man on a vintage motorcycle waving at me as he whizzed by. Was that my John Denver?

Oddly, I did not want the reading to end. I have since had other readings with Nova, who continues to amaze me with her second sight. I have learned more about my Mother and gained more insight into why she made the choices she did.

I left the reading with a renewed feeling of hope for a better tomorrow. Until my time comes, I will choose—like Maredia Pace Bowdon, my Other Southern Mother—to experience my own "normal" and continue tap dancing on my own. I head forth on my individual soul journey in a never-ending quest for love and happiness!

Playlist Song #47:
"You Learn," by Alanis Morissette.

Playlist Song #48:
"Love and Happiness," by Al Green.[46]

EPILOGUE

Life can only be understood backwards,
but it must be lived forwards.
Soren Kierkegaard

I have relived several eras from my past. I choose to believe I have learned a little more each time. I continue to work on letting go, not wishing to experience any more toxicity in my current reality. The old ways of being are over. People are not made bitter by life itself, but by their interpretation of it.

I have encountered many "whitewashed tombs." Embracing one's dark shadow is not easy, the fears being more than real. I am finally experiencing the awakening of my purpose in life, more than twenty-four (twenty-one plus three) years after my three "Cs"—my cancer and my cave period plus COVID.

I am continually trying to be a better person—to serve the collective. Deep compassion and empathy for the pain of others is a rare dimension that has emerged from my own life's experiences.

I have a rare gift for tolerance and the capacity to see more than one "truth." I have merged my two warring parents—the yin and the yang—within me, which I credit to my continuing Libran search for balance.

The renewed hope of my individual transformation may not resonate with everyone, but I hope it does with you. I continue searching for my "Heart of Gold," as Neil Young sang in 1972—the year of my high school graduation. I have learned that the greatest of these is God's love. I am thankful to have found Dr. Faith along the way.

Alone with my own faith and these higher beings, I am finishing this story—my "brain dump"—in a hotel room at the Marriott Delta in South Burlington, Vermont. I come here every few months to regroup spiritually, nourish my creativity, and write my stories. It is where my life turned around.

How fitting it is that I am finishing my writing on a beautiful but cold spring day in March 2023, almost twenty years after my cancer—and two years after this process began. I am still a romantic and naïve enough to believe in a good love story ending well, although I have yet to completely experience mine. As Bob Dylan sang in 1963, "Don't Think Twice, It's All Right."

Playlist Song #49:
"Don't Think Twice, It's All Right," by Bob Dylan.

Can romance and reality coexist? Yes, this is my life as it is. As I said at the beginning, I have no regrets. I say goodbye only "for now," because I believe all souls are forever connected.

My life has involved a complex learning curve of letting go—although my learning curve with men has been more complicated than most. We learn things and we forget, sometimes too easily, especially in today's world of instant gratification. Certain men have taught me a lot about myself, beginning with my Father; and a few men continue to teach me now. We all have much learning to do. Jeff would say it is all God's plan.

I believe all our futures are determined by a marvelous plan for each person, which culminates in the hope of finding love and one's own level of happiness. Yes, I will surely continue on my spiritual path, constantly learning and turning my words into song, because music transforms and heals—even though there were sad moments when there was no music.

Today, though, I have eventually found the music again and started dancing to it. The beautiful educator Maredia Pace Bowdon taught me much about life. Life is a continual learning process. As I said at the beginning, we learn from both the joy and the sadness, the rights and the wrongs, the good and the bad.

I have lived my life fully *and* "way beyond the GRITS"—after all, life is about what is normal to you and how *you* deal with it. Good luck with that!

ACKNOWLEDGMENTS

To all of my bee's knees...

I dedicate this book to Maredia Pace Bowdon, my Other Mother—the truest of Southern women. She believed in me. She constantly reminded me "who I am" and that I am loved. She made me a better person, proudly supporting my writing. I know you entered heaven with your arms spread wide, proclaiming "I'm here!" To Maredia: I will always "keep my sunny side up"! I *promise* never to reveal the real story behind that saying.

I also dedicate this book to my son, E., the only male I have truly been able to commit time to. I have no regrets. Son, I hope my story does not shock you too much.

I wish to acknowledge my Louisiana heritage and all the people who grew up "with a drink in my (their) hand," as Eric Church sings—in particular, those in my hometown of Shreveport, Louisiana. I will especially remember the laughter and sadness of my high school and college years. More recently, I have fond memories from my high school's fiftieth reunion.

To Jeff: I am glad my Father did not shoot you. You are the only man who continues to amaze me after fifty years. I appreciate your love for your family. I hope you feel "my quiet love" for you. Please beware those "thirsty women"!

To Leesa: my Mother will always blame YOU for everything. It is okay to eat the chalazae (pronounced: cuh-LAY-zuh) part of the egg. It is not the baby chick.

To Jimmy Mac: we had such great fun! Our dating experiences were filled with lifelong lessons as well as much laughter. Hope to see you at the next reunion!

To all of my other friends from elementary, junior, high school, and college: do not be afraid to embrace your shadow! It has many facets—and some may even help you grow. I say to you: "Without the shadow we cannot pursue the light."

Next, I acknowledge the many friends, young and old, who I have met at various stages of my life's journey—thanks to my gypsy soul and the God above who made it happen. You span many states: Texas, Florida, Vermont, Maine, Colorado, South Carolina, and, finally, New Hampshire. "All these places had their moments / with lovers and friends I still can recall," as the Beatles sang in their song "In My Life." To you, I say: be authentic and not afraid to step into your truth. Learn to love genuinely.

To Nina Sartorelli, aka Nova: thank you for "conjuring up" Karen Williams. Thank you for listening to my endless stories for hours on end. You have given me so much good advice. You ARE beautiful and gifted in every way.

And, finally, I wish to mention my "Northern Stars"—two handsome and intelligent New England men. We share so much past karma. Your intelligence challenges my thinking and you both make me question my integrity. I met both of you to learn the lessons you are here to teach me.

To my first Northern Star, "a sensitive man." You represent the extroverted side of my Father. To you, I say: "I know; I understand; I do care. I want you in my life. *We both have a broken road.*" You, alone, spurred my desire to write this book. Meeting you awakened my creativity, as words flowed effortlessly onto the page. Various emotions I have not acknowledged for more than fifty years (and have yet to fully deal with) emerged. You are shameless yet unforgettable. Your big hands help me to feel safe. I want you to live, to be alive, to "cultivate your own culture"—but also to be aware of, as you would say, the "lion's head." I hope you are not still ghosting me when I finish this book.

To my second Northern Star: it took a journey of a "thousand years" to find you. You represent the introverted side of my Father. To answer your question: Yes, I will continue to do my "redneck shit" for the rest of my life!

ENDNOTES

All web addresses were last accessed in October 2024.

1 *106 degrees Fahrenheit.*
   According to *Weather Underground*: see https://www.
   wunderground.com/history/daily/us/la/Shreveport/KSHV/
   date/1954-8-13.

2 *Biblical story of David and Goliath.*
   For related discussion, see Malcolm Gladwell's *David and
   Goliath: Underdogs, Misfits, and the Art of Battling Giants*
   (2013).

3 *Legislative act of concubinage.*
   Act No. 87, Section 1. House Bill No. 4. Acts Passed by *The
   General Assembly of the State of Louisiana at the Regular
   Session*, May 1908, Approved July 1, 1908. Article published on
   the front page of *The Caucasian* newspaper in Shreveport,
   Louisiana, May 19, 1910.

4 *Life insurance.*
   For further details, see Diana Murphy's article "A Brief History
   of Life Insurance" from November 2018 (available at https://
   www.ethoslife.com/life-insurance/history-of-life-insurance/)

and Jeremy Hallet's article "A Primer on the History of Life Assurance" from July 2015 (available at https://www.quotacy.com/history-of-life-insurance/).

5 *Articles about husbands cheating.*
See, for example, those by Ann Landers collected into her early book *Since You Asked Me* (1961).

6 *Mayhaw jelly.*
For more information about mayhaw berries, see the Louisiana Mayhaw Association's website: https://mayhaw.org. According to the LSU AgCenter article "The Mayhaw: Out of the Swamp and Into the Orchard" (available at https://www.lsuagcenter.com/~/media/system/2/f/9/d/2f9d18664800f6184f43b7df0ae57b4a/pub2484mayhaw2.pdf), the mayhaw is a red to deep red berry approximately three-quarters of an inch in diameter. It is primarily used for making jelly, but is also present in syrup, butter, various dishes, and wine. The berries can also be frozen for later use.

7 *Shreve Town on Texas Avenue.*
For further details, see the article "Shreveport: A Brief History," with details provided by Eric J. Brock (available at https://www.shreveportla.gov/618/History-of-Shreveport).

8 *Vince Lombardi.*
For further details, see the Wikipedia article (https://en.wikipedia.org/wiki/Vince_Lombardi) as well as Cliff Cristl's article "The 1960s Packers: A Product of Vince Lombardi's Prejudice-free Culture" from February 2021 (available at https://www.packers.com/news/the-1960s-packers-a-product-of-vince-lombardi-s-prejudice-free-culture).

9   *Average cost of a house.*
    See Jane Kenney's article "Here's How Much a House Cost the Year You Were Born" from January 2019 (available at https://doyouremember.com/91242/how-much-house-cost-year).

10 *Herby K's "Shrimp Buster."*
    As mentioned on the website: https://herbyks.net/.

11 *Original Tabasco sauce.*
    For further details, see the history of the brand available on its website: https://www.tabasco.com/tabasco-history.

12 *The wife of my father's friend.*
    See the article "Mobile Press-Register 200th Anniversary: Mobile Had Its Share of Sensational Murders through the Decades" from June 2013: https://www.al.com/live/2013/06/mobile_press-register_200th_an_25.html. See also the episode of "Conversations with Jeff Weeks" with guest Phyllis Hain that was also broadcast in 2013: https://www.pbs.org/video/conversations-jeff-weeks-conversations-jeff-weeks-phyllis-hain/.

13 *Starseed.*
    For further details, see the Aura Health Team's article "What Is a Starseed?" from February 2024 (available at https://www.aurahealth.io/blog/what-is-a-starseed-exploring-the-meaning-of-this-cosmic-term) as well as "An Introduction to Starseeds" (available at https://www.centreofexcellence.com/what-is-a-starseed).

14 *Invisible ink.*
Quotation and information taken from the article "Man Knowledge: The History of Invisible Ink," by Brett and Kate McKay, originally published in September 2011 and last updated in June 2021: https://www.artofmanliness.com/character/knowledge-of-men/man-knowledge-the-history-of-invisible-ink/.

15 *Delta Kappa Epsilon or the DEKES.*
A prominent fraternity that was founded on June 22, 1844, at Yale University. For further information, see the website: https://dke.org/about/organization-history/.

16 *Streaking trend.*
For further details, see Frederic D. O'Brien's article "That Streaking Fad," in American Heritage, from April 1999: https://www.americanheritage.com/streaking-fad.

17 *Streaking as reaction.*
See the article "Why Was the Country So Obsessed with Streaking in the 1970s?" from October 2016: https://www.metv.com/lists/why-was-the-country-so-obsessed-with-streaking-in-the-1970s.

18 *Louisiana drinking age.*
For further information, see Tara I. Chang's article "Lower Drinking Age Has Minors Speaking Cajun," in *The Harvard Crimson*, from March 1996: https://www.thecrimson.com/article/1996/3/16/lower-drinking-age-has-minors-speaking/.

19 *Boz Scaggs.*

A music performer who explores "the rock, blues, and soul genres" in a pop-oriented way and "was a renowned guitarist in the Steve Miller Band, as well as having a successful solo career," according to https://www.songkick.com/artists/86623-boz-scaggs. His album, *Silk Degrees* (1976), which featured performances from several members of Toto, reached number two on the Billboard 200 chart, was certified five times platinum, and contained three top 40 singles: "It's Over," "Lowdown," and "Lido Shuffle." The single "Lowdown" won a Grammy Award for Best R&B song in 1977.

20 *"Cotton-Eyed Joe."*

For further information, see Elizabeth Manson's article "The History of Cotton Eyed Joe Dance" from September 2017: https://ourpastimes.com/the-history-of-cotton-eyed-joe-dance-12214420.html.

21 *Hippy Hollow.*

Travis County Commissioners passed an ordinance restricting admittance and "park usage" to those over eighteen years of age. This was challenged by naturist families, whose German and Czech cultures had encouraged nude sunbathing in the nineteenth century. The Appeals Court ruled in their favor, before the U.S. Supreme Court refused to hear the case in 2001 (*Central Texas Nudists v. Travis County*). The current website is hippiehollow.com. Many articles about this iconic park are available online, which make for interesting reading.

22 *Illustration.*

The illustration by Cate Lowry appears in Michelle Facio's article "Hippie Hollow Park Promotes Body Positivity, Acceptance" from July 2021: https://thedailytexan.com/2021/07/15/hippie-hollow-park-promotes-body-positivity-acceptance/.

23 *Muzak.*
For further details, see Greg Collard's article "Muzak—From the Elevator to the Future" from May 2009, available at https://www.npr.org/2009/05/14/104133884/muzak-from-the-elevator-to-the-future. The article notes that the Austin Muzak franchise was owned by Lyndon B. Johnson and further suggests that Muzak is still trying to "shake" its longstanding "elevator-music reputation," having made its mark on American culture by producing generic-sounding songs for office buildings, retail stores and dentists. Muzak now provides clients with mixtapes of popular recordings.

24 *Tequila worm.*
See Laura Studarus's article "Everything You Need to Know About Tequila Worms" from March 2020: https://10best.usatoday.com/interests/drinks/tequila-worm-should-I-eat/.

25 *Zippo.*
See "Our History" on the Zippo website: https://www.zippo.com/pages/then-now.

26 *John Lennon's "supposed" last words.*
See Dave Lifton's article "The Last Time John Lennon Saw His Beatles Bandmates" from December 2020: https://ultimateclassicrock.com/last-time-john-lennon-saw-beatles/.

27 *San Francisco fire.*
Quotation taken from *Mountains and Molehills; or Recollections of a Burnt Journal* by Frank Marryat (1855), p. 174. For further information about the fire, see the "Early History of the San Francisco Fire Department" on the Museum of the City of San Francisco website: https://sfmuseum.org/hist1/fire.html.

28 *Saturn return.*
For further details, see Molly Hall's article "The Saturn Return and Its Significance in Astrology" from May 2019: https://www.liveabout.com/what-is-the-return-of-saturn-206368. Molly Hall also wrote the book *Knack Astrology: A Complete Illustrated Guide to the Zodiac* (2010).

29 *The Baths.*
See the article "Explore the Baths on Virgin Gorda" by Scotti Shafer: https://www.theoutbound.com/british-virgin-islands/chillin/explore-the-baths-on-virgin-gorda.

30 *Little Dix Bay and Pelican Smash.*
For further information, see https://www.rosewoodhotels.com/en/little-dix-bay-virgin-gorda/experiences/60-years and https://www.mrandmrssmith.com/luxury/rosewood-little-dix-bay.

31 *"Tropical playground."*
See Elise Taylor's article "Little Dix Bay—The Caribbean Getaway Beloved by Queen Elizabeth—Makes Its Triumphant Return" from January 2020: https://www.vogue.com/slideshow/rosewood-little-dix-bay-reopens.

32 *Tortola.*
Quotation taken from Andrew Cooper's article "Top Ten Things to Do in Tortola," originally published in April 2022 and updated in May 2023: https://www.oceanblisscharters.com/post/tortola-day-trip-top-10-things-to-do-in-tortola.

33 *Blackbeard.*
"One of history's most infamous pirates, Blackbeard, was based on Tortola during the 1700's," according to the article "British Virgin Islands—History and Culture," available at https://www.iexplore.com/articles/travel-guides/caribbean/british-virgin-islands/history-and-culture. There has recently been a resurgence of interest in Blackbeard's treasure: see the episode "Blackbeard's Lost Treasure" from the series *History's Greatest Mysteries*, on the History Channel, for further information.

34 *Maredia Pace Bowdon.*
For the obituary, see https://www.shreveporttimes.com/obituaries/spt081035.

35 *"Total Eclipse of the Heart."*
See Alli Patton's article "Did You Know? The Blood Sucking Truth behind Bonnie Tyler's 'Total Eclipse of the Heart'" from November 2022: https://americansongwriter.com/did-you-know-the-blood-sucking-truth-behind-bonnie-tylers-total-eclipse-of-the-heart/.

36 *Fibromyalgia.*
For further information about fibromyalgia, see the pages on the Mayo Clinic's website: https://www.mayoclinic.org/diseases-conditions/fibromyalgia/symptoms-causes/syc-20354780.

37 *Tom's Place.*
See Michael Mayo's article "Remember Tom's Place BBQ in Boca? Its Famed Ribs are Back-in Boynton" from September 2019: https://www.sun-sentinel.com/2019/09/11/remember-toms-place-bbq-in-boca-its-famed-ribs-are-back-in-boynton/.

WAY BEYOND THE GRITS | SIDNEY KATE

38 IEPs.

For further information, see the article "History of the Individualized Education Program (IEP)" from April 2024: https://easchools.org/history-of-the-individualized-education-program-iep.

39 504 Plan.

For further information, see the US Department of Education's "Parent and Educator Resource Guide to Section 504 in Public Elementary and Secondary Schools" from December 2016: https://www.ed.gov/sites/ed/files/about/offices/list/ocr/docs/504-resource-guide-201612.pdf.

40 Agency for Health Care Administration.

For further information, see the "Health Care Policy and Oversight" page on the Department of Health website: https://ahca.myflorida.com/health-care-policy-and-oversight.

41 FDA caution.

See the "Information for Patients About Dermal Fillers" on the FDA website: https://www.fda.gov/medical-devices/aesthetic-cosmetic-devices/dermal-fillers-soft-tissue-fillers.

42 Botox.

See Malena Amato's article "Botox Through the Decades," available at https://www.malenaamatomd.com/botox-through-the-decades/.

43 Botox as filler.

See Melissa Morrison's article "On the Front Lines: What's New in Botox and Facial Fillers," in *Missouri Medicine*, vol. 107, no. 6 (2010), pp. 379–382. https://www.ncbi.nlm.nih.gov/pmc/articles/PMC6188240/.

44 Vermont Turnaround.

See https://www.cowtalesdrivereducation.com/test-prep.html.

45 *Flynn Theatre.*

For further information, see John K. Killacky's article "History Space: The Flynn at 35," in the *Burlington Free Press*, originally published in September 2016: https://www.burlingtonfreepress. com/story/news/local/2016/09/16/history-space-flynn/89589192/.

46 *Al Green.*

According to an article at *Song Bar* from March 2017 (available at https://www.song-bar.com/song-of-the-day/al-green-love-and-happiness), this song "describes a fraught scenario of a telephone call at 3 a.m." The article proceeds to relate that "In his earlier years, the now Reverend Al Green was something of a heartthrob lothario until a girlfriend, Mary Woodson White, assaulted him before killing herself at his Memphis home in 1974."

ABOUT THE AUTHOR

Sidney Kate was born in Louisiana in 1954.

She believes our past experiences shape our future decision making and that learning is a lifelong endeavour. She shares her personal life experiences in hopes her stories not only entertain but transport history to the present. Her main intention with this book is to help heal those who struggle with similar issues in today's not so normal world. Know you are not alone...

She currently lives a quiet life in the Northeast. She plans to continue writing her stories but in the fiction genre.